Innovation Networks
and Clusters

The Knowledge Backbone

P.I.E. Peter Lang

Bruxelles · Bern · Berlin · Frankfurt am Main · New York · Oxford · Wien

Blandine LAPERCHE, Paul SOMMERS
& Dimitri UZUNIDIS (eds.)

Innovation Networks
and Clusters

The Knowledge Backbone

© P.I.E. PETER LANG S.A.,
Éditions scientifiques internationales
Brussels, 2010
1 avenue Maurice, B-1050 Brussels, Belgium
info@peterlang.com; www.peterlang.com

Printed in Germany

ISBN 978-90-5201-602-3
D/2010/5678/16

*CIP available from the British Library, GB
and the Library of Congress, USA.*

Bibliographic information published by "Die Deutsche Nationalbibliothek"
"Die Deutsche Nationalbibliothek" lists this publication in the "Deutsche National-bibliografie"; detailed bibliographic data is available on Internet at <http://dnb.d-nb.de>.

Acknowledgements

The chapters included in this volume were presented at the Pacific North Regional Economic Conference (PNREC) / Spirit of Innovation conference on Innovation networks (Tacoma-Seattle, Washington, May, 2008), organised by the PNREC committee, the Research Network on Innovation (http://rri.univ-littoral.fr) and the Industry and Innovation Research Unit (Lab.RII, http://rii.univ-littoral.fr), University of Littoral (France).

Many institutions supported the organisation of this event and the publication of this volume. We would especially like to thank Seattle University, the Universities of Littoral and Poitiers (France) the IGS group (Institute of social management/Institut de Gestion Sociale, Paris), Northwest Energy and Conservation Council, the Consulate General of Canada in Seattle and the Community and Economic Development of the City of Tacoma.

We offer our deep appreciation to all members of the scientific committee of this conference for their help in the selection of chapters and the construction and publication of the book. We also thank Maria Lorek for her help in the preparation of the final manuscript.

Table of Contents

The Knowledge Base
of Innovation Networks

Blandine LAPERCHE and Dimitri UZUNIDIS

At first beyond the scope of economics, the notion of a network is increasingly used to describe the many links created between independent companies, as well as between them and other institutions. As a matter of fact, these new organisational forms continue to develop. There are several reasons for this rapid development: the globalisation of the economy and the strategies of firms contribute to the building of links to other firms around the world. The opening up of national markets to competition creates a global market on which firms compete. In order to win, they are encouraged, if not obliged, to cooperate with other firms (whether big or small) and with other institutions (universities, local authorities, non-profit institutions).

Moreover, the growing complexity of modern technology considerably increases the diversity of competences that have to be mastered in order to create, produce and commercialise new and/or improved products. The cost of innovation rises continuously, which in turn increases the financing needs of enterprises. It therefore becomes difficult for a single firm to hold all the necessary resources and competences to adapt to the evolutions of the market. Even if a firm were able to do so, its specialisation advantages would vanish because of the growing problems of coordination arising from its big size. This aspect is all the more important as harsh competition exists between firms for the reduction of costs.

Finally, technological convergence implies the creation of various forms of cooperation between different skills in order to benefit from new synergies. Horizontal and vertical networks between public and private actors of innovation are the result of the increase in the amount of capital invested in R&D, the pressure of competition on opened-up markets and the increase of the cost of innovation[1]. However, while the

---

[1] On collaborative innovation processes see B. Laperche, D. Uzunidis and N. Von Tunzelmann (eds.), *The Genesis of Innovation. Systemic Linkages between Know-*

facts seem to show that networks are well established as the major institution of contemporary capitalism, they remain insufficiently defined by economic analysis and their economic consequences, notably in the field of innovation, are not well assessed.

In this book, the contributors aim to show that networks can be characterised as "knowledge factories" and knowledge boosters that feed the internal processes of innovation (collaborative innovation) or the external processes of innovation, created by the propagation effects that come from inter-firm collaboration. In this perspective, innovation induces the development of merchant relationships, but also non-merchant ones, prior to a confrontation in the markets. An example of this are the links established between the scientific milieu and other enterprises through information swaps. This means that networks are at the origin of the creation of new knowledge, tacit and codified, which will be used in innovation processes. Networks are therefore the knowledge backbone of contemporary innovation processes. For a long time now, technical progress and *a fortiori* knowledge have lost the exogenous and residual form they had in the neoclassical production function, and the endogenous growth theories have shown that they are the result of planned (public and private) investments. However, in the current context of collaborative innovation, it seems necessary to go a step further, showing how knowledge is generated within networks involving a variety of public and private institutions.

These externalities have to be integrated in the notion of networks (the process of integrating outsourcing). The network is therefore organised around three poles: the scientific pole, whose main function is to produce knowledge; the technical pole, more oriented towards the elaboration of devices, and mobilising resources to apply knowledge to production in order to obtain anticipated results; and finally the market pole, which shapes demand. However, the economic consequences of the development of networks do not only refer to the creation of new knowledge, and of new entrepreneurs exploiting it. The web created by the links between firms of different sizes and institutions is also a "knowledge trap". The collaborating organisations and institutions develop complex strategies aimed at appropriating core knowledge, which is essential to their current and future competitiveness, and thus design a hierarchy within the networks, where leaders and laggards cooperate and compete. Networks are systems in a state of constant evolution.

---

ledge and the Market, Edward Elgar, Cheltenham, 2008 and on the impact of finance on Innovation processes, see B. Laperche and D. Uzunidis (eds.), *Powerful Finance and Innovation Trends in a High-Risk Economy*, Palgrave Macmillan, London, 2008.

Some of the authors of this book focus specifically on the functioning and the identification of clusters. To innovate, the network produces scientific, technical and organisational knowledge. At the other end of the chain, the needed knowledge to implement innovation processes is developed thanks to the geographical proximity of actors. This notion of proximity – first analysed by Alfred Marshall, who pointed out the "industrial atmosphere" existing within industrial clusters – has been recently rediscovered and refined in economic theories and policies. For about 40 years, the approach of innovation based on proximity (and, more precisely, the concept of cluster, considered as innovative milieu) has demonstrated its pertinence as a kind of model of decentralised economic growth, but also of the accumulation of the technological competencies of enterprises (knowledge pool). This approach is part of an interactive vision, which insists on the importance of the networks of actors, public and private, at a level – the local economy – recognised as pertinent for the study of the origins of various innovative networks. The study of the immediate environment of enterprises helps us to understand their innovation dynamics, but also their capacity to build scientific and technological relationships and to appropriate themselves, thanks to cooperative relationships, the knowledge produced by this geographically-situated milieu. In other words, location matters, and clusters cannot be instantaneously generated from scratch. Many ingredients need to be present, over some decades, to build a competitive cluster, which will differ from a mere aggregation of firms thanks to the quality of the network built.

The systemic nature of the relationships that characterise an economic and social milieu explains what favours or hinders the act of innovation. An innovative milieu, considered to be an innovation system, describes the relationships between institutions (scientific, technological, industrial, commercial, financial, political), whether private or public (enterprises, research and engineering laboratories, government agencies, training centres, etc.). More often than not these relationships consist of financial and informational flows and of individual's movements. The aim of such a system is to produce innovations (new products, new services, etc.), spread by entrepreneurs acting in innovative start-up, as well as in bigger enterprises. This structure of the milieu does not only refer to economic interactions but also takes into account social structures at the origin of innovative behaviours. Institutions (state and local authorities, non-profit organisations) play a significant role in the organisation and the evolution of socio-economic structures. In turn, the innovative milieu contributes to the innovative performances of enterprises and of regions through the supply of scientific and technical resources.

This approach, of linking territories with innovation networks, influences national competitiveness policies throughout the world. The first well-known clusters were in the Silicon Valley and on Route 128 outside Boston, but they are now flourishing in all industrial and emerging countries. Many Europeans countries have also developed cluster initiatives. This is, for example, the case in France with the "Pôle de Compétitivité" policy, which encourages the creation and growth of clusters throughout the country. This is also the case in Canada, Japan, South Korea, China, etc., as illustrated in some of the chapters of this volume. Even in the United States, clusters are still at the centre of innovation policies, as shown by President Obama's recent call for a new federal effort to support regional innovation clusters[2].

Innovation Networks and Clusters as Knowledge Boosters

The first part of the book explains how innovation networks (territorially localised or not) can be considered as knowledge factories. This means they are at the origin of the production of new knowledge that will be transformed and used in common as well as in separated production processes. This characteristic of networks as knowledge factories gives incentives to further investment in the production of knowledge and allows us to define innovation networks as knowledge boosters, ensuring the cumulativeness of the innovation process.

In chapter 1, Abdelillah Hamdouch makes a critical analysis of the most visible pieces of literature on innovation clusters and networks. He suggests some possible pathways for a better grounding for the analysis of clustering and networking phenomena within innovative or creative fields. Besides defining the notions of clusters and innovation clusters or networks, a core topic within the literature relates to the analysis of the logic behind the emergence, structuring and evolution of innovative activities within various geographic areas. But despite the large amount of effort deployed, there are no consensual views among academics on the various key issues, conceptual and analytical, especially with regards to the spatial/geographical boundaries of an innovation cluster and the nature and intensity of the actors' interaction that characterise it. The whole picture is also blurred as a persistent "disciplinary segregation", which prevents the integration of the most valuable and converging insights that could be drawn from the various complementary social science perspectives. Abdelillah Hamdouch suggests that innovation

---

[2]   Sallet J., Paisley E., Masterman J., *The Geography of Innovation. The Federal Government and the growth of regional innovation clusters*, Center for American progress, sept. 2009.

clusters are the result of the dynamic articulation of various circles of relationships between actors, which he calls "multi-scaled networks".

Chapter 2 focuses on the dynamics of networking innovation at the company level. Blandine Laperche explains that within the innovation network developed by the big firm, intellectual property rights play crucial roles, not only in terms of strategy but also in terms of organisation. Laperche shows that IPRs have a growing 'coordination role', making the relationships between the fragmented parts of the networked enterprise easier. The coordination role is also gaining ground in the context of collaborative innovation (innovation networks). Reducing the cost of cooperation, IPRs support the creation of innovation networks. The second role is the 'incentive/defensive role' aimed at protecting and giving incentives to the constitution of the networked firm's innovation potential, called here 'knowledge-capital'. In other words, IPRs secure innovation networks and therefore support them in their function of knowledge boosters. The third role is an offensive one, as IPRs largely contribute to define the place of the firm(s) (owner(s) of the IPRs) within the innovation network to which it (they) usually belong(s). The chapter concludes by stressing the relationships between the roles of IPRs for networked enterprises and the strengthening of IPRs on a global level.

In chapter 3, Francis Munier shows that something other than contractual relationships boosts or hinders innovation processes. He studies the specific management of Chinese firms, called Guanxi, based on the network of relationships among various parties that cooperate together and support one another. Ever since China's new period of openness, it seems that a contradiction has appeared between the constraints of corporate governance and the cultural and traditional behaviour in business. As a consequence, most Western analysis considers that Guanxi is merely a form of corruption and should therefore be eliminated. The originality of Francis Munier's work is to frame these questions in the context of recent concepts such as communities of practice and espistemic communities. Based on these concepts, the author considers that the firm can be analysed from a dual perspective: cognitive and organisational. The first one belongs to the Guanxi logic and the second one to corporate governance. According to these frameworks, Francis Munier points out that Guanxi provides an innovative network in order to enhance and spread knowledge.

Many forms of entrepreneurship are described in strategic management literature. For high-tech firms, the most fitting forms of entrepreneurship are the so-called plural form and the network/distributed form of entrepreneurship. These forms are often overlapping, and in many cases, for high-tech firms, they probably evolve continuously from one form into the other. In chapter 4, Thierry Burger Helmchen develops a representation of the dynamics between the two forms and uses a longitudinal case study on a small high-tech firm to test its relevance. In particular, he looks at the cause and consequence relationship of the network position as a determinant of the firm's business model/market innovation capability and the technological/product innovation capability.

The knowledge Pool and Clustering Innovation

The second part of the book clearly takes a territorial point of view and studies how clusters, propelled by the quality of the innovation networks they enclose, can be characterised as knowledge pools into which the local actors will be able to draw to reinforce their individual and collective competitiveness. This part also includes analyses of the quality of the networks built within clusters, which may help their identification.

In chapter 5, Maryann Feldman focuses on the importance of local factors in the emergence of innovation. After recalling the main definitions and characteristics of innovation and knowledge, she highlights the importance of the existence, in a particular location, of an ecology of actors and institutions (big firms and small entrepreneurs, incitative public policies) to explain the emergence and prosperity of innovative clusters. This alchemy between actors and institutions creates a social dynamic within a location and defines a spatially-bounded community of interests around a nascent technology or emerging industry.

Today, economists consider the regional economy as a geographical and economic platform for the organisation of production and, as a consequence, an opportunity to create new activities, goods and services, new employment and sources of income. In chapter 6, Sophie Boutillier and Dimitri Uzunidis examine the role of synergic relationships (spatial, organisational and cognitive – named proximity) in the innovation and entrepreneurial processes. The density of these relationships reinforces the capability of a local economy to generate small independent enterprises. But in the context of contemporary capitalism, the entrepreneur, as the owner and the manager of a small enterprise, has a specific function: he is not a hero (as Schumpeter noted) but he is a socialised entrepreneur. The former is at the origin of the development of big industries and new areas of activities; the latter is the result of the financial strategies and industrial policies of the major actors of the economy (big firms, financial institutions, central and local public administrations, etc.). As a result, Sophie Boutillier and Dimitri

Uzunidis analyse the "resource potential" of the entrepreneur as a necessary condition to business creation. This potential – composed of capital, knowledge and social relations – can give value to the entrepreneur's function. In this case, the relations of proximity, applied to the territorial level of analysis, must be characterised by the logic of collaboration, confidence and reciprocity.

The intensity of proximity relationships differ according to the characteristics of the different scientific and technology fields, as shown in chapter 7. In this chapter, Catherine Beaudry and Andrea Schiffaeurova study Canadian biotechnology and nanotechnology clusters with a focus on the importance of collaboration networks for innovation creation. Using information contained in the USPTO registered patents, the authors examine Canadian biotechnology and nanotechnology innovation networks and describe the collaborative behaviour of the inventors. They find that most of the collaborative activity that involves Canadian biotechnology and nanotechnology inventors takes place inside clusters. Canadian inventors who decide to build cooperation ties outside their clusters usually prefer to do so with collaborators from abroad, mainly from the US. The authors then examine the structural properties of the local collaboration subnetwork within each cluster and relate them to the efficiency in the spread of knowledge and innovation creation in that cluster. The comparative analysis between biotechnology and nanotechnology innovation networks reveals that the biotechnology network is larger and more developed than the nanotechnology one. It is also less fragmented due to the scientific nature of the biotechnology specialisation fields, which are often overlapping. Nanotechnology, in contrast, includes many quite disparate fields, where the inventors work in more separated groups.

Chapter 8 compares cluster structures identified through a statistical analysis of input-output data to other clusters identified by regional governmental organisations in the Puget Sound region (Washington, USA). Paul Sommers and William B. Beyers demonstrate explicit analytical procedures for classifying clusters that might lead to cluster initiatives based on clusters emerging from the statistical analysis. They argue that use of an explicit analytical procedure has many advantages, including identifying clusters that neither a regional governmental organisation nor a major city government has identified, and providing insights into potential difficulties likely to be encountered by regional cluster initiatives based on clusters identified in other ways.

FIRST PART

INNOVATION NETWORKS AND CLUSTERS AS KNOWLEDGE BOOSTERS

CHAPTER I

Conceptualising Innovation Networks and Clusters

Abdelillah HAMDOUCH

1. Introduction[1]

Since the mid 1990s, an increasing amount of research has been devoted to the study of innovation clusters and networks. Scholars from various fields such as economics (especially industrial economics and 'new' economic geography), as well as economic sociology and strategic management, have engaged in continuous investigations, either theoretical/conceptual, methodological or (mostly) empirical. One important and common challenge of these research efforts has been to provide in-depth analyses of the spatial dimensions and mechanisms (mainly at the national or regional level) underlying the clustering and networking phenomena in prominent high-tech sectors, notably in biotechnology, information & communication technologies (ICT), nanotechnologies, new materials, and the space and defence industries.

This academic interest in innovation clusters and networks analysis has been accompanied and encouraged by the growing conviction expressed since the late 1990s by many governments and international organisations (notably the OECD and the EU) that national competitiveness in a global economy lies paradoxically, as Porter (1998) puts it, in

---

[1] This chapter is a revised/refined version of an earlier draft first presented in November 2007, at the 19th EAEPE Conference in Porto (see Hamdouch, 2007). It has also been discussed in a revised form at the PNREC 2008 Conference (Tacoma-Seattle, May 2008), at two research seminars, respectively in Paris (*Research Network on Innovation*, October 2007) and Annecy (IREGE – Université de Savoie, March, 2008), and at the International Conference on Competitiveness Clusters (Liège, March 2009). Finally, valuable comments have been kindly provided by some researchers belonging to my personal "research networks". This entire "buzz" resulted in useful remarks and suggestions that helped me improve the initial versions of the chapter on various crucial points. Special thanks to Rachel Bocquet, Olivier Brossard, Catherine Comet, Jerry Courvisanos, Olivier Crevoisier, Marc-Hubert Depret, Blandine Laperche, Didier Lebert, Frank Moulaert, Jim Sawyer, Bénédicte Serrate, Paul Sommers, André Torre, Pasquale Tridico and Dimitri Uzunidis. The usual caveats apply for any eventual remaining errors or omissions.

"local things". Following this conviction, most governments in developed, emerging or developing countries have engaged in, more or less, active cluster policies, but with differentiated achievements and success. Along with these policies, national or regional governments and international organisations have supported and funded a large set of academic research in order to enlighten their choices and actions in favour of innovative sectors and regional development and competitiveness.

Among the numerous research issues addressed in the literature, the analysis of the logic (scientific/technological, economic/financial, historical/institutional) behind the emergence, structuring and evolution of innovative activities within various geographic areas (metropolitan areas, regions, countries) appears to be a core topic. In most works, the emphasis is (explicitly or implicitly) placed on two central issues. The first one relates to the nature and the intensity of the relationships between the key actors involved in innovative activities (especially in high-tech sectors): universities and research labs, firms, funding organisations and public/governmental institutions. The second (and partly related) issue concerns the relevant spatial/geographical scaling of innovation clusters and networks. Of course, behind these issues also lies the conceptual challenge of defining what a "cluster" is in general, and what is an "innovation cluster" or an "innovation network" in particular.

However, despite a large amount of research effort and the yielding of some valuable results, all these issues are still hotly debated. In fact, when carefully examining the extensive literature that is available, one can only conclude that there are no consensual views among academics, as well as only a few well-documented 'stylised facts', either at the conceptual/theoretical or methodological/empirical level. The definition of what a cluster really is (specifically, an innovation cluster or network), and what its spatial/geographical boundaries could be, as well as its conditions of emergence and evolution, have not been clearly and coherently established. By the same token, the literature displays a large variety of analytical/theoretical/methodological approaches and a persistent "disciplinary segregation" which blur the picture even more.

Through a critical *and* constructive study of the most visible pieces of this literature, the aim of the chapter is to highlight the various dimensions and implications of the issues at stake, while providing at the same time some "reading keys" of the conceptual and analytical challenges that these issues raise. The chapter is structured as follows: section two tries to disentangle the various definitions and conceptual approaches of the notion of "cluster" as stated in general terms, and discusses the analytical and operational difficulties it entails. This discussion is crucial, as it underlies some of the key analytical problems one encounters when turning specifically to the notions of "innovation clusters" and "innovation networks". As shown in section three, important indeterminacies remain regarding these notions, yet some useful insights and stimulating ideas can be drawn from several works. Building on the discussions developed in sections two and three, section four is aimed at clarifying some key conceptual and analytical issues related to the dynamics underlying innovation clusters and the formation and structuring of networks. Here I also make some suggestions on how these dynamics could be (potentially) better conceptualised through the notion of "multi-scaled networks", though the notion is only embryonic and requires further analytical elaboration. Section five concludes the chapter by pointing out some important challenges that are still to be tackled if one truly wants to demonstrate that innovation clusters and networks are relevant phenomena for innovation dynamics analysis.

2. What is a cluster, *really*?[2]

When scanning the large amount of literature that has been written on "clusters" in recent years, to try to identify what could be the essence and the foundations of the notion, the result is quite frightening: there are as many different definitions of what a "cluster" might be as there are authors or publications – even if, very often, the differences are only marginal or anecdotic.[3] Furthermore, whatever the definition encountered, the notion of cluster remains rather fuzzy in its theoretical "contours" (see Martin, Sunley, 2003, who even talk of a "chaotic concept"). This lack of clarity and conceptualisation gets even worse as the notion of cluster is frequently confused with many other notions or concepts, which are supposed to be "neighbouring". These are then used as equivalents or even synonyms of the term "cluster" without systematic and due clarification or justification. Notions such as "network", "value chain", "industrial district", "local production system", "innovative milieu", "regional system of innovation", "new industrial space", "scientific/ technological park", "pôle de compétitivité" (the "French and Belgian touch"), all "float" together in the literature on clusters and cluster policies.[4] Some distinctions are also frequently encountered, which adds

---

[2] This section builds partly on Hamdouch (2008a).

[3] I will not go into a detailed (and somehow vain) exercise of listing all the authors and definitions. Large samples of these notions and their various conceptions have already been compiled by others and can be found for example in Martin and Sunley (2003, p. 10-13), and in Preissl and Solimene (2003, Ch. 3).

[4] To take just an example, Nooteboom (2004, p. 2-3) says in a straightforward manner: "Apparently, clusters and industrial districts are more or less synonymous" and that

to the general confusion, as the criteria used for such distinctions are rarely specified: "industrial district" *vs.* "innovation district"; "industrial cluster" *vs.* "innovation cluster"/"technological cluster"/"knowledge cluster"; "production network" *vs.* "innovation network"; "industrial region" *vs.* "learning region", and so on.

In fact, it is difficult even for specialised academics to swim in such troubled waters. Yet, fortunately, some valuable syntheses and critical attempts have been proposed, which contribute to a conceptual and analytical clarification of the various notions and approaches in the literature (see den Hertog, Roelandt, 1999; Martin, Sunley, 2003; Moulaert, Sékia, 2003; Preissl, Solimene, 2003, Ch. 3; Bekele, Jackson, 2006). These authors also provide a useful examination of old and recent theories of industrial location and regional/territorial development, ranging from the "canonical" theories (Marshall, Weber, Hoover, Lösch, Jacobs etc.) to contemporary approaches rooted in: economic geography (especially the "Californian School"); economics (new geographical economics, endogenous growth theories, new industrial organisation theories, evolutionary theories, regulation theories); economic sociology (social networks theories); and managerial literature (especially strategic management, with Porter as a prominent representative).[5]

As my focus in this chapter is only on the "cluster literature" (only the literature using explicitly the term "cluster" and focusing on the study of "clusters"), and due to space limitations, I do not go into the analysis of these various approaches. I will instead go back to the notion of "cluster" *per se* and try to identify the content and features it is supposed to exhibit. Despite the wide variety of cluster definitions in the literature, it seems to me that the spectrum of the different conceptions could be considerably reduced if we were able to select only few relevant, discriminating criteria. As a matter of fact, after a careful screening of non-redundant features included in the various definitions proposed, two criteria appear to be particularly important. The first one is related to the *territorialised* vs. *non-territorialised* conception of the cluster notion. The second decisive criterion corresponds to *the focus vs. non-focus of the notion on activities or industries strongly based on innovation.*

"presumably, the notions of 'innovation clusters' and 'regional innovation systems' are close synonyms". But as Moulaert and Sékia (2003) show, among others, these notions are quite distinct concepts as they relate each to a different theory of territorial development.

[5] See also Scott (2004) for a useful discussion on the evolution pathways during the last decades of economic geography theories and their increasing insemination today by the so-called "new geographical economics".

On this basis, the full range of cluster definitions fall, more or less, under two main lines of conception. The first one turns around Porter's works and the many authors that, broadly speaking, follow his approach. The second line, which is clearly more heterogeneous, is in tune with the OECD approach and/or follows "reticular" conceptions of clusters. Of course, a series of nuances, subtleties and incremental differences persist amongst the various definitions of clusters. Still, the two identified lines of cluster conception are quite likely to reflect most of the definitions of clusters encountered in the literature because they have also been the most influential (especially the Porter approach) in the academic field, as well as in political circles (see Martin, Sunley, 2003).

I examine these two conceptions and stress their shortcomings and the main conceptual and analytical problems they entail.

Porter's approach and its various ambiguities

While it is difficult to trace the origins of the notion of "cluster" with precision, it is undoubtedly Michael Porter who popularised it in his 1990 book *The Competitive Advantage of Nations* (see Porter, 1990), and then later elaborated on it in a number of his publications (see especially Porter, 1995, 1998a, 1998b, 1998c, and 2000).

First, Porter (1998c, p. 78) defines in a very general manner what he means by "clusters":

> Clusters (are) critical masses – in one place – of unusual competitive success in particular fields. (...) Clusters are geographic concentrations of interconnected companies and institutions in a particular field. Clusters encompass an array of linked industries and other entities important to competition.

Then he indicates the features that he believes make the cluster an efficient form for the spatial organisation of industrial activities:

> Clusters promote both competition and cooperation (...). Competition can coexist with cooperation because they occur on different dimensions and among different players. Clusters represent a kind of new organizational form in between arm's-length markets on the one hand and hierarchies, or vertical integration, on the other. A cluster, then, is an alternative way of organizing the value-chain. Compared with market transactions among dispersed and random buyers and sellers, the proximity of companies and institutions in one location – and the repeated exchanges among them – fosters better coordination and trust. Thus clusters mitigate the problems inherent to arm's-length relationships without imposing the inflexibilities of vertical integration or the management challenges of creating formal linkages such as networks, alliances, and partnerships. A cluster of independent and informally linked companies and institutions represents a robust organiza-

tional form that offers advantages in efficiency, effectiveness, and flexibility (*ibid.*, p. 79-80).

In this conception, the cluster is meant as a *specific spatial industrial organisation* based on two main dimensions: (a) the links between actors in terms of geographical proximity, of complementarities and the building of trustworthy relationships; and (b) the existence of both competitive and cooperative interaction between co-localised firms. It is the combination of these two dimensions that induces, according to Porter, a greater competitiveness of the firms and industries located within a cluster (when compared to those operating in other organisational settings).[6]

This approach has been widely acknowledged and appropriated (with some nuances and variations) by many scholars and by national or regional policy-makers, probably due to its simplicity and *a priori* convincing flavour. However, besides the fact that most of Porter's assertions on the supposed direct links between industrial clustering and competitiveness are, on the whole, neither theoretically nor empirically demonstrated (see Martin, Sunley, 2003, for a detailed critical account), the notion of cluster as presented (and marketed) by Porter raises numerous key questions and analytical difficulties.

1) The first difficulty is related to the *identification of the relevant borders of the geographical space defining a cluster*. Here, Porter varied significantly from one of his writings to another, but in the end settled on a very vague spatial bounding of the cluster. In his first approach, Porter (1998c, p. 79) defines these boundaries with no spatial reference at all:

> A cluster's boundaries are defined by the linkages and complementarities across industries and institutions that are most important to competition.

---

[6] As Porter himself admits (see Porter, 1998a), his conception was to a large extent initially inspired by Alfred Marshall's "industrial districts" conception – but with no further explicit emphasis put on the key elements he picked up from his famous predecessor of a century or so ago. In fact, the two key dimensions of clusters, as emphasised by Porter, overlap clearly and comprehensively with those stressed by Marshall, though with different wording: "When an industry has thus chosen a locality for itself, it is likely to stay there long: so great are the advantages which people following the same skilled trade get from near neighbourhood to one another. The mysteries of the trade become no mysteries; but are as it were in the air (...) Good work is rightly appreciated; inventions and improvements in machinery, in processes and the general organisation of the business have their merits promptly discussed; if one man starts a new idea it is taken up by others and combined with suggestions of their own, and thus it becomes the source of further new ideas" (see Marshall, 1903, Book IV, Ch. X, p. 152-153). For a renewed and enlightening presentation of industrial districts in the contemporary Italian context, see Beccatini (1990).

In another article, two years later, Porter (2000, p. 16) provides a different definition, including a spatial, though very permissive reference:

> A cluster is a geographically proximate group of interconnected companies and associated institutions in a particular field, linked by commonalities and complementarities. The geographic scope of a cluster can range from a single city or state to a country or even a group of neighbouring countries.

As one can easily notice, this spatial bounding of the cluster is not totally clear. The first definition stresses *organisational and competitive borders rather than spatial borders*, whereas the second definition envisages *all geographical scopes* as being relevant spatial cluster boundaries, including the entire country or even a group of geographically close countries. Thus, this conception departs from Marshall's 'industrial districts' approach, while at the same time moving towards more *reticular conceptions of the cluster* (see below). But then, what distinguishes the notion of *cluster* from the more general notion of *network*?

2) In his "territorialised" conception of clusters, Porter poses the existence of an *array of inter-related industries* (and other entities and institutions) that are important for competition (see Porter, 1998c, p. 78). Yet this supposed interindustrial feature of the cluster also remains unclear. Does it refer to *vertical industrial complementarities*? In this case, it would overlap with the "value chain" (an eminently 'Porterian' notion) conception of the cluster as proposed by the OECD definition (see below), or more simply with the concept of "filière de production", which was developed in France in the early 1980s (see Monfort, 1983). Or does it relate to *horizontally different but co-localised industries*? This would then correspond to a conception of industrial location close to classical or more recent theories of urban and regional agglomeration in which co-localised firms and industries benefit from common markets of input factors and from the existence of a pooled basin of labour force and competences.

In both cases, the notion of "cluster" would lose much of its (alleged) specificity. Besides, the idea that the cluster's industrial diversification – and therefore that the diversity of activities and competences in the same place would augment the individual innovativeness of the firms located within the cluster – is challenged by some authors. For example, Baptista and Swann (1998) show that if a firm is actually more likely to innovate if the labour resources linked to its sector are available within its regional location space, there is no robust relationship between the cluster's degree of industrial diversification and the total innovative propensity of the firms.

3) The third difficulty is related to the way Porter characterises the links between the firms (and other organisations and institutions) within

a cluster. For him, these links are *informal*, and it is precisely for this reason that clusters are seen to be more efficient and flexible modes of industrial organisation than pure market relationships, or even vertical integration, alliances, partnerships and networks (see above the citation from Porter, 1998c, p. 78-79). But, paradoxically, these latter *formal modes of industrial collaboration* (along with more informal inter-organisational and inter-personal relationships) appear to be precisely the key building blocks of most industrial and innovation networks. This is especially the case when the mobilisation of strong complementarities between specialised firms (and between the latter and other kinds of actors like research centres, universities or funding organisations) is crucial for industrial and commercial operations and for innovation processes. Indeed, these formal, collaborative forms are generally most needed when innovation processes entail access to funding resources and to new knowledge and competence fields, and then when collaborative R&D raises crucial issues regarding appropriation and patenting.[7]

4) As a matter of fact, Porter's approach does not make any distinction between clusters according to the nature of the sector or activities considered. Indeed, traditional and mature sectors on the one hand, and innovative or high-tech sectors on the other – especially science-based sectors – are not differentiated at all in the 'Porterian' cluster approach. Moreover, Porter (1998c, p. 85-87) goes as far as denying any relevance in the distinction between high-tech and low-tech industries. The importance of R&D and innovation processes seem then to be clearly underscored by Porter, yet these processes are actually at the core of sectors whose dynamics are intensively based on the development and the exploitation of new knowledge and competence bundles (like in bio-technology or nanotechnology).[8]

The reticular conceptions of clusters

Following the line of the studies initiated by the OECD (1999, 2001), an *essentially reticular conception of clusters* has emerged and been spread throughout the academic sphere in recent years:

> Clusters are characterised as networks of production of strongly interde-
> pendent firms (including specialised suppliers), knowledge producing agents
> (universities, research institutes, engineering companies), bridging institu-

---

[7] This pattern is clearly demonstrated for most sectors where innovation is the key engine for firm competitiveness and market competition, as it is the case for pharmaceuticals and biotechnology, for example (see Hamdouch, Perrochon, 2000a, 2000b; Hamdouch, Depret, 2001).

[8] See Hamdouch (2008b) and Hamdouch and He (2009) for analyses and illustrations of these dynamics in the case of pharmaceuticals and biotechnology.

tions (brokers, consultants) and customers, linked to each other in a value-adding production chain (OECD, 1999, p. 5).

Within the OECD stream of works, den Hertog and Roelandt (1999) have enriched this approach by including the *possibility of strategic alliances* between firms, but also between the latter and universities and research institutions.

Here, *there are the strong institutional and inter-organisational links between interdependent actors that define the network within a value-chain.* But the links envisaged are apparently only of a formal form, leaving aside all more informal interactions between organisational or individual actors. Yet these more informal links require a certain *topo-logic proximity* of the actors (see Dahl, Pedersen, 2004; Nooteboom, 2004). Contrary to Porter (and many others), the OECD approach is not very explicit on this issue, even if it stresses the frequently localised, but "open"[9] nature of clusters:

> In a knowledge-based economy, these clusters of innovative firms form around sources of knowledge. They are based on a sophisticated infrastructure in which knowledge is developed, shared and exchanged, and are characterised by highly concentrated and effective links between entrepreneurs, investors and researchers. Clusters can take a variety of forms, depending on their main technological and commercial areas of specialisation. In most cases they operate within localised geographical areas and interact within larger innovation systems at the regional, national and international level. With globalisation, dynamic clusters are becoming key factors in a country's capacity to attract the international investment that generates new technological expertise, to interest investors in innovation (venture capital, etc.) and to benefit from the international mobility of skilled personnel (OECD, 1999, p. 5).

Another approach, with a purely reticular conception of the cluster, goes far beyond that of the OECD in two combined directions: first, because it merges all possible spatial scopes within a global undifferentiated framework; second, because it completely dematerialises the cluster by assimilating it with a virtual innovation network based on a cross-learning process among electronically connected actors. Hence, Passiante and Secundo (2002) talk of "the global virtual learning environment" and defend the following hypothesis: in a global informational economy, learning, which is at the heart of innovation processes, takes place increasingly within virtual networks.

---

[9] Indeed, this spatial openness of the cluster is rightly emphasised here, as I think it truly constitutes a key feature of clustering and networking dynamics within innovative industries (see below in the next paragraphs, and the detailed discussions in sections 3 and 4).

On the one hand, one can easily agree that this dimension of dematerialised exchanges of information and (codified) knowledge between distant actors is nowadays of unquestionable importance. In particular, it introduces the potentially advantageous possibility of "open" clusters and networks and of valuable connections and exchanges with actors or partners located in various, more or less distant spaces. This "openness" of the cluster or network is particularly crucial when innovation processes entail some logic of "exploration": searching for and capturing new knowledge pieces (see Nooteboom, 2004).

But, on the other hand, one must stress that electronic networks are not really adapted to the exchange of tacit knowledge (see Preissl, Solimene, 2003). To be effectively exchanged, tacit knowledge requires spatial proximity and physical, material interaction (see Dahl, Pedersen, 2004). Besides, even the electronic exchange of *codified knowledge* between distant actors (especially if not yet published or legally protected) usually requires a *minimum of previous direct or physical contacts* that initiate mutual recognition and cross-identification of the potential "corresponding" actors, and also allows the establishment of a trustworthy basis for further relationships.

In any case, even an essentially reticular approach of (loose) clusters with distant actors exchanging goods, services, technologies, knowledge, etc, would need to call for some *spatial dimension* (though not identified by a specific, singular geographical area). This would mean *geographical landmarks*, allowing each of the interacting actors to know where his or her partners are located and what the institutional, political and social specificities (and potential consequences) of that location are.[10] In other words, e*ach actor has a specific geographical location that is almost entirely not neutral*. Indeed, in a context of a capitalist-driven economy where profit-seeking behaviour is the rule, no person (or organisation) will exchange anything of economic value to somebody else if, as a minimum basis for possible exchange or economic transaction, he or she (a) does not know where the distant counterpart is located, and (b) is not confident with this location. This means that the "geographical identity" of the actors matters, especially when crucial knowledge or technologies are to be shared or exchanged.

However, this does not mean that the interacting actors necessarily or systematically have to be co-located in the same geographical area. Indeed, as Owen-Smith *et al.* (2002) have convincingly demonstrated through the case of the Boston biotech cluster, firms from this area have

---

[10] This idea is in tune with that of the "institutional embedding" of actors interacting within a cluster or network (Nooteboom, 2004); see section 3.

developed strong relationships with "external" partners in the Bay area of San Francisco, in the New York City area, and abroad. This case shows that the relevant spatial scale of a cluster may be variable and "multi-territorialised" over several regions or even countries. Furthermore, in the latter configuration of multi-national locations of various partners, some authors have come to talk of "*Global Innovation Networks*" *(GIN's)* (see Ernst, 2006), which reflect the effects of the increasing internationalisation of R&D activities of large firms and the growing structural relationships among production and research centres ("clusters", indeed) localised in different countries.[11] I shall return to this in section 4.

To conclude this section, it seems clear to me that if the notion of "cluster" is to be recognised, and the analysis of the spatial organisation of production and innovation activities is to have some use, it still has to be clarified and refined. This is precisely the pathway opened up by the concepts of "innovation clusters" or more generally of "innovation networks", especially in high-tech sectors.

3. Conceptual Approaches of Innovation Clusters and Networks: a Review and Discussion

The critical study in "Territorial Innovation Models" by Moulaert and Sékia (2003) is particularly illuminating as they identify six main models: 'Local Production Systems', 'Innovative Milieux', 'Learning Regions', 'Regional Innovation Systems', 'New Industrial Spaces', and 'Spatial Clusters of Innovation'. But they qualify the latter model as being a "residual category, with little affinity to regional economics but close to Porter's clusters of innovation" (p. 291).

On the grounds of the various analytical difficulties that the cluster notion entails (see above), one can only but agree with this statement. But, on the other hand, it is hard to dismiss it purely and simply as a possible pathway for analysing clustering and networking dynamics and the spatial organisation of innovation activities. First of all, because the

---

[11] In the Chinese case, for example, Liu and Buck (2007) and Hamdouch and He (2009) clearly show how "*international technology spillovers*" are becoming important in high-tech sectors (especially in ICT) due primarily to the increasing direct investments engaged by multinational companies for building production and research facilities in China, but also thanks to the ongoing building of strong relationships between Chinese firms and research centres with North-American and European partners. These links are particularly strong and dense with the Silicon Valley thanks to the "Returnees" phenomenon: the moving back to China (but the same holds for India and Taiwan) of Chinese (Indian, Taiwanese) students and migrants (see Saxenian, 1999, 2006; Bresnahan *et al.*, 2004).

five other territorial innovation models also present several important (yet probably more limited) deficiencies and shortcomings, as Moulaert and Sékia (2003, p. 295) clearly recognise:

> The conceptual superficiality of the TIM [Territorial Innovation Models] literature is a consequence of several factors such as the immediate links with regional economic competition policy (many TIM were written to legitimize it), the general trend in today's scientific practice of 'fast theory building' and the confusion of analytical modelling with normative modelling (…).

To be sure, the cluster approach could not be well ranked in the TIM based on this different criteria! But, and this is my second "defending" argument, the notion of cluster could become useful if clarified and refined on more robust analytical grounds, especially if it is explicitly articulated (together with the notion of network) with innovation issues. My final argument in defence of a cluster approach is maybe the simplest: the popularity and widespread use of the cluster reference amongst academics (most of the empirical work on innovation spatial dynamics use explicitly the term[12]) and in policy-making arenas (the "sacred" terms here are "cluster policy" or "cluster initiative") should force one to examine how to turn this loose and problematic notion of "cluster" into something more analytically grounded and empirically more "tractable" and meaningful.

This is the path I try to pave here, though the specific literature on innovation clusters is not as prolific as the more general literature on clusters in providing definitions of the notion. Indeed, only a few useful definitions have been proposed (although with various wordings and denominations), and most of them rather overlap or complement each other. I discuss here several of these definitions in order to identify what could be the main features and dimensions that appear to be important components of an innovation cluster.

---

[12] This is especially the case for empirical works on biotechnology (which represents a large share of the literature), on ICT sectors and (more recently) on nanotechnology. It is impossible to cite here all the numerous empirical works on innovation clusters and networks. I just refer to some important works (other references will be signalled in the sequel of the text when relevant): Saxenian (1994, 1999, 2006); Swann and Prevezer (1996); Castilla *et al.* (2000); Ahuja (2000); Depret and Hamdouch (2000); Cooke (2001, 2002); Zeller (2001); Owen-Smith *et al.* (2002); Powell *et al.* (2002); Feldman (2003); Waluszewski (2004); Chiaroni and Chiesa (2006); Robinson *et al.* (2007); etc.

Strong collaboration and links are not enough

A first, rather general (although somehow deficient) definition is used here as an *illustration of what should be avoided* if one really wants to identify what makes the specificity of innovation clusters and networks vis-à-vis clusters, broadly speaking. As a "negative" of a photograph, it serves also to point out some key dimensions that should be checked for getting the "positive" of the picture. This definition is due to Simmie and Sennet (1999) in their attempt to analyse "innovation in the London metropolitan region" (*sic*):

> We define an innovative cluster as a *large number* of interconnected industrial and/or service *companies* having a *high degree of collaboration*, typically through a *supply chain*, and operating under the *same market conditions* (p. 51; emphasis added).

This definition rests, as one can easily see, on very general features that could a priori define any kind of cluster. Indeed, if a "high degree of collaboration" may truly play a key role in innovation clusters (see below), the other features overlap with those highlighted by Porter or the OECD in their generic definitions of clusters (see above section 2). Even worse, besides the fact that there is no explicit reference to innovative activities at all, this definition suffers from several restrictions and deficiencies:

- It restricts collaboration to that between firms, and then excludes all other important organisations that are usually key players in innovative clusters, especially universities and research centres.

- It talks of a "large number" of companies as a key feature of these clusters, but with no precision on what the threshold for this "number" should be.

- It considers the "supply chain" as the central locus of inter-firm collaboration, which is doubly misleading: (a) Only vertical connections are considered, thus ignoring all horizontal relationships (including those between direct or potential rivals); (b) The supply chain relates to productive and commercially linked processes, not to innovation processes, which is not truly the right way to proceed if one wants to talk about "innovative clusters"...

- There is no explicit indication on the spatial scope or dimensions of the "innovative cluster". Why then talk of a "cluster" at all?

- Finally, the reference to the expression "the same market conditions" is vague and even intriguing. Does it refer to "institutional conditions" (laws, regulations, political and administrative settings, etc.) or to "competitive conditions" of the 'market' in question? In both cases, a spatial or geographically relevant bounding of the market should be indicated, but is not (see above). Still, the expression is in any case misleading in two ways. Firstly, the interconnected companies may well be operating in different but complementary activities, and then at least partly belong to different markets. Secondly, innovation processes take place for the most upstream or outside markets, and the collaborations between firms (and between the latter and other organisations) in these processes rely precisely on other modes of interaction and coordination (R&D agreements, licensing, alliances, partnerships, and informal relationships) than primarily on market mechanisms.

This critical discussion clearly points out crucial dimensions that should be carefully considered in an accurate exercise of defining "innovation clusters".

Technological and functional links: Is it the whole story?

A more interesting and analytically detailed approach – corresponding to what seems to me being a *"technological-functional"* conception of innovation clusters – has been proposed by Preissl and Solimene (2003). At a first glance, their definition (*ibid.*, p. 61) appears to be rather simple or even very general:

> A cluster is a set of interdependent organisations that contribute to the realisation of innovations in an economic sector or industry.

According to the authors, this definition is based on two key principles: (a) clusters represent a relevant phenomenon for the achievement of innovations; (b) thus, the analysis of clusters constitutes a useful tool if one wants to capture the main features characterising recent evolutions in innovation processes.

But things become much more interesting as the authors (*ibid.*, p. 61-62) go on to detail what seem to them to be the crucial features of innovation clusters involved in their definition. I summarise (and comment) on their key ideas in the following terms:

- Clusters *are not* conceived as geographical agglomerations. This does not mean, however, that there are no potential benefits possibly stemming from geographical proximity. Rather, what is emphasised here is the fact that for some innovation processes or projects it is the quality of the technological expertise of the partners that matters (rather than a mere geographical closeness). Hence, thanks to the development of efficient electronic communication tools, innovative firms can possibly benefit from the competences of rather geographically distant partners that are the most valuable for their very specific projects.

- The definition proposed by Preissl and Solimene adopts an explicit *sectoral perspective*, relating to the idea that each specific industry is characterised by complex and idiosyncratic processes of knowledge creation in technological fields that are relevant to this singular industry, and typically not to other industries.[13]
- The cluster is defined as an entity that contributes to *innovation outcomes at the collective or aggregate level* – and not only for some specific firms that belong to it. Thus, an innovation cluster must be interpreted as a *bundle of resources that constitutes a potential base (a "reservoir") for innovative projects and activities*. These resources can then be activated or mobilised by *certain* innovative firms belonging to the clusters, typically through cooperative arrangements. From this point of view, an innovation cluster within a given industry comprises *sub-sets of inter-related firms (and organisations) within specific innovation projects or processes*. Hence, these sub-sets of firms and organisations can assimilate to *innovation networks* that form and operate within the innovation cluster.[14]
- Finally, this definition comprises *all the actors* that contribute to the innovation dynamics within a cluster. This concerns universities and public or private research organisations, but also industrial firms or service providers whose activities are not necessarily R&D intensive.

As such, this approach appears well "calibrated" for the analysis of innovation clusters, and above all in high-tech or science-based sectors. Still, it rests on somehow *excessive technological and functional grounds*, as it surprisingly lacks a clear integration of some key dimensions highlighted by Nooteboom (2004) and Scott (2006) (see below) along with many others (including Porter, the OECD and the various general approaches of clusters; see above). Indeed, the social and institu-

---

[13] While clearly contrasting with approaches (such as the Porter one, or Scott, 2006 one; see below) that assume a rather industrial diversification of a cluster, Preissl and Solimene are in tune with a number of studies on innovation clusters/networks in high-tech sectors like biotechnology (see e.g. Owen-Smith *et al.*, 2002) or nanotechnology (see Robinson *et al.*, 2007) where clustering dynamics are essentially sector-driven. Yet, as these studies also show, co-location and geographical proximity are often crucial in the initial phases of cluster/network formation and development.

[14] This idea is very important: an innovation cluster is not a whole homogeneous, undifferentiated ensemble of actors, but rather a systemic and structured entity. It also points to the fact that clusters and networks of innovation are obviously overlapping phenomena, at least in the specific way Preissl and Solimene put it. I shall elaborate more on this in the next section and show that this overlap is of a more general essence and operates on various organisational and spatial inter-related scales.

tional dimensions of actors' interactions and embedding, and the role of *informal interactions* and of *interpersonal relationships*, are roughly underscored or even ignored. By the same token, the roles of various institutions that usually have an impact on the formation, the functioning and the development patterns of an innovation cluster are not clearly stressed in this approach. Such institutions are typically funding organisations (banks, venture capital companies, 'business angels', public funding agencies, etc.), law companies (especially those specialised in property rights issues), regulation entities (standardisation committees, ethical commissions, etc.), and so on. Yet these institutions are greatly differentiated across countries, across regions and across cities. Their impact on innovation dynamics is therefore likely to be quite variable from one location to another.[15] This stresses again the necessity to take explicitly into account the specific geographical locations of the actors involved in a clustering dynamic.

Exploration networks

A third approach, which I could qualify as a *"socio-cognitive" conception* of clusters and innovation clusters, is much more analytically grounded than the previous one, and offers a truly interesting angle for the specification of innovation clusters (and networks). This approach, due to Nooteboom (2004), combines three sets of "ingredients":

- *The notion of "embedding"*. Here, Nooteboom (2004, p. 3) distinguishes between "three kinds of embedding: *institutional embedding, structural embedding* and *relational embedding*. Institutional embedding concerns the impact of regulation and norms of conduct, taxes, subsidies, the legal system, infrastructure, schooling, research, labour market, etc. Structural embedding derives from the social network literature. Structural features of networks are size (…), density (…), centrality (…), and stability (…). Relational embedding appears in the social network literature in the notion of 'strength of ties', but is developed in more detail in the literature on alliances or inter-organisational relations (…). In other words, I propose that *an adequate understanding of clusters requires a combination of geography, social networks and inter-organisational relations*" (my italics here).

---

[15] See, among others: Castilla *et al.* (2000); Cooke (2001); Zeller (2001); Owen-Smith *et al.* (2002); Powell *et al.* (2002); Eto (2005); Feldman and Martin (2005); Autant-Bernard *et al.* (2006); Depret and Hamdouch (2006, 2007); Hamdouch and Moulaert (2006); Lynskey (2006); Scott (2006); Hamdouch and He (2009). Feldman and Martin (2005) even talk of a "jurisdictional advantage" of certain countries, regions or cities, which could explain their attractiveness for firm location and their positive role in initiating and sustaining spatial clustering dynamics of innovative industries.

- *The notion of "cognitive distance"*. This notion "(...) derives from a social constructivist view of knowledge, according to which perception, interpretation, understanding and value judgment entail mental constructions on the basis of mental categories developed in interaction with the physical and social world. As a result, *different people, and different organisations, which have developed their cognition along different paths of development and in different conditions, will perceive, interpret and evaluate the world differently*" (*ibid.*, emphasis added).

- *The distinction between "exploitation" and "exploration"*, as derived from James March's (1991) work. Exploitation corresponds to "the efficient employment of current assets and capabilities", while exploration means "the development of novel capabilities" (see Nooteboom, 2004, p. 5).

Although Nooteboom states that "(t)he economic success of regions and clusters requires success in both exploitation and exploration (...)", he recognises, straightforwardly, that this double condition "is a paradoxical task" as exploitation "often requires the maintenance of a stable organisational structure (...) in unambiguous terms of clear standards, in a narrow organisational focus, while exploration requires the reverse: the loosening of structure for novel reconfigurations, shifting meanings and deviation from existing standards, in a wide focus" (*ibid.*).

Nooteboom then goes on to build a detailed analytical approach, describing the conditions and features of a "cycle of discovery" process through which the exploitation logic and the exploration logic can combine in time and space, depending on "how exploration may be based on experience in exploitation, and how to ensure that the outcome of exploration will be exploitable" (*ibid.*).

I do not enter here into the discussion about this idea of "cycle of discovery". Suffice to say it is quite questionable, as it seems to me that:

- Alternatives to this model exist, e.g. *multi-scaled clusters and networks* where, at the same time, the logic of exploitation may prevail on some spatial scale, whereas the logic of exploration may entail the commitment of some actors in open-ended (exploratory) and innovation-oriented relationships, with partners delineated by different geographical locations (see below)[16];

- It is not at all certain that the two logics should *necessarily* be combined and articulated in a timely and cyclical way: the exploitation logic may well be continued and sustained for a very long period of time through incremental changes, and then maybe change radically when

---

[16] Nooteboom (2004, p. 5) himself recognises that "clusters, to the extent that they entail stable relations, need outside ties for ongoing innovation".

new structural conditions arise.[17] By the same token, the exploration logic may be continually renewed through "edge investments" towards sustaining scientific and applied knowledge, pioneer development and innovation, while exploitation activities may be 'off-shored' to a certain extent to other "partner" locations. This is exactly what has been depicted by Saxenian (1999, 2006) for the Silicon Valley (SV) in recent years, where the SV, California, remains at the front-edge of ICT, while at the same time being strongly related to "New Silicon Valleys" in China, Taiwan and India for manufacturing operations (but also, and increasingly, design and development). See also Bresnahan *et al.*, 2004; Poon *et al.*, 2006; and Hamdouch and He, 2009.

Following these remarks, it seems to me that the exploitation *vs.* exploration logics could be a fruitful analytical tool for characterising innovation clusters and networks where the dominant logic should be that of exploration, while industrial clusters and networks correspond essentially to an exploitation principle. Admittedly, this simplified assimilation may be criticised. Yet, Nooteboom himself distinguishes between "networks for exploration" and "networks for exploitation". And when looking at the way Nooteboom develops his analytical framework and specifies the main features for each of the two categories of networks (see table 1), the differentiation between the two logics of networking (or clustering) is so clear that the simplification operated here appears rather acceptable.

---

[17] See, for example, the remarkable essay by Edward Glaeser (2005) showing how Boston was only able to "reinvent" itself three times in its long history between 1630 and today: in the early 19th century; in the late 19th century; and in the late 20th century. According to Glaeser, the "secret" resides in *human capital* and its capacity to adapt to new, radical circumstances: "(…) in all of its periods of reinvention, *Boston's human capital has been critical*. Skills connected with sailing ships enabled the city to reinvent itself as a global maritime centre in the early 19th century. Yankee technology and Irish labour fuelled industrialisation. And, today more than ever, Boston's skills provide the impetus for economic success in technology, professional services and higher education. Boston's experience certainly suggests that *human capital is most valuable to a city during transition periods when skills create flexibility and the ability to reorient towards a new urban focus*" (see Glaeser, 2005, p. 122; my emphasis). For a more general, enlightening discussion on economic regional evolution and the possibility to escape path dependency and lock-in through a "regional path creation", see Martin and Sunley (2006).

Table 1: Key distinctive features of 'Networks for exploration'
vs. 'Networks for exploitation'

Network features:	'Exploration' Logic	'Exploitation' Logic
Network structure:		
Density	High	Low
Stability	Low	High
Centrality	High	Often high
Strength of ties:		
Scope	Wide	Narrow
Investment in mutual understanding	High	Low
Duration	Limited*	Often long
Frequency of interaction	High	Low
Trust/openness	High	Generally low

* "Especially when technology is systemic".
Source: Adapted from Nooteboom (2004), Table 2, p. 24.

Indeed, in terms of *network structure parameters*, "networks for exploration" show a high density of connections, a low centrality of actors and a low stability of the network. *"Strength of ties" parameters* are also clearly discriminating. In particular, one must notice that networks for exploration entail a wide scope of open ties based on a priori trustworthiness. The "values" attributed to the other parameters are more questionable. For example, it is not certain that the "frequency of interaction" should be high when exploration is at stake but low when the network has an exploitation configuration. It may well be exactly the reverse: frequency of interaction with the same actors when exploring for new knowledge (if, for example, some "knowledge providers" appear to be less promising than expected, or if they "defect"), whereas the frequency of interactions may well prove high if exploitation entails recurrent transactions with the same partners. The same assessment holds for the "duration" of ties: they can obviously be high if collaborating actors are for example working together on basic research in new technological areas or in new scientific fields, which usually demand time and perseverance (like in biotechnology and in nanotechnology). As a matter of fact, some parameters are probably more sensitive to the exact nature of the activities at stake and to the specific configuration of interaction (precisely according to the types of actors' embedding and to the prevailing "cognitive distance" between the interacting actors) than to the mere broad nature of the network.

In any case, the approach proposed by Nooteboom is very interesting and useful as it opens up a genuine route for the characterisation of innovation clusters and networks.

Creative fields

Finally, a fourth interesting and truly useful approach, which I qualify here as a *socio-institutional-evolutionary conception* of innovation clusters, is that of "creative fields", proposed by Scott (2006). To begin with, the author provides (p. 3) three differentiated, but complementary definitions of what he means by "creative field":

Definition 1: "The notion of a field of creative forces can be used to describe any system of social relationships that shapes or influences human ingenuity and inventiveness and that is the site of concomitant innovations. An adjunct idea is that this field will rarely be frozen in time and space, but that the very innovations it triggers will also act back upon it, thereby causing changes in its organisation and operational logic".

Definition 2: "A more specific identification of the creative field (…) is that is comprises all those instances of economic effort and organisation whose *spatial and locational* attributes, at whatever scale they may occur, promote development – and growth-inducing change".

Definition 3: "To narrow the focus yet more, the creative field (…) is represented by sets of industrial activities and related social phenomena forming geographically-differentiated webs of interaction giving rise to diverse entrepreneurial and innovative outcomes. An intrinsic element of this definition is that both the field on the one side and its effects on entrepreneurship and innovation on the other are reflexively intertwined with one another".

Then Scott recognises that this concept overlaps partly with notions such as "innovative milieu", "learning region", "regional innovation system", but declares that his main focus is on "agglomerated economic structures such as industrial districts, regional productive complexes, and urban economic systems. Phenomena like this, he continues, are almost always characterised by dense networks of firms and multifaceted local labour markets, and (…) these are the settings within which entrepreneurial and innovative energies flourish *par excellence* in the new economy (…)" (Scott, 2006, p. 3).[18]

Finally, for Scott, a distinctive feature of his concept is that "the idea of the creative field goes far beyond specific applications in the domain of the economy". He continues: "Developments in the spheres of culture

---

[18] In his mind, this focus on agglomeration phenomena does not mean that "wider spatial frameworks of industrial activity and their implications for entrepreneurship and innovation, including, in the limit, the global" (*ibid.*, p. 3) are not important, as he claims in several parts of his article (for example in p. 7). But this recognition seems to me rather superficial, as Scott is clearly focusing on the socio-institutional creative dynamics as they are territorialised within specific geographical locations, notably cities and regions for him.

and science, too, can in part be understood in terms of arguments that are essentially variations of the notion of the creative field" (*ibid.*).

All in all, one can only strongly agree with most or nearly all of Scott's statements cited above.[19] In particular, the notion of "creative field" seems to me to be very fruitful as it potentially embraces the key idea that any domain of human activity (including the social, artistic and aesthetic fields) is susceptible to novelty, inventiveness and innovation within and across various spatial scales – as has already been emphasised by different authors (see e.g. Moulaert, Sékia, 2003; Moulaert *et al.*, 2005).

Yet, the various definitions provided by Scott deserve some analysis and discussion. First of all, each of the three definitions offers a distinctive angle of analysis or a specific emphasis, though all valuable. The first definition highlights, among other traits, the idea that the creative field "is the site of *concomitant innovations*", which stresses the *systemic nature of innovativeness within the 'field'*, and then rightly departs from a mere firm-centred approach of innovation in the vein of most of the literature promoting the idealised figure of the individual entrepreneur or innovator. It also emphasises the *dynamic intrinsic nature of the innovative field* as it insists on its spatial and temporal coordinates and on the *feedbacks* that innovation outcomes are likely to entail for the field itself, in terms of structure and organisation. Here again, this approach throws discredit on frequent static and poor innovation cluster conceptions which are made up of simplistic "success stories".

The second definition insists on the *variety of actors involved in creative activities*, which then severely disqualifies narrow conceptions of the "innovative engine" as being solely fuelled by (mostly) private companies, such as the one discussed in the beginning of this section.

Finally, the third definition points out the *spatially, institutionally and socially embedding characteristics of the actors involved* (see also above the approach developed by Nooteboom) and insists on the *diverse but intrinsically related or connected* nature of the activities concerned (Scott talks of "sets of industrial activities"). This approach sheds a crude light on the vacuity of all marketed (and usually "moneyed"; see Martin, Sunley, 2003) "friendly" advice that there may be "recipes" for initiating and/or promoting innovative or competitive cluster policies on the (false) grounds of presumably previous successful cases or experiences (on this, see also Bresnahan *et al.*, 2004).

---

[19] Yet, of course, I do not really adhere to all the ideas developed in Scott's paper. In particular, the evolutionary process he describes for network formation and development seem to me rather mechanical and simplistic.

Another positive assessment of Scott's approach is that *it truly focuses on innovation dynamics* as it takes place within *specific fields and spaces*, whatever the wordings and spatial spaces that may be envisaged (fields, networks, clusters, districts, cities, metropolitan areas, regions or even countries or the global arena). In this sense, the approach proposed by Scott clearly distinguishes itself with 'a-spatial' and non-specific oriented conceptions of the clustering and networking conceptions (see above).

If I were to express one, yet important regret regarding Scott's approach, it would be this: while the author alludes to possible multiple spatial scales and to "multiscalar interdependencies" (see Scott, 2006, p. 17) as key features of creative fields, his analysis rests on quite allusive settlements. As we shall see in the next section, these "multi-scaled" organisational and spatial attributes of innovation clusters and networks could be rather general features of innovative (creative) inter-acting actors, and not only contextual, occasional or specific ingredients, especially when genuine innovative activities are at stake.

To conclude, it seems to me that while the various definitions and approaches discussed in this section (and also in the previous one) provide quite valuable insights on what may be the key features of clusters and especially of innovation clusters, the whole picture remains rather dispersed and thus there is a need for some kind of synthesising effort. Besides, several crucial issues regarding the analytical grounds of the notion and its empirical investigation are still pending, and therefore deserve some clarification.

4. Crucial Pending Issues and Suggested Pathways for Further Research

The idea I defend here is that innovation clusters and networks are not "conceptual illusions" or "panacea" (see Martin, Sunley, 2003) as they truly display concrete, detectable features and dynamics. Indeed, I think that these notions could genuinely prove to be helpful (and potentially relevant) for our comprehension of the spatial and organisational dynamics underlying innovation processes, but at the (affordable) price of a serious effort towards a better conceptual and methodological grounding of the analysis.

Of course, given the limited space allowed here, it is impossible to give an extensive account of all the facets that this analytical improvement entails. Rather, I shall focus only on some selected, yet key issues that one can derive from the work examined in the previous sections and from other important pieces of the literature.

I will therefore organise the discussion under six main headings:

1. Fixing the notion of innovation cluster in a synthetic way
2. Outlining the debate about the originating dynamics and the initiating/impeding "forces" that drive innovation cluster formation and sustainability
3. Clarifying key issues related to the spatial scaling of innovation clusters and networks
4. Analysing the nature and the strength of the ties among the actors
5. Identifying the structure configurations of innovation clusters/networks
6. Deriving and outlining the hypothesis of "multi-scaled networks" as potentially being the foundational principle of innovation clusters.

Fixing the notion

Building on the previous discussion of the varied definitions examined in sections 2 and 3, it seems to me possible and useful to outline a synthetic definition that captures the key features of innovation clusters (more generally, of innovation networks):

> An innovation cluster comprises an ensemble of various organisations and institutions (a) that are defined by respective geographic localisations occurring at variable spatial scales and within specific institutional environments, (b) that interact formally and/or informally through inter-organisational and/or interpersonal relationships and networks that are regular or more occasional, (c) and that contribute collectively to the achievement of all kinds of innovations within a given industry or domain of activity, i.e. within a domain defined by specific fields of knowledge, competences and technologies.

This definition is rather flexible, as it means that only the three sets of conditions are being simultaneously verified. It could then correspond to a large variety of spatial, institutional and organisational concrete configurations of innovative dynamics. Moreover, it does not prejudge the spatial topography of the interacting actors, nor does it impose any constraint on the way they may interact (cooperate or compete). Finally, it does not stipulate any specific paths of cluster emergence, structuring, evolution and performance.

Indeed, as we shall now see, the way innovation clusters (and networks) are susceptible to emerge, become structured and potentially evolve is rather complex, varied and quite uncertain.

Neither miracles nor chimera

One of the most vigorous debates in the literature turns around the originating dynamics and the initiating/impeding "forces" that drive innovation cluster formation and sustainability. For the most part, the views expressed turn around the opposition between "top-down" and "bottom-up" processes (see e.g. Bresnahan *et al.*, 2004; Fromhold, Fromhold-Eisebith, 2005), or in even more crude terms, between "spontaneous clusters" and "political clusters" (see Chiaroni, Chiesa, 2006).

What I want to stress here is that these binary views are misleading. Indeed, innovation clusters are neither "chimera" – in the sense of a purely artificially designed creation by way of a *deus ex machina* concretising some strong strategic or political will – nor "miracles" stemming from a deterministic chaos, or alternatively yielded by some mysterious force or even by pure chance. Indeed, the very processes underlying clustering and networking phenomena within and across innovative fields often operate in *hybrid forms that combine an array of various mechanisms*. These mechanisms range, in a continuum, from rather decentralised and somehow self-organising dynamics to more collective and institutionalised actions and policies. They comprise, among various other possibilities:

- *Science and technology driven logics*, like in biotech clusters (see Owen-Smith *et al.*, 2002; Powell *et al.*, 2002), or *technology and manufacturing driven logics* like in ICT (see Saxenian, 1994; Bresnahan *et al.*, 2004);

- *"Genealogical" chains of spin-offs*, like in the historical development of the Silicon Valley (see Castilla *et al.*, 2000);

- *"Historical" accidents or path-dependent processes* (for an in-depth presentation and discussion as well as many examples of these processes, see Martin and Sunley, 2006[20]);

- *The possible catalytic role of "returnees" and of "Argonauts"*, as in the case of the "New Silicon Valleys" in Asia and elsewhere (see Saxenian, 1999, 2006);

- *The specific initiating role of an "institutional entrepreneur"*, like in the case of the development of a nanotechnology cluster in Grenoble (see Robinson *et al.*, 2007);

- And, of course, yet at different degrees of political or institutional "voluntarism", the *very large array of local, regional or national actions, policies and initiatives* (for accounts of these initiatives and

---

[20] Other examples are the case of Uppsala in Sweden (see Waluszewski, 2004) or again the case of Boston (see Glaeser, 2005).

policies, see for example Sölvell *et al.*, 2003; Ketels, Sölvell, 2006; OECD, 2007).

I will not go any further on this discussion, as the topic is truly endless. Yet, one additional remark seems to me important: while on the one hand – as now widely agreed in the literature – no one policy-maker can simply decide "by fiat" to create an innovation cluster almost from scratch (or at the risk of later experiencing a likely and painful failure[21]), on the other hand, one cannot hastily conclude that every voluntarism or policy measures towards helping the start or the development of an innovation clustering process should be banished (see, among others: Luukkunainen, 2001; Bresnahan *et al.*, 2004; Fromhold, Fromhold-Eisebith, 2005; Scott, 2006). Therefore, the central issue should be about which relevant incentive and coordination mechanisms could be designed and implemented by the various public and institutional actors interested in the development of an innovation cluster[22] – as long as other important conditions are met, such as a critical mass of competences, strong inter-organisational complementarities, a diversity of actors, an entrepreneurial culture, and so on. (For extended accounts of these conditions and various sectoral illustrations of their impact see e.g.: Saxenian, 1994, 2006; Audretsch, 2001; Fromhold and Fromhold-Eisebith, 2005; Gordon and MacCann, 2005; Martin and Sunley, 2006; Scott, 2006; and Robinson *et al.*, 2007).

Spatial scales

The brief discussion above shows that clustering and networking processes are by no means simple, as they follow no clear "fairways": they are likely to be driven *both* by "invisible hands" and by "visible hands"; and they may develop as a "legacy of the past" or emerge as an attempt towards exploring a new and promising "creative field", or combine both paths by following some transitional dynamics.

---

[21] An interesting illustrative case, analysed by Orsenigo (2001), is the failure of the development of a biotech cluster in Lombardy. The failure of the Multimedia Corridor Project in Malaysia (see Bunnell, 2002) is another, yet more striking example.

[22] In this respect, the original and successful case of the BioReggio contest, launched in the 1990s by the German Federal Government in order to encourage the formation/development of biotech clusters, is quite interesting in that it clearly illustrates how adapted incentives and balanced coordination schemes between and across the federal/regional levels can yield positive outcomes (see Dohse, 2000; Zeller, 2001). By contrast, the policies engaged in Japan and France for the creation of clusters in high-tech sectors display rather mitigated and uncertain results, probably because they have been mainly designed at the central level, yet in different forms (see respectively Eto, 2005; and Gaffard, 2005).

I shall now discuss the way these processes are also likely to display different spatial/geographical scaling and configuration patterns as well as various 'tying' and relational paths of actors.

Although, admittedly, the localisation of activities within a geo-graphically-bounded space (a city, a metropolitan area or a region) is neither a sufficient ground nor a systematic condition for the existence of an innovative cluster, one should nevertheless recognise the fact that the firms and other actors involved in interacting in innovation proc-esses or common projects are, for their part, necessarily located some-where. It is then the *spatial configuration* of the various individual localisations of the interacting actors within innovation activities that matters, rather than their mere spatial co-location or their geographical proximity. Besides, if the geographical proximity of actors can certainly play a key role in many innovation processes, in most situations it must also be combined with other forms of proximity if it is to generate location spillovers and agglomeration-positive externalities. Therefore, as many works have repeatedly shown, organisational, cognitive and institutional dimensions of proximity are usually at least as (and some-times even more) crucial for innovation networking and collaboration as geographical proximity (see among others: Rallet, Torre, 1995, 2001, 2007; Audretsch, Feldman, 1996; Feldman, 1999, 2003; Depret, Hamdouch, 2006, 2007).

Moreover, the geographic proximity alone (though more or less pos-sibly supplemented with other dimensions) of truly innovative firms and "knowledge organisations" (such as universities and research centres) by no means indicates the very existence of an innovation cluster. Indeed, as clearly demonstrated in a detailed comparative study of eight high-tech regional agglomerations in the United-States, the impact of these organisations on the development of innovating firms depends crucially on the "alignment" between the research competence fields of the universities and the industrial specialisations of the firms, even if they are located in the same area (see Paytas *et al.*, 2004).[23] Equally impor-tant is the availability of efficient systems for the coordination and the cooperation of the various "actors of innovation" and the reach of balanced compromises between centralised and decentralised levels of decision-making processes (*ibid.*). Once again, this analysis shows that

---

[23] In line with this idea, see also the concept of "regional industrial identity" proposed by Romanelli and Khessina (2005). This approach highlights the importance of the way the internal or external actors of the cluster build on specific representations of the capacity of a region to promote the development of certain activities, and on the way these representations can influence the actors' decisions about the nature and the localisation of their investments.

the existence (or the sustainability) of an innovation cluster requires both an institutional and organisational proximity and what I call a "cognitive impedance" of the actors (see also Nooteboom, 2004; Depret, Hamdouch, 2006, 2007).

By contrast, more or less geographically distant actors can engage in "strong links" and manage sustained interactions within a productive and/or innovation process that requires continued collaborations or exchanges with close-complementary partners in terms of knowledge, competences or expertise (Ernst, 2006; see also Preissl and Solimene, 2003, as already pointed out in section 3).

By the same token, as stressed by Bresnahan *et al.* (2004), if the local availability of a university and of high-skilled human capital (both technical and managerial) may truly help with the emergence and the development of an innovation cluster, it is neither a sufficient nor a compulsory condition as "the supply of skills can come from outside the region" (p. 847). This may be the case when "there can be different sources of skills in different regions" (*ibid.*) within a country, or even when regional innovative firms can attract high-skilled labour from abroad (as happened in the Silicon Valley in the 1980s and 1990s). Finally, as the authors show, most of the "nascent clusters" ("New Silicon Valleys") in China, Taiwan and India have greatly benefited from the technical and managerial skills of US-educated returnees.

In sum, beyond mere geographical proximity, it is the actors' ability to engage in valuable relationships with specific partners that matters, whatever the distance there may be between them. Yet, as I have already stressed above, the geographical origin and localisation of each of the interacting actors is also crucial in one's decision as an actor to engage or not in a relationship with a certain potential partner. Hence, while the spatial distance (or closeness) between actors is not *per se* as crucial in all circumstances, the *topography* of the actors according to their respective geographical localisations should constitute a key dimension of our understanding of how an innovative cluster (or network) with specific dynamics of emergence, structuring and evolution operate, and on how the prevailing governance modalities of the cluster emerged and might have fostered (or, conversely, impeded) its very development and achievements.

It is precisely here that the discussion about the nature and the strength of the ties between the actors should shed some light on how various forms of "proximities" among the actors can be more or less decisive.

The varied nature and strength of ties

Let me briefly synthesise some of the key issues at stake. First of all, besides *formal inter-organisational links* between interacting actors within and/or across innovation clusters and networks – which may prove crucial when appropriation and patenting issues are at stake (see above, section 2) – many network analysts (economists, but for the most part sociologists) have stressed the decisive role of both *informal links* (either at inter-organisational or inter-individual level) and *inter-personal ties* (see among others: Granovetter, 1973; Saxenian, 1994; Walker *et al.*, 1997; Castilla *et al.*, 2000; McKelvey *et al.*, 2003; Dahl, Pedersen, 2004; Owen-Smith, Powell, 2004; Casper, Murray, 2005; Cassi, Zirulia, 2005; Goyal, 2005; Casper, 2007). These links or ties play a doubly decisive role: (a) they create what I call the "cement" (in terms of trust and mutual understanding; see also above the discussions in sections 2 and 3) that is required for a flexible and adaptive coordination of the actors within an innovation cluster or within the various networks it generally comprises; (b) these ties are the very foundations of innovation clusters and networks as "opportunity creators" (see Preissl, Solimene, 2003; Dahl, Pedersen, 2004; Paytas *et al.*, 2004; Cassi, Zirulia, 2005).

This discussion points immediately to another lively debate among the sociologists of networks: in order to have the best conditions for novelty and innovation, what should be the "strength" of the ties between the actors? Briefly speaking, three main arguments have been proposed. I outline them for the specific context of innovation networks:

(a) *The "social capital" or the "network closure" argument* (see Coleman, 1988, 1990). The idea is that the social capital of an actor (for example a start-up) builds on the high connectivity and cohesion of the network (which facilitates trust and the exchange of knowledge, and therefore collective learning). Hence, the actors who enjoy the highest social capital are also the most likely to create new ties and potentially benefit from a new knowledge or a new source of economic advantage (or, more broadly speaking, in sociological and political terms, of an enhanced "power" position) through new partnerships.

(b) *The "structural holes" argument* (see Burt, 1992, 2001, 2005). The idea is that the actors that are the most structurally constrained (which have dense and "closed" networks, with only a few or indirect ties) are also the less likely to attract new partners – either because they display lower returns due to their constrained strong relationships with eventually powerful actors or because they are seen as engaged in routine rather than innovative activities. In any case,

Burt's argument, on general grounds of network analysis, is that actors who are "brokers" between rather loosely connected actors (here lay the "structural holes") enjoy a powerful position. In an innovation context, the idea is that diversified and "open networks" stimulate the creativity of the actors as they give access to more varied information while at the same time they are less constraining for their members, which is also favourable for innovation.

(c) *The "strength of weak ties" argument* (see Granovetter, 1973). While compatible with Burt's view, the argument here is somehow different because the "weak ties" in question relate essentially to informal or occasional relationships. Therefore, as I interpret it in the context of an innovation network, the idea is that weak ties may be crucial when uncertainty is at stake, as it could reveal new unforeseen opportunities, new knowledge and cutting-edge innovation fields or, more simply, new and potentially fruitful relationships.

The first *vs.* the two latter arguments are apparently opposite. Yet Burt (2001) offers a somewhat "operational" compromise between his view and Coleman's: closure and social capital are then meant to be important for network consolidation and functioning, and for "absorbing" eventual opportunities yielded by structural holes, while the latter could build further potential, valuable new ties (as sources for new knowledge insights or innovation possibilities).[24] This reminds us of the "exploitation-exploration" articulated pathway logic proposed by Nooteboom (2004), yet in very different terms. Burt's approach is related mainly to inter-personal networking analysis whereas Nooteboom's one is mainly dealing with broader socio-economic inter-organisational interactions – notwithstanding the fact that sociological analysis of networks preceded by more than a decade the interest of economists or management specialists in these topics. With regard to Granovetter's "strength of weak ties" argument, it seems to me that it may potentially be the most stimulating notion for the analysis of innovation clustering and networking dynamics in such science-based fields like biotechnology or nanotechnology in which the future paths for technological achievements are at best "promising" (for the first one) or embryonic (for the latter field).

---

[24] Indeed, no conclusive assessments have been provided on general grounds in favour or, conversely, in negative support of these opposing theses. In the specific case of networks in biotechnology, the same authors in two different papers arrive at contradictory conclusions: Shan, Walker and Kogut (1994) find rather supportive results in favour of the structural holes argument, while Walker, Kogut and Shan (1997) find results that support the social capital and network closure argument...

Network structure configurations

The controversy surrounding the openness *vs.* closeness of networks, and their respective merits regarding innovation, leads us onto another inquiry topic emanating from a different and yet surprisingly "distant" scientific field: statistical physics. Building on the sociological work on social networks that developed in the Granovetter and White tradition[25], scientists like Watts, Strogatz, Girvan, Newman and several others (see especially Watts, Strogatz, 1998; Albert, Barabasi, 2002) have built what Watts (2004) labelled as a "New Science of Networks"(NSN). This NSN consists of developing powerful algorithms in order to detect *topological regularities within digital as well as real social networks*. This is where this approach connects to the previous discussion, as four main categories of networks are distinguished. The first two categories relate to the traditional polarised hypotheses of "Random Networks" *vs.* "Regular networks", whereas the two latter are genuinely new (intermediary) configurations highlighted by the NSN, drawing from the analysis of "real networks":

- *Random Networks*: The distribution of the links between the nodes (actors) and the path lengths connecting them are completely random (which corresponds somehow to the image of the "pure competitive market" in economics, or to that of a generalised "anarchy" in organisation and political science);

- *Regular Networks*: All the nodes (actors, organisations, institutions) are connected with neighbour or more distant nodes in a similar way (all nodes have the same "degree", i.e. the same number of connections, and the same path length, i.e. the same average distance with other nodes) with certainty (absence of any randomness), at the image of a totally integrated community or team amongst "equals";

- *Small World Networks* (SWN): Most of the nodes are interconnected through short paths with a high coefficient of connectivity (transitivity). This is a dense, rather homogeneous network, yet some nodes may have fewer/more and/or closer/longer connections. This means that SWN allow both for a (small) dose of randomness for the connections and some degree of topological differentiation amongst the actors;

- *Scale Free Networks* (SFN): As for SWN, SFN emphasise the importance of short path lengths and the weight of the transitivity coefficient between nodes (actors) as displayed by most real networks.

---

[25] See Granovetter (1973, 1979, 1985, 1992); White (1981a, 2001); White and Harary (2001). For useful studies of this literature, cf. Swedberg (1994), Flap (2002), and Borgatti and Foster (2003).

But here the role of these parameters derives from hypothetical dynamics of entries/exits of nodes (actors) within/from the network (evolutionary properties of a graph according to its "demography"); SFN are usually "heterogeneous".

Clearly, the first form of networks is an extreme, rather hypothetical situation as it has little to do with the social world. Regular networks are more likely to illustrate some specific, though not so spread out real social situations. They reflect, in my opinion, an extreme, specific case of "cohesive networks" (according to Coleman's terms).

Our interest here is rather with the two other networking structures highlighted by Watts and Strogatz (1998). It seems to me then that "small world networks" (SWN) are somehow analogues to Coleman's "cohesive networks", while "scale free networks" (SFN) are obviously echoing Burt's idea of "structural holes". As to Granovetter's idea of "strength of weak ties", I think it lies in between the two network configurations; indeed, it does not disqualify strong ties (as those in SWN) while stressing at the same time the key role of more remote and/or occasional/random ties (as those in SFN).

This debate around the openness/closeness of innovation networks is not merely a technical or theoretical issue. It is at the very heart of the understanding of how the "morphogenesis" (see Cohendet *et al.*, 2003) of networks and clusters – their emergence, structuring and evolution processes – may impact on innovation dynamics within a given industry. The pending question is then how various forms of ties and network structures combine with specific spatial/geographical scales to form particular networking and clustering configurations within and across given creative fields.

"Multi-scaled networks": The key foundational components of innovation clustering dynamics?

The notion of *multi-scaled networks* I propose here builds on the previous discussions in the chapter. It is aimed at designing an alternative way of conceiving innovation clusters that attempts to go beyond the various splits and distinctions regarding both the spatial/geographical scaling of an innovation cluster and the nature and strength of ties between the interacting actors it comprises. But I do not proceed from scratch. Rather, my idea is to put together the various insights gathered into an enlarged analytical framework.

The point I want to emphasise is that multi-scaled networks may well constitute a crucial key for our understanding of how innovation clusters come to form, and how they may structure and evolve. At the moment this approach is only an exploratory research hypothesis within my ongoing work on innovation clusters and networks, so I will only briefly outline it here.

My idea is that *innovation clusters build on the development of variously scaled and structured networks that dynamically combine, superpose or overlap in various configurations.* Put in other words: *innovation clusters are meant as the result of the dynamic articulation of various "circles" and time-space scales of relationships between the actors.*

Either formal or informal, some of these relationships could be rather dense, close and recurrent, therefore producing "strong ties", "local cohesiveness" and "social capital" (as in Coleman's analysis) in a "small-world network" (see Watts, Strogatz, 1998). This configuration also fits with what Nooteboom (2004) calls a "network for exploitation" of already identified and concretely valorised technological or market opportunities. Yet, the exploitation logic can go along with a continuous stream of incremental innovations (either technological, organisational, commercial, institutional or social) stemming from collective learning processes in the close and regular interactions of actors.

By contrast, other relationships could be more occasional, smoother and more distant through "weak ties" that can potentially turn to be useful or even decisive (see Granovetter, 1973) in providing advantages (in terms of new knowledge flows, new technologies or new market opportunities). This 'tying logic' is much in tune with the idea of "Networks for exploration", as highlighted by Nooteboom (2004).

Yet other different relationships can emerge from unforeseen events or build on rather random processes, following therefore a somehow "scale-free" networking dynamics (see Watts, Strogatz, 1998; Albert, Barabasi, 2002). These relationships could then only concern certain "privileged" actors (benefiting of "structural holes" or brokerage positions; see Burt, 1992, 2000). The latter category could correspond to several different paths. First, the scale-free networking logics may simply and generally fit in with the idea of genuine discovery, chance, "serendipity" or "nice surprise" (for example in a neo-Austrian perspective of entrepreneurship; see Kirzner, 1997) in meeting some new valuable contact person or a new technological or market opportunity. The second possible path is related to "genealogical effects" and "serial entrepreneurs", through chains of spin-offs from existing firms (see Saxenian, 1994; Castilla *et al.*, 2000; Feldman, 2003; Feldman, Romanelli, 2006). A final possibility is what Castilla *et al.* (2000, p. 220-221) call "Networks of Access and Opportunity" which are built through chains of direct and indirect acquaintances rather than on close relationships (as illustrated by the Silicon Valley's very "fluid" labour market).

Of course, all of these possible networking paths can occur on any spatial scale. Indeed, the openness of some innovation networks and clusters towards interregional, national or international relationships clearly illustrates this idea of multiple "circles" of relationships (see among others: OECD, 1999; Owen-Smith *et al.*, 2002; Bresnahan *et al.*, 2004; Gay, Dousset, 2005; Ernst, 2006; Roijakkers, Hagedoorn, 2006; Saxenian, 2006). This openness may be necessary not only for the access by the actors to some key resources, knowledge or competences (see Bathelt *et al.*, 2004), but also because it may be useful both for benchmarking purposes and for the detection of new possible "futures".

The idea of multi-scaled networks still requires due formalisation on stronger analytical grounds. Yet, the hypothesis that the actors could potentially connect to each other and interact in rather different but complementary ways in innovative or creative fields appears rather plausible, as echoed by a number of works examined in the chapter. Therefore, the real variety of possible networking forms – through concomitant but differentiated relationships – may truly be a fruitful pathway for conceptualising clustering dynamics.

As a first, tentative integration exercise, table 2 summarises the key networking configurations suggested in this section and outlines, more broadly, a typology of the networking dynamics that could potentially be used as an analytical basis for understanding the emergence and structuring patterns of innovation clusters on various spatial and relational scales.

Table 2: Innovation Networking Configurations for Clustering Dynamics: A Tentative Analytical Typology

Features / Network Configurations	Rationales for Networking	Spatial scales	Types of relationships	Forms of proximity	Examples
Networked Firm: *"The Godfather and its Lieutenants"*	Dispatching of the R&D process of a large firm among its own subsidiaries and/or subcontractors/partners	Usually local or regional; Increasingly multinational and/or global	"Hub and Spokes"; hierarchical relationships; mainly formal links	Organisational, geographic, cognitive	IBM in Albany (New York), Airbus in Toulouse, Boeing in Seattle, etc.
Loose networks: *"Potential mutual attraction"*	Exploration behavior; tiny R&D projects that could (potentially) become concrete and successful, or mere random new contacts	Any scale	"Weak ties"; promoting and valorising informal ties; exploiting "structural holes"	"Occasional" or "Transitory"	Conferences, symposia, fairs, etc. (see Rallet, Torre, 2007)
Research Consortium: *"Temporary Concubinage"*	Strong project "constrained" complementarities and uncertainties; pooling resources, and possible losses /potential returns	Various scales, increasingly continental or global	Strong, but flexible ties	Cognitive, technological, "strategic"	The SNP consortium in biotechnology (see Hamdouch, Depret, 2001)
Pool of R&D Subcontractors/CRO/ University specialised labs for Large firms: *"Close Families"*	Tapping in a common pool of competences; reducing costs	City, metropolitan area or region	"Regional alignment"; formal, but also informal/ weak relationships; close interactions	Organisational, geographic, institutional	Côte d'Azur Region, many clusters in the US, in Germany, in India, etc. (Zeller, 2001; Paytas *et al.*, 2004)
Innovative Milieu/District: *"Many Cousins and Friends"*	"It's in the air"; specialisation and complementarities in addressing common client's needs	Local or regional	Informal relationships; emulation, imitation and collaboration; formalised collaboration	Cognitive/cultural, geographic, organisational	Italian Districts in Emilia-Romana (see Beccatini, 1990), Watch Industry in the Jurassic Arc (see Berset, Crevoisier, 2006); etc.

Technological Platform: *"The Common House"*	Availability of costly infrastructure; sharing costs; synergetic projects (transversal technologies)	Local, metropolitan area; or regional area; sometimes transnational	Contractual ties; crucial role of an "Institutional entre-preneur" in initiating and coordinating the platform	Cognitive, technological, institutional, "strategic"	Nanotechnology in Grenoble (see Robinson *et al.*, 2007)
Scientific/Technological Park, "Technopole": *"The Elite Club"*	Gathering together basic and applied research and Higher-Education; facilitating knowl-edge transfers and innovation ("Translational research")	Local, metropoli-tan or regional areas	Contractual and non contractual ties	Cognitive, institutional, "political"	Many examples: Sophia-Antipolis, (see Longhi, 1999), Shanghaï (see Hamdouch, He, 2009)
Network of Unexpected Entrepreneurs: *"Orphans Solidarity"/ Emergent "Creative Field"*	The lack or the off-shoring of R&D large labs; exploiting former social links; valorising entrepreneurship capabilities	Variable, but mainly local, or metropolitan/ regional areas	Informal, then mixed with more formal relationships	Relational, geo-graphic, "Existential", cognitive/cultural, institutional	Upsalla in Biopharmaceu-ticals (see Waluszwski, 2004)
"Genealogical Networks" or "Serial Entrepreneurs": *"Fathers and Sons"*	Valorising creative capabili-ties and potential new ideas from/and with the "mothering enterprise"; new business opportunities related to those of the "nurturing" company	Mainly local, metropolitan or regional scales, but remote connections are often also of crucial importance	Formal/informal	Relational, geographic, "strategic", cognitive/cultural, institutional	Silicon Valley, San Francisco Bay Area, Biotechnology in Boston, the Puget Sound region (see Castilla *et al.*, 2000; Owen-Smith *et al.*, 2002, etc.)
Parent/Connected Networks: *"Twins, Clones and Argonauts"*	Exploiting and developing R&D and (for the most) expertise and production complementarities through "ubiquitous" entrepreneurs	"Glocal", "multilocated"	Formal/informal	Cognitive, cultural, "strategic"	"New Silicon Valleys" in China, India, Taiwan, etc. (see Bresnahan *et al.*, 2004; Saxenian, 2006)
Global Innovation Networks: *"Polyglot Families"*	Strong complementarities in R&D and gathering of global R&D and production dispersed capabilities, competences and skills	Continental/global, "multi-scaled"	"Network of Networks"	"Strategic", organisa-tional, cognitive	Gene Therapy (see Hamdouch, Depret, 2001), ICT (see Ernst, 2006), etc.

5. Conclusion: The Challenges Ahead

The aim of this chapter was to examine the vast literature devoted to the study of clustering/networking dynamics in innovation or creative fields and to see if this literature has been able to capture the essentials of the phenomenon. I have shown that if some useful insights and analytical results can be derived from a number of works, the picture is not as positive as one might have expected. The notions of "clusters" and "innovation clusters" (or "innovation networks") are far from being unified and grounded in solid analytical frameworks. Also, some key issues relating to the clusters' spatial/geographical scaling, and to the nature and the forms of actors' interaction within innovation clusters (and networks), are still pending, although widely debated in the literature.

Moreover, one can only but recognise that, by and large, our comprehension of the mechanisms underlying the dynamics of emergence, structuring and evolution of innovation clustering and networking phenomena rests on partial, fragmented and rather fragile theoretical and analytical grounds. Yet, as I have tried to show, along with others, there are obviously some promising pathways for improving these grounds but at the price of departing from (explicit or implicit) normative postures and "fast theory building" (see Moulaert, Sékia, 2003, p. 295). Therefore, strong efforts towards better conceptualisation and sound analytical work are required. The challenge is also to be able to overcome cross-disciplinary boundaries, which are often rather artificial and counterproductive. Indeed, if economists, sociologists, economic geographers, organisation scientists and probably others have followed different paths for the analysis of innovation clusters and networks, their (partial) respective achievements appear to me rather complementary or even converging.

This observation holds particularly for the way actors' relationships and network structures are conceptualised and analysed by various social scientists. As my discussion of this key topic in section 4 shows, there are obviously substantial overlaps and "bridges" between the remarkable intuitions and insights provided in: the sociological work on social networks; the in-depth work of economists and organisation scientists on knowledge creation/diffusion and learning processes; the emphasis placed by economic geographers and other social scientists on the key role of institutions and the institutional embedding of the actors within specific geographical spaces; and the network structuring and its changing features, as highlighted by the "New Science of Networks".

Building on this, and on my discussion about the spatial/geographical scaling and configuration of innovation clusters and networks, I have suggested the idea of "multi-scaled networks" as a potential (yet embry-onic) analytical tool for understanding how innovation clusters' dynam-ics of emergence and structuring operate and how they lead to spatial, institutional and organisational-specific configurations in a given crea-tive field.

My conviction is that it is only through these efforts towards better analytical grounding and strong interdisciplinary integration that social scientists might be able to prove that clustering and networking proc-esses are neither illusions nor mysterious phenomena, but rather consti-tute real structuring forces of innovation dynamics within and across creative spaces.

Bibliography

Ahuja, G., "Collaboration networks, structural holes and innovation: A longitu-dinal study", in *Administrative Science Quarterly*, 2000, 45 (3), p. 425-455.

Albert, R., Barabasi, A.-L., "Statistical mechanics of complex networks", in *Review of Modern Physics*, 2002, 74 (1), p. 47-97.

Audretsch, D., Feldman, M., "Knowledge spillovers and the geography of innovation and production", in *American Economic Review*, 1996, 86 (3), p. 630-640.

Autant-Bernard, C., Mangematin, V., Massard, N., "L'influence de l'environnement régional sur la création et la croissance des PME de biotech-nologie", in *Éducation & Formation*, 2006, 73, p. 47-64.

Baptista, R., Swann, P., "Do firms in clusters innovate more?", in *Research Policy*, 1998, 27, p. 525-540.

Bathelt, H., Malmberg, A., Maskell, P., "Clusters and Knowledge: Local buzz, global pipelines and the process of knowledge creation", in *Progress in Hu-man Geography*, 2004, 28 (1), p. 31-56.

Beccatini, G., "The Marshallian Industrial District as a Socio-economic Notion", in G. Beccatini, F. Pyke and W. Sengenberger (eds.), *Industrial Districts and Inter-firm Co-operation in Italy*, International Institute for Labour Studies, Geneva, 1990.

Bekele, G. W., Jackson, R. W., "Theoretical Perspectives on Industry Clusters", *Regional Research Institute*, Research Paper 2006-5, West Virginia Univer-sity, 2006, 26 p.

Berset, A., Crevoisier, O., "Circulation of competencies and dynamics of regional production systems", in *International Journal on Multicultural Socie-ties*, 2006, 8 (1), p. 61-83.

Borgatti, S. P., Foster, P. C., "The network paradigm in organizational research: A review and typology", in *Journal of Management*, 2003, 29 (6), p. 991-1013.

Bresnahan, T., Gambardella, A., Saxenian, A.,'Old Economy' Inputs for 'New Economy' Outcomes: Cluster Formation in the New Silicon Valleys, in *Indus-trial and Corporate Change*, 2004, 10 (4), p. 835-860.

Bunnell, T.G., "Multimedia utopia? A geographical critique of high-tech development in Malaysia's Multimedia Supercorridor", in *Antipode*, 2002, 34, p. 265-295.

Burt, R. S., *Structural Holes*, Harvard University Press, Cambridge (MA), 1992.

Burt, R. S., "Structural Holes versus Network Closure as Social Capital", in N. Lin, K. S. Cook, and R. S. Burt (eds.), *Social Capital: Theory and Research*, Aldyn de Gruyter, 2001.

Burt, R. S., *Brokerage and closure. An introduction to social capital*, Oxford University Press, New York, 2005.

Casper, S., "How do technology clusters emerge and become sustainable? Social network formation and inter-firm mobility within the San Diego biotechnology cluster", in *Research Policy*, 2007, 36, p. 438-455.

Casper, S., Murray, F., "Careers and Clusters: Analyzing the Career Network Dynamic of Biotechnology Clusters", in *Journal of Engineering and Technology Management*, 2005, 22, p. 51-74.

Cassi, L., Zirulia, L., "The opportunity cost of social relations: on the effectiveness of small worlds", *Bocconi Working Papers*, No. 175, Bocconi University, 2005.

Castilla, E., Hwang, H., Granovetter, E., Granovetter, M., "Social Networks in Silicon Valley", in C. Moon-Lee, W. F. Miller, M. Cong Hancock and H. S. Rowen (eds.), *The Silicon Valley Edge*, Stanford University Press, Stanford, 2000, p. 218-247.

Chiaroni, D., Chiesa, V., "Forms of Creation of Industrial Clusters in Biotechnology", in *Technovation*, 2006, 26, p. 1064-1076.

Cohendet, P., Kirman, A. P., Zimmermann, J.-B., "Émergence, formation et dynamique des réseaux: modèles de la morphogenèse", in *Revue d'Économie Industrielle*, 2003, 103, p. 15-42.

Coleman, J. S., "Social capital in the creation of human capital", in *American Journal of Sociology*, 1988, 94 (Supplement), p. 95-120.

Coleman, J. S., *Foundations of Social Theory*, Harvard University Press, Cambridge (MA), 1990.

Cooke, P., "Biotechnology clusters in the U.K.: lessons from localisation in the commercialisation of science", in *Small Business Economics*, 2001, 17, p. 43-57.

Cooke, P., "Biotechnology Clusters as Regional/Sectoral Innovation Systems", in *International Regional Science Review*, 2002, 25 (1), p. 8-37.

Dahl, M. S., Pedersen, C. O. R., "Knowledge flows through informal contacts in industrial clusters: myth or reality?", in *Research Policy*, 2004, 33, p. 1673-1686.

Den Hertog, P., Roelandt, T. J. A., "Cluster analysis and cluster-based policy making: the state of the art", in T. J. A. Roelandt and P. den Hertog (eds.), *Cluster Analysis and Cluster-based Policy: New Perspectives and Rationale in Innovation Policy*, OECD, Paris, 1999.

Depret, M.-H., Hamdouch, A., "Innovation Networks and Competitive Coalitions in the Pharmaceutical Industry: Emergence and Structures of a New

Industrial Organisation", in *European Journal of Economic and Social Systems*, 2000, 14 (3), p. 229-270.

Depret, M.-H., Hamdouch, A., "Échelles spatiales, formes de proximité et logiques institutionnelles: Esquisse d'une approche co-évolutionnaire des dynamiques de changement technologique dans la pharmacie et les biotechnologies", *Cinquièmes Journées de la Proximité: La proximité, entre interactions et institutions*, Bordeaux, 2006, 28-30 June, 31 p., http://beagle.u-bordeaux4.fr/conf2006/program.php.

Depret, M.-H., Hamdouch, A., "Changements technologiques, logiques institutionnelles et dynamiques industrielles: Esquisse d'une approche co-évolutionnaire appliquée à l'industrie pharmaceutique et aux biotechnologies", in *Innovations*, 2007, 25, p. 85-109.

Dohse, D., "Technology Policy and the Regions: The case of the BioRegio Contest", in *Research Policy*, 2000, 29, p. 1111-1133.

Ernst, D., *Innovation Offshoring – Asia's Emerging Role in Global Innovation Networks*, East-West Center Special Reports, 2006, No. 10, July, 48 p., http://www.EastWestCenter.org.

Eto, H., Obstacles to emergence of high/new technology parks, ventures and clusters in Japan, in *Technological Forecasting & Social Change*, 2005, 72, p. 359-373.

Feldman, M. P., "The new economics of innovation, spillovers and agglomeration: a review of empirical studies", in *Economics of Innovation and New Technology*, 1999, 8, p. 5-25.

Feldman, M. P., "The locational dynamics of the US biotech industry: knowledge externalities and the anchor hypothesis", in *Industry and Innovation*, 2003, 10 (3), p. 311-328.

Feldman, M. P., Martin, R., "Constructing jurisdictional advantage", in *Research Policy*, 2005, 34, p. 1235-1249.

Feldman, M. P., Romanelli, E., "Organizational legacy and the internal dynamics of clusters: the U.S. human Bio-Therapeutics Industry", 1976-2002, *Cinquièmes Journées de la Proximité: La proximité, entre interactions et institutions*, Bordeaux, 28-30 June 2006, 31 p. http://beagle.u-bordeaux4.fr/conf2006/program.php.

Flap, H., "No man is an island: the research programme of a social capital theory", in O. Favereau and E. Lazega (eds.), *Conventions and Structures in Economic Organisation*, Edward Elgar, Cheltenham (UK) - Northampton (MA, USA), 2002, p. 29-59.

Fromhold-Eisebith, M., Eisebith, G., "How to institutionalize innovative clusters? Comparing explicit top-down and implicit bottom-up approaches", in *Research Policy*, 2005, 34, p. 1250-1268.

Gaffard, J.-L., "Vers une nouvelle politique industrielle", *Lettre de l'OFCE – Observations et diagnostics économiques*, 2005, 269 (December), p. 1-8.

Gay, B., Dousset, B., "Innovation and network structural dynamics: Study of the alliance network of a major sector of the biotechnology industry", in *Research Policy*, 2005, 34, p. 1457-1475.

Glaeser, E. L., "Reinventing Boston: 1630-2003", in *Journal of Economic Geography*, 2005, 5, p. 119-153.

Gordon, I. R., McCann, P., "Innovation, agglomeration, and regional development", in *Journal of Economic Geography*, 2005, 5, p. 523-543.

Goyal, S., "Learning in networks: a survey", in G. Demange and M. Wooders (eds.), *Group formation in economics: networks, clubs, and coalitions*, Cambridge University Press, Cambridge, 2005.

Granovetter, M., "The strength of weak ties", in *American Journal of Sociology*, 1973, 78, p. 1360-1380.

Granovetter, M., "The theory gap in social network analysis", in P. W. Holland and S. Leinhardt (eds.), in *Perspectives on Social Network Research*, Academic Press, New York, 1979, p. 501-518.

Granovetter, M., "Economic action and social structure: the problem of embeddedness", in *American Journal of Sociology*, 1985, 91, p. 481-510.

Granovetter, M., "Economic institutions as social structures", *Acta Sociologica*, 1992, 35, p. 3-11.

Hamdouch, A., Innovation Clusters and Networks: A Critical Review of the Recent Literature. *The 19th EAEPE Conference*, Universidade do Porto, 2007, 1-3 November.

Hamdouch, A., "Concetti e analisi sul cluster: la letteratura per conoscere lo spazio fisico delle aggregazioni di innovazione", in *Archivio di Studi Urbani e Regionali*, Franco Angeli, Milan, 2008a, 92, p. 30-48.

Hamdouch, A., "Start-up biotechnologiques et dynamique des *clusters* et réseaux d'innovation dans la biopharmacie: Une revue de la littérature empirique", in *Journal des Entreprises Familiales*, 2008b, 1(3), p. 7-43.

Hamdouch, A., Depret, M.-H., *La nouvelle économie industrielle de la pharmacie. Structures industrielles, dynamique d'innovation et stratégies commerciales*, Elsevier, Paris, 2001.

Hamdouch, A., He, F., "R&D Offshoring and clustering dynamics in pharmaceuticals and biotechnology: key features and insights from the Chinese case", *Journal of Innovation Economics*, 4, Special Issue, *Networking, Innovation and Clusters*, A. Hamdouch (ed.), December 2009, p. 95-117.

Hamdouch, A., Moulaert, F., Knowledge Infrastructures, Innovation Dynamics and Knowledge Creation/Diffusion/Accumulation Processes: A Comparative Institutional Perspective, Special Issue: "The Knowledge Infrastructure: Analysis, Institutional Dynamics and Policy Issues", F. Moulaert and A. Hamdouch (eds.), *Innovation – The European Journal of Social Science Research*, 2006, 19 (1), p. 25-50.

Hamdouch, A., Perrochon, D., "Formes d'engagement en R&D, processus d'innovation et modalités d'interaction entre firmes dans l'industrie pharmaceutique", in *Revue d'Économie Industrielle*, 2000a, 93, p. 29-50.

Hamdouch, A., Perrochon, D., "Les dynamiques d'interaction entre firmes dans les secteurs intensifs en R&D", in C. Voisin, A. Plunket et B. Bellon (eds.), *La coopération industrielle*, Economica, Paris, 2000b, p. 179-194.

Ketels, C., Sövell, Ö., *Clusters in the EU-10 new member countries*. Report, Europe INNOVA Cluster Mapping, Centre for Strategy and Competitiveness, Harvard Business School, 2006, 69 p.

Kirzner, I., "Entrepreneurial Discovery and the Competitive Market Process: An Austrian Approach", in *Journal of Economic Literature*, 1997, XXXV (4).

Liu, X., Buck, T., "Innovation performance and channels for international technology spillovers: Evidence from Chinese high-tech industries", in *Research Policy*, 2007, 36, p. 355-366.

Longhi, C., "Networks, collective learning and technology development in innovative hightechnology regions: the case of Sophia Antipolis", in *Regional Studies*, 1999, 33 (4).

Luukkunainen, S., "Industrial clusters in the finnish economy", in OECD 2001, p. 273-287.

Lynskey, M.J., "Transformative technology and institutional transformation: Coevolution of biotechnology venture firms and the institutional framework in Japan", in *Research Policy*, 2006, 35, p. 1389-1422.

March, J.G., "Exploration and exploitation in organizational learning", in *Organisation Science*, 1991, 2 (1), p. 101-123.

Marshall, A., *Elements of Economics of Industry* (First Volume of *Elements of Economics*), Third Edition (First Edition, 1892), Macmillan and Co., Limited, London, 1903.

Martin, R., Sunley, P., "Deconstructing clusters: chaotic concept or policy panacea?", in *Journal of Economic Geography*, 2003, 3, p. 5-35.

Martin, R., Sunley, P., "Path dependence and regional economic evolution", in *Journal of Economic Geography*, 2006, 6, p. 395-437.

McKelvey, M., Alm, H., Riccaboni, M., "Does co-location matter for formal knowledge collaboration in the Swedish biotechnology-pharmaceutical sector?", in *Research Policy*, 2003, 32, p. 483-501.

Moulaert, F., Sékia, F., "Territorial Innovation Models: A Critical Survey", in *Regional Studies*, 2003, 37 (3), p. 289-302.

Moulaert, F., Martinelli, F., Swyngedouw, E., Gonzalez, S., "Towards Alternative Model(s) of Local Innovation", in *Urban Studies*, 2005, 42 (11), p. 1969-1990.

Nooteboom, B., "Innovation, Learning and Cluster Dynamics", Discussion Paper No 44, Tilburg University, April, 2004, 24 p.

OECD, *Boosting Innovation: The Cluster Approach*, OECD, Paris, 1999.

OECD, *Innovative Clusters: Drivers of National Innovation Systems*, OECD, Paris, 2001.

OECD, *Competitive Regional Clusters. National Policy Approaches*, OECD, Paris, 2007.

Orsenigo, L., "The (Failed) Development of a Biotechnology Cluster: The Case of Lombardy", in *Small Business Economics*, 2001, 17, p. 77-92.

Owen-Smith, J., Powell, W.W., "Knowledge Networks as Channels and Conduits: The Effects of Spillovers in the Boston Biotechnology Community", in *Organisation Science*, 2004, 15 (1), p. 5-21.

Owen-Smith, J., Riccaboni, M., Pammolli, F., Powell, W., "A comparison of U.S. and European University-Industry Relations in the Life Sciences", in *Management Science*, 2002, 48 (1), p. 24-43.

Passiante, G., Secundo, G., "From Geographical Innovation Clusters to Virtual Innovation Clusters: The Innovation Virtual System", *ERSA Conference 2002*, Dortmund, August 2002.

Paytas, J., Gradeck, R., Andrews, L., *Universities and the Development of Industry Clusters*. Report prepared for the Economic Development Administration of the U.S. Department of Commerce, Pittsburgh, Carnegie Mellon Center for Economic Development, 2004, 102 p., http://www.smartpolicy. org.

Poon, J., Hsu, J.-Y., Jeongwook, S., "The geography of learning and knowledge acquisition among Asian latecomers", in *Journal of Economic Geography*, 2006, 6, p. 541-559.

Porter, M. E., *The Competitive Advantage of Nations*, The Free Press, New York, 1990.

Porter, M. E., "The Competitive Advantage of the Inner City", in *Economic Development Quarterly*, 1995, 11 (1), February.

Porter, M. E., "The Adam Smith Address: Location, Clusters and the 'New' Microeconomics of Competition", in *Business Economics*, 1998a, 33 (1), p. 7-13.

Porter, M. E., *On Competition*, Harvard Business School press, Boston, 1998b.

Porter, M. E., "Clusters and the New Economics of Competition", in *Harvard Business Review*, November-December, 1998c, p. 77-90.

Porter, M. E., "Location, competition, and economic development: Local clusters in a global economy", in *Economic Development Quarterly*, 2000, 14 (1), p. 15-34.

Powell, W.W., Koput, K.W., Bowie, J.I., Smith-Doerr, L., "The Spatial Clustering of Science Capital: Accounting for Biotech Firm-venture Capital Relationships", in *Regional Studies*, 2002, 36 (3), p. 291-305.

Preissl, B., Solimene, L., *The Dynamics of Clusters and Innovation*, Physisca-Verlag, Heidelberg and New York, 2003.

Rallet, A., Torre, A. (eds.), *Économie industrielle et économie spatiale*, Bibliothèque de Science Régionale, Economica, Paris, 1995.

Rallet, A., Torre, A., "Proximité géographique ou proximité organisationnelle? Une analyse spatiale des coopérations technologiques dans les réseaux localisés d'innovation", in *Économie Appliquée*, 2001, LIV (1), p. 147-171.

Rallet, A., Torre, A. (eds.), *Quelles proximités pour innover?*, L'Harmattan, Paris, 2007.

Robinson, K. R., Rip, A., Mangematin, V., "Technological agglomeration and the emergence of clusters and networks in nanotechnology", in *Research Policy*, 2007, 36, p. 871-879.

Roijakkers, N., Hagedoorn, J., "Inter-firm R&D partnering in pharmaceutical biotechnology since 1975: Trends, patterns, and networks", in *Research Policy*, 2006, 35 (3), p. 431-446.

Romanelli, E., Khessina, O. M., "Regional Industrial Identity: Cluster Configuration and Economic Development", in *Organisation Science*, 2005, 16 (4), p. 344-358.

Saxenian, A., *Regional advantage. Culture and Competition in Silicon Valley and Route 128*, Harvard University Press, Cambridge (MA), 1994.

Saxenian, A., The Silicon Valley-Hsinchu Connection: Technical Communities and Industrial Upgrading. Mimeo, University of California at Berkeley, 1999, 27 September, p. 34.

Saxenian, A., *The New Argonauts: Regional Advantage in a Global Economy*, Harvard University Press, Cambridge (MA), 2006.

Scott, A., "Entrepreneurship, Innovation, and Industrial Development: Geography and the Creative Field Revisited", in *Small Business Economics*, 2006, 26, p. 1-24.

Shan, W., Walker, G., Kogut, B., "Interfirm cooperation and startup innovation in the biotechnology industry", in *Strategic Management Journal*, 1994, 15, p. 387-394.

Simmie, J., Sennett, J., "Innovation in the London metropolitan region", in D. Hart, J. Simmie, P. Wood and J. Sennett (eds.), *Innovative clusters and competitive cities in the UK and Europe*, Working Paper No. 182, Oxford Brookes School of Planning, 1999.

Sölvell, Ö., Lindqvist, G., Ketels, C., *The Cluster Initiative Greenbook*. Report presented at the 6th Global TCI Conference, Gothenburg, 2003, September, 92 p., http://www.cluster-research.org).

Swann, P., Prevezer, M., "A Comparison of the Dynamics of Industrial Clustering in Computing and Biotechnology", in *Research Policy*, 1996, 25, p. 1139-1157.

Swedberg, R., "Markets as Social Structures", in N. Smelser and R. Swedberg (eds.), *Handbook of Economic Sociology*, Russel Sage Foundation, Princeton, 1994, p. 255-282.

Walker, G., Kogut, B., Shan, W., "Social capital, structural holes and the formation of an industry network", in *Organisation Science*, 1997, 8 (2), p. 109-125.

Waluszewski, A., "A Competing or Co-operating Cluster or Seven Decades of Combinatory Resources? What's Behind a Prospering Biotech Valley?", in *Scandinavian Journal of Management*, 2004, 20, p. 125-150.

Watts, D.J., "The "new" science of networks", in *Annual Review of Sociology*, 2004, 30, p. 243-270.

Watts, D.J., Strogatz, S.S., "Collective dynamics of "small world" networks", in *Nature*, 1998, 393, p. 440-442.

White, H. C., "Production markets as induced role structures", in S. L. Leinhardt (ed.), *Sociological Methodology*, Jossey-Bass, San Francisco, 1981, p. 1-57.

White, H. C., *Markets from Networks*, Princeton University Press, Princeton, 2001.

White, D. R., Harary F., "The cohesiveness of blocks in social networks: connectivity and conditional density", in *Sociological Methodology*, 2001, 31, p. 305-359.

Zeller, C., "Clustering biotech: a recipe for success? Spatial patterns of growth of biotechnology in Munich, Rhineland and Hamburg", in *Small Business Economics*, 2001, 17, p. 123-141.

CHAPTER II

Networking Innovation and Intellectual Property Rights

The Enterprise's Knowledge Capital

Blandine LAPERCHE

"Put simply, patents and copyrights are often the crown jewels in a high tech company's collection of assets" C. Shapiro (2003, p. 391).

1. Introduction

Despite the diversity of organisational models that can be found in the economic reality (see Berger, 2005; Lung, 2008), there is no doubt that the organisation and management of activities through networks have gained ground. In particular, big hierarchical firms seem to be part of past history, being replaced by the 'networked enterprise'. Today, most companies are increasingly concentrated on a very small part or on small parts of the value chain: conception/design of new products (final products, or intermediary goods), production (of pieces or final assembling); commercialisation (services). Also, at each step of the value chain (conception, production, commercialisation), most firms try to reduce the ownership of assets to the core activities (the most profitable but also often the most risky) and use contractual relations to manage the rest of the activities.

This type of organisation has been well studied in sociology (see Castells, 1996; Mariotti, 2004) and in economics and management of innovation and of organisations, certainly because it seems to be particularly adapted to the economic context characterised by the globalisation of competition based on innovation (see notably Porter, 1990; Chesnais, 1994; Uzunidis *et al.*, 1997; Sturgeon, 2002; Langlois, 2002; Gaffard, 2003; Baudry, 2004; Berger, 2005).

At the same time, in the field of economics and management of innovation, intellectual property rights (IPRs) have obtained the status of "assets" (see the quotation at the start of the introduction) showing their crucial role in innovation strategies, as well as in innovation policies (see Foray, 2004; Scotchmer, 2004; Shapiro, 1998, 2001, 2003; Lévêque, Ménière, 2004).

In this chapter, based on a review of academic literature, we want to better understand the functions of intellectual property rights (IPRs) in the particular case of the networked enterprise building innovation networks. IPRs are often studied in relation to innovation dynamics and strategy, notably focusing on the strategic roles of IPRs (an incentive/ defensive role, which is aimed at protecting and thus giving incentives to the constitution of the firm's innovation resources; an offensive role, aimed at defining the place of the firm in competition). The organisational functions of IPRs and particularly their role in the coordination of activities are more rarely studied. We consider that intellectual property rights may play this role in the networked enterprise, making the relationships between all the fragmented parts of the networked enterprise easier. Moreover, this coordination function is revealed to be fundamental in a context of collaborative innovation, i.e. the construction of innovation networks. This chapter thus offers a new point of view on the strategic but also on the organisational functions of IPRs, particularly in the case of the networked enterprise.

Part 2 comes back to the origin of the networked enterprise and defines its main characteristics. It also defines IPRs and presents their strategic roles as they appear in the literature. Part 3 presents the 'coordination' and the 'incentive/defensive' functions of IPRs in the networked enterprise, which are gaining ground in a context of collaborative innovation. Part 4 presents the 'offensive role' of IPRs, which largely contributes to define the place of the networked enterprise (as a leader or a follower) within the networks of firms to which it usually belongs. Finally, Part 5 concludes the chapter by stressing the fact that the new forms of organisation of enterprises largely explain the recent evolution of IPRs legislation.

2. The Organisation of the Networked Enterprise: Origin and Definition

2.1. A dual vision of the firm: knowledge and transactions

Among the theories of the firm, we cannot detect a theory specially dedicated to the networked enterprise. The traditional theories of the firm mostly focused on the objectives of the firm (conflict between profit maximisation in the neoclassical approach of the firm and the existence of multiple objectives reflecting the complexity of the organisation in the behavioural and managerial approaches). The question of the boundaries of the firm, first posed in Ronald Coase's contribution in

1937, which opposed market and hierarchy, became more topical from the 1970s. This was a period that coincided – in the economic reality – with the organisational difficulties faced by the hierarchical mode of organisation of enterprises. The existence of transaction costs, but also of bureaucratic costs thus began to explain the size of enterprises and the related "make or buy" choice (see Willamson, 1975, 1985). The agency theory (see Jensen, Meckling, 1976) and the theory of property rights (see Alchian, Demsetz, 1972) have adopted a radical, individualist approach to the firm, with it being viewed as a 'nexus of contracts' and thus being a 'legal fiction'. With this approach, the networked enterprise does not exist: there are only contracts that link individuals who own various production means. The competence-based approach of the firm[1], which relies on the vision of the firm as a complex organisation, a 'processor of knowledge', helps us to understand how the objective of knowledge creation and diffusion is achieved, associating the internal organisation of the firm and the access to external resources (see Cohendet, Llerrena, 2005). Following the logic of these authors, we see that the transaction approach of the firm (where it is viewed as a 'processor of information' (see Fransman, 1994), focusing on the allocation of resources according to the level of transaction costs) and the competence-based approach of the firm can be complementary and not a substitute – what is called a 'dual' vision of the firm. The firm, considered as an organisational device, simultaneously allocates and creates resources. In this vision, the characteristic of the economic context, and the attention given to the activities (core competences, non-core competences, peripherical activities) will determine the importance given to knowledge creation (associated with core competence and a challenging economic context) and to transaction costs (mostly important for peripherical activities and a stable economic context). This is this dual vision of the firm that we retain to study the origin and the organisation of the networked enterprise. Such an approach necessitates coming back to the economic context that largely contributes to explaining the evolution of the organisational structures of the enterprise.

2.2. *From the hierarchical to the networked enterprise*

The study of economic history allows us to highlight the evolution of the firm's organisation from the integrated company (at the beginning of the 20th century) to the multidivisional company (from the 1960s on; see Chandler 1977, 1990), where the units that could be located abroad were

---

[1] Including the evolutionist approach, the resource-based theory, the strategic competence-based approach and the social-anthropology of learning approach (see Cohendet, Llerena, 2005).

functioning as 'quasi firms'. The reasons for the evolution of the firm's organisation lies in a mix of economic, social and technological factors (see on this point, Kapàs, 2008). The main explanations of the emergence of a new form of enterprise, the networked enterprise[2], are also related to a set of economic, social and technological factors, which are a) the crisis of the Fordist model of production, b) the deregulation of markets and c) the diffusion of information technologies.

The crisis of the Fordist model of production begins at the end of the 1960s and is characterised by the saturation of markets for undifferentiated goods. In a more open environment, big integrated firms bear increasing "bureaucratic costs" and have difficulties to adapt. The necessity to adapt to a changing and diversified demand grows and shows the main change in the competition grounds, from the price in the Fordist model of production to innovation in the flexible model of production. Innovation – that is new combinations in the terms of Schumpeter (1911, 1942) – has become a fundamental objective of the firm, imposed by competition. This idea is commonly shared by business theories (see Porter, 1990; Tidd *et al.*, 2005; Uzunidis, 2004) and the competence-based theories of the firm (see above), defining the firm as a 'processor of knowledge', and making the link between the creation of knowledge and the diffusion of innovation.

The opening up and liberalisation of markets, which began at the end of the 1970s, were aimed at fighting against the economic crisis characterised by the conjunction of inflation and unemployment. These policies have been developed and disseminated through international organisations (WTO, IMF and World Bank) (see Michie, 2003; Milward, 2003). The liberalisation of markets (goods and services, labour, finance) has opened new markets up to firms but has also made the organisation of the production process on an international scale easier, not only through the creation or purchase of new subsidiaries (internal and external growth) in different countries but also through the signature of contracts with suppliers and subcontractors located in different parts of the world.

Thanks to the progress and the spread of information technology, the global management of production – in real time – becomes possible. In

---

[2]   Many names are given to this new form of organisation of activities: project-based company, modular enterprise, hollow corporation, etc. Several processes known as vertical disintegration, outsourcing/offshoring etc. also define these new forms of organisation. This diversity of names also reflects the many differences that exist between the organisations of firms, more or less close to the multidivisional enterprise. As a matter of fact, the networked enterprise is more a complement than a substitute to the multidivisional firm (see Berger, 2005).

fact, information technology binds the scattered units of the enterprise. The use of modern information technology reduces the cost of data transfer and facilitates the location of units abroad, as well as national and international partnerships. Information and communication technologies are also fundamental in the mobilisation and the integration of fragmented and diversified forms of localised knowledge and competences (see Cohendet *et al.*, 1999).

A large modern corporation can be described as a network of units linked together with the aim of producing goods and services (final or intermediary production). Some of the units are owned by a central firm (usually a holding company) and the other kinds of activities are linked by contract (partnerships, subcontracting, licensing, franchising).

In the networked enterprise, the central firm focuses on its 'core' activities (usually the ones that will reinforce its innovation capacity and more globally the ones at the basis of the definition of the firm's strategy). These core activities are wholly owned by the central firm (which is coherent with the vision of the firm as a processor of knowledge). The achievement of the other activities (for example, the production of parts of the final products, the commercialisation of final goods) is mainly managed through contracts with other more or less independent entities (subcontractors, licences, franchises etc.). The fully outsourced activities mainly concern the ones that deal with the implementation of the firm's strategy (here, the transaction costs are the main governance criteria). As a consequence, the value of firms increasingly relies on intangible assets (IPRs and other components of the knowledge capital, see below) compared with tangible ones (see Serfati, 2008). Therefore, the central firm can be considered as a designer or an architect of a global network. The expression "network architect" is, for example, used by the Renault Group to describe its main activity.

Networked enterprises have gained greater flexibility, thus enabling them to adjust to the evolution of the demand. The networked enterprise associates internal and external flexibility. Internal flexibility deals with the management of work within the company: the enterprise focuses on a stable core of managers in R&D, financial and administrative departments. It uses diverse forms of work and contracts of employment (in terms of working time, salaries, place of work, job content) to manage the other employees. Associated with this greater internal flexibility are increased options in the ways firms manage their assets at the international level (external flexibility). The globalisation of corporate strategies refers to their liberty or flexibility in the management of human, financial, scientific and technical assets on an international level. Networked enterprises are organised on a global level, according to the competitive advantages of potential host territories. Holding companies are located in areas with low or even zero taxation. Research and development laboratories are set up in areas where financial, scientific and technical resources are abundant. Production plants select attractive countries in terms of specialisation and labour costs as well as transport infrastructures. Goods are marketed in all financially solvent areas worldwide. The pertinence of the dual vision of the firm can be seen in the productive strategy developed by the networked enterprise, which simultaneously tries to develop its innovative capacity (which implies new investments) and to reduce its production costs (through the rationalisation of its production process and of its structure; see Uzunidis *et al.*, 1997).

The strategy of rationalisation is all the more important that finance has gained a major role in the management of firms (see Plihon, 2002; Aglietta, Rébérioux, 2004; Gaffard, 2003; Michalet, 2007). The different steps of financial market deregulation and liberalisation have produced an interconnected global market. New types of investors (pension funds, insurance companies, investments funds) are investing in big enterprises worldwide. Due to their main activity (e.g. managing employee's pension funds), they feel less concerned by the development of such companies (e.g. their technological performance or the size of their staff) than by the amount of the dividends to be received. Their fluctuating behaviour, dependent on the level of the price earning ratio, has important implications in the management of such corporations. In particular, the objective of profit maximisation, linked to the increase of the shareholder's value, becomes one of the most important (see Laperche, 2006). The "profitability imperative" is the result of this new context. It means that in order to keep the precious new institutional investors, managers of big globalised corporations have to boost shareholder value. The increase of the shareholder value will, moreover, be profitable to them, as they have often become, due to the stock options plans, shareholders of the companies they manage. This profitability imperative is a powerful reason for the erratic boundaries of networked enterprises, which are transformed by processes of mergers/acquisitions and outsourcing/offshoring.

2.3. The definition and role of IPRs in the literature

IPRs include industrial property rights: patents, trademarks, industrial models and the protection of trade secrets. They also include copyright protection. The patent is a temporary monopoly (which lasts 20 years) given to an inventor, as an acknowledgement of the invention, whether a product or a process in all fields of technology, provided that it is new, involves an inventive step and is capable of industrial application. A trademark protects words, names, symbols, sounds, or colours that distinguish goods and services from those manufactured or sold by others and it indicates the source of goods. Trademarks, unlike patents, can be renewed forever as long as they are being used in commerce. A design patent may be granted to anyone who invents a new, original, and ornamental design for an article of manufacture. Trade secret laws protect individuals and businesses against the misappropriation of trade secrets by improper means. Copyrights protect works of authorship, such as writings, music, and works of art that have been tangibly expressed.

The many works dealing with the functions of intellectual property rights in enterprises give us the possibility to draw up a list of the main aims that encourage firms to use them (see for synthesis Gallini, 2002; Scotchmer, 2004; Hanel, 2006).

Table 1: The reasons of the resort to intellectual property rights (in particular to patents)

Protection against imitation (copy dissuasion and/or lawsuits in case of counterfeiting)
Incentive to invest in R&D by making investments profitable (production and commercialisation of protected products and/or signature of licence agreements)
Negotiation means (in partnerships and/or with financing institutions)
Image / reputation of the enterprise
Assessment of internal performance / Valuation of the enterprise
Blocking competitors / reinforcement of entry barriers

These aims are well studied in the literature and they will be explained in more details in the rest of the chapter, applied to the particular case of the networked enterprise. What is important to mention here is that the hierarchy of the objective is not unchanging. It varies, according to many factors such as the size of the enterprise, the sector, the type of protected creation, the more or less innovative character of the enterprise, the market structure and the intensity of competition (see Hanel, 2006).

In the dual networked firm, focused on the reduction of organisational and production costs and on the creation of new knowledge, we can make the hypothesis that the roles of coordination and of incentives will be strong.

3. The Coordination Role and the Incitative/Defensive Roles of IPRs in the Networked Enterprise

3.1. The coordination role of IPRs

Contemporary economic theory stresses the role of property rights in the coordination of activities and in the allocation of resources. The Coase theorem (see Coase, 1960; Stigler, 1966) suggests that negotiation leads to an effective allocation of resources when property rights are clearly defined and when there is no other obstacle to the transaction. The transaction cost theory (see Williamson, 1975, 1985) and the theory of uncompleted contracts (see Hart, Moore, 1990) stipulate that, in presence of specific assets and incomplete contracts, vertical integration leads to more efficient transactions and organisational forms.

However, the networked enterprise means the reintroduction of market in the functioning of the enterprise – compared to integrated firms, where hierarchy (based on the ownership of physical assets) is considered an alternative to market. This reintroduction of market reveals transaction costs, which are caused by the imperfection of markets: information searches, finding suppliers, negotiation of contracts and the execution of contracts.

According to this reasoning, and taking account of the growing importance of the ownership of intangible assets, compared to the ownership of physical assets in the networked enterprise (see Serfati, 2008), we can consider the hypothesis that IPRs – like certification and logistics integration (see Baudry, 2004) – would play an important role in the coordination of activities, clarifying the relationship, and thus reducing the transaction costs between the central firm and the different units that compose the networked enterprise.

As a matter of fact, the ownership of trademarks, for example (and this also goes for patented inventions or designs), acts as a sign of the quality of the central firm or potential suppliers' products and services. In other words, trademarks may increase the reputation of the central firm and of potential suppliers that would be chosen thanks to the IPRs they own. In the case of subcontracting and in franchising contracts, licences[3] allow the different units to use the patented invention, or the protected trademark or design usually owned by the central firm. Licences are usually considered to be responsible for productive efficiency: to create proprietary products efficiently; to allow others to use the intellectual property as inputs towards innovation (research tools); to

---

[3] A licence is an agreement whereby the owner of intellectual property authorises another party to use it.

resolve blocking situation; and to enable the development of complementary inventions (see Sctochmer, 2004, p. 162). IPRs allow the
diffusion of technology within the enterprise and creates incentives for
the production of specific assets. In the case of R&D partnerships,
where specific assets are jointly built (co-contracting or contracts between the central firm and a research lab, for example), shared patents
reduce the possibility of opportunist behaviour (hold-up situations)
between the co-contractors.

In other words, the possession of IPRs may facilitate exchanges by
reducing transaction costs, as in the Coase theorem. However, it does
not mean that the allocation of resources will be efficient in every case
as the transaction costs do not completely disappear, a situation that
would only occur in a context of pure and perfect competition. That is to
say that the choice of whether or not to outsource activities will depend
on the comparison between the transaction costs and the gains of exchange, where IPRs play an important role.

The coordination function of IPRs is all the more important as, in recent years, innovation has become a collaborative process, linking
together several firms and institutions. The building of the networked
enterprise's innovation capabilities, its 'knowledge capital' is achieved
through innovation networks.

In the dual networked enterprise, the coordination function of IPRs
(reduction of transactions costs) and their role of incentives (for the
creation of new knowledge) appear to be linked.

3.2. From coordination to incitation
in the context of collaborative innovation

Collaborative innovation means that the process of knowledge creation is the result of partnerships between the units of the same firm
(more or less independent of the central firm), but also between several
networked enterprises and several kinds of institutions (see Hamdouch
et al., 2008). Collaborative innovation mainly results from an economic
context based on global competition, where innovation performance and
profitability imperatives are associated.

To better understand this collaborative innovation process within the
networked enterprise, we define the "knowledge capital" as the set of
scientific and technical knowledge and information produced, acquired,
combined and systematised by one or several firms for productive

purposes.[4] "Knowledge capital" (see figure 1) refers to the accumulated knowledge of one or several linked firms (embedded in the individuals – know-how, competences – machines, technologies and routines of the enterprise) which is continuously enriched by information flows and used in the production process or, more globally, in the value creation process. Thus, it is a dynamic concept – a process – that defines the knowledge accumulated by one or several firms and continuously enriched and combined in different ways, and eventually used or commercialised. This productive aim – the creation of value – is the main characteristic that turns knowledge into 'capital'.

Figure 1: The 'knowledge capital' (Laperche, 2007)

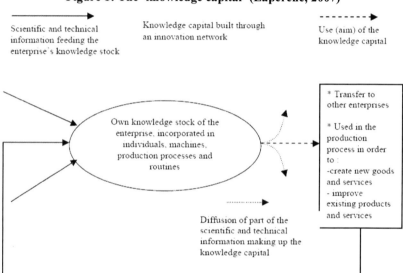

A firm may use its "knowledge capital" in a value creation process by: a) simply selling this knowledge base to another enterprise (e.g. the selling of a computer programme) – the "knowledge capital" (embodied in the software) is transferred to another enterprise which can use it in its production process; b) introducing this "knowledge capital" in its own production process – in this case, the 'knowledge capital' can be considered as a means to produce or improve goods and services, and as a tool for reducing the completion time of the production process.

---

[4] Theoretically, the notion of "knowledge capital" is based on the definitions and/or on the economic developments of three key concepts/notions: knowledge, firm and capital (see Laperche, 2007).

The formation of this knowledge capital is today achieved on a global scale. This can be assessed by the growing importance of international R&D partnerships between firms (see Archibigu, Iammarino, 2002; Hagedoorn, 2002), patents and technology flows (see OECD, 2003), and globalisation of R&D (UNCTAD, 2005; OECD, 2008).

Moreover, networked firms are increasingly developing their knowledge bases, thanks to the innovation networks in which they are involved. The issue of networks is now considered as a challenge in the economics of innovation, which starts "from the recognition that innovation and industry are highly affected by the interaction of heterogeneous actors with different knowledge, competencies and specialisation, with relationships that may range from competitive to cooperative, from formal to informal, from market to non-market" (see Malerba, 2006, p. 15).

As a matter of fact, the formation of the enterprise's "knowledge capital" implies the gathering of different types of inputs: human resources (researchers, engineers); tangible resources (machines, tools) and intangible ones (patents, software, information). The enterprise has to produce and appropriate scientific and technical knowledge in order to expand the knowledge base it has already accumulated. Different means are used by the enterprise: in-house means (investment and management of human resources, R&D and tangible and intangible resources) and external means. External means can be divided into two categories: equity relations (for example, joint venture) and non-equity relations (contracts with firms and other institutions and more informal contacts). (see table 2)

Table 2: Means of formation of the firm's "knowledge capital"

In-house means (Rosenberg, 1990; Cohen, Levinthal, 1990)	External Means (see Jaffe, 2000; Mowery *et al.*, 2001; Tidd *et al.*, 2005; Antonelli, 2005)

- Investment in Human Resources
- Investment in and management
  of R&D and means of production
  (tangible and intangible)
	Equity relations:
	- joint venture
	- purchase of innovative enterprise
	Non equity relations:
	- Contracts with other firms (including licensing)
	- Contracts with institutions: e.g. university
	  research labs (including licensing and hiring of
	  short term researchers)
	- More informal contacts

This strategy of having a collective constitution of knowledge capital can be seen in high-tech sectors and in apparently more traditional ones. The case of the Lafarge Group illustrates this: its research centre is located at L'Isle d'Asbeau, near Lyon, and was, in the year 2000, the top world research centre in terms of employees and budget in the field of building material. It also cooperates with other enterprises (Bouygues and Rhone Poulenc, and Rodhia since 1994) and with research Labs (Polytechniques, INSA Lyon and Toulouse, Universities of Berkeley, Princeton, Massachussets institute of Boston US, of Laval and Sherbrooke Canada and Polytechnique of Lausanne) – see Barjot, 2007. The evolution of IBM from a hardware manufacturing company to a global service provider has depended on a strong evolution of its collaborative network, which has taken part in the adaptation of its knowledge capital. In the case of IBM, the network – and the characteristics of the relationships within the network – has been used to facilitate the strategic positioning of the firm (see Dittrich *et al.*, 2007). It is also through the constitution of a network of partnerships, linking small and big companies, universities and research centres that Monsanto achieved in the 1970s-1980s its strategic shift from chemistry to vegetal biotechnology.

The purpose of all these strategies is to reduce the cost, risk and length of technical progress and hence increase the short term return on investment in the scientific and technical fields. This purpose is all the more important that the complexity of technological development increases, which implies a collective process that is able to innovate faster and with less risks. Due to the profitability imperative, the big enterprise develops external means of formation of the knowledge base, which are both less risky and less costly. This does not mean, however, that the firm does not make in-house investment any more, as this kind of investment is crucial to understanding and absorbing the scientific and technical development achieved by other institutions on their own base. This trend shows that the formation of "knowledge capital" is built collectively: several institutions (big or small enterprises, research laboratories, etc.) take part in its formation.

The collective constitution of the knowledge capital thus involves the use of tools to ensure the coordination within the networked enterprise and between the central firm and its partners (networks of firms). We can advance the argument that IPRs take a greater part in this coordination process. The sharp increase of licence agreements in the past decade supports this idea: in a recent survey of firms in OECD countries, approximately 60% of respondents indicated that they had experienced an increase in both inward and outward patent licensing over the past decade and more than 70% expected inward licensing to increase further in the next five years (see Sheehan *et al.*, 2004).[5] Whereas some empiri-

---

[5] The type of IPRs agreement may depend on the type of commitment between the partners. Whereas licence agreements may be used in exploitation strategies that involve an important exchange of information, exploration strategies may rely on a

cal studies show the importance of property rights protection over transaction cost considerations in the decision to outsource (see Gooroochurn, Hanley, 2007), according to us, IPRs also have a role in the reduction of transaction costs in collaborative strategies (including outsourcing). As a matter of fact, IPRs clarify the relationships between the co-contractors (coordination), and therefore, by reducing transaction costs, give incentives to the collective building of knowledge capital, by protecting the tangible and intangible elements that constitute it. In the networked enterprise, the coordination role of IPRs is linked to their more traditional defensive/incitative roles. The temporary monopoly conferred by industrial property rights gives the possibility to go to court in case of infringement. IPRs thus secure merchant relations and give an incentive to joint investment efforts and to the internal transfer of technology. Within the networked enterprise, IPRs are a tool used by firms to replace the control based on the ownership of tangible assets by a control based on the ownership of intangible assets.

The coordination function is also visible through the relationships with investors. IPRs give a value to R&D investments, in a context where profitability has become an imperative. Filing and holding patents transform potential inventions into valuable assets, which can give confidence to investors and shareholders concerning the profitability of the firm's investments.

However, if we come back to the first role assigned to IPRs (protection of invention and creations), some limits have been put forward (see Gallini, 2002). For instance, patents spread too much information and are costly (direct and indirect costs). Copyright protection implies the capacity to provide proof of being the first creator, etc. To reduce the limits of IPRs, enterprises use joint tools of protection; in other words, they build a portfolio of protection tools, notably associating 'lead time' with traditional IPRs protection tools (see Levin *et al.*, 1987; Cohen *et al.*, 2000). This leads us to the offensive role of IPRs within innovation networks. Here again, the coordination functions are associated with the offensive role of IPRs.

---

lower commitment (as shown by Dittrich *et al.*, 2007 in the case of IBM), notably at the beginning of the project (trade secrets could be used first – however, if from exploration strategies are generated new technologies, these ones would surely result in shared patents or cross licences).

4. The Offensive Role of IPRs: Coordination and Leadership within Innovation Networks

4.1. Patent pools as a solution to 'a patent thicket'

The innovation strategies of networked firms lead to a blurred distinction between the networked enterprise and the innovation network to which it belongs. As a matter of fact, the constitution of the knowledge capital implies contractual relations between the central firm and units and partners. The partners may be small and medium enterprises specialised in technological fields but they may also be big enterprises and competitors of the networked firm as a whole. These kinds of alliances are meant to share the cost of development of new products and processes and to reduce the time needed for their conception. These alliances often lead to an important number of patents that can be owned separately by the different partners or be shared. Whatever the chosen solution, the development of a new technique leads to an important number of patents, a "patent thicket" in the words of Shapiro (2001), which can block the use or even the final production by a subcontractor who would have to sign too many costly licences. The number of infringements and litigations also increases. These situations have become much more common with the growing number of very restricted patents delivered notably by the USPTO since the 1980s (see Gallini, 2002). A good example of the blocking impact of a patent thicket in the biotechnology sector is the case of Golden Rice, a variety of rice produced through genetic engineering to biosynthesise beta-carotene, a precursor of pro-vitamin A in the edible parts of rice. While created at the university of Zurich, Golden Rice uses technological means protected by patents. For its exploitation, licences had to be negotiated with more than 70 patent owners (see Joly, Hervieu, 2003).

Some legal solutions are proposed to conciliate the incentives to innovate and the dissemination of knowledge, such as compulsory licensing, non-exclusive licences, modifying the duration and the breadth of patents (see O'Donoghue *et al.*, 1998; Scotchmer, 2004). But another type of solution to these restrictions has been found in the way firms manage their industrial property rights. Some studies have shown that building patent pools, could be a solution to the blocking of knowledge or could prevent litigation (see Clark *et al.*, 2000; Shapiro, 2001; Choi, 2003; Scotchmer, 2004). According to C. Shapiro, 'Virtually, every patent licence [and by extension cross licences and patent pools], can be viewed as a settlement of a patent dispute' (2003, p. 392) [...] added by us. This was, for example, the solution chosen to solve the problem of the exploitation of the Golden Rice, the case we referred to above (see Bonneuil *et al.*, 2006).

A patent pool can be defined as: "an agreement between two or more patent owners to license one or more of their patents to another or third party". Or, more precisely, as: "the aggregation of intellectual property rights which are the subject of cross-licensing, whether they are transferred directly by patentee to licensee or through some medium, such as a joint venture, set up specifically to administer the patent pool" (see Clark *et al.*, 2000, p. 4). Patent pooling is not new, as shown by the cases of the Manufacturers' Association formed in 1914 and the radio broadcast pool undertaken by RCA in 1920 (see Scotchmer, 2004, p. 174-176). This practice was often regarded as a threat to competition (notably in the US under antitrust laws), but in the two cases mentioned above, the US navy supported patent pools for defence purposes.

In fact, two cases may be distinguished: when patent pools, or cross licences, concern technology substitutes, they are considered as part of a strategy of 'cartelisation' (see Shapiro, 2001, p. 139 gives the example of the laser eye surgery attempted by summit technology Inc and VisX Inc). In these cases, patent pooling can encourage the development of monopolistic behaviour (such as high prices, imposition of "invalid" technologies, technology Malthusianism). When patent pools concern complementary pieces, they may be considered positively, as a solution to resolve blocking situations (the famous cases of MPEG 2 video compression technology, DVD standard and DVD video are often cited in the literature). The strong link between 'cartelisation' and patent agreements justifies, according to Shapiro, the development of antitrust limits to patent settlements, based on the consumer benefit of such agreements (see Shapiro, 2003).

At the same time, since the beginning of the 1980s, discussions have gained ground on the positive impact of patent pooling, and led to the *Antitrust guidelines for the licensing of intellectual property* in 1995 (issued by the US Department of Justice and the Federal Trade Commission), which recognises that 'patent pools can have significant procompetitive effects' (see Clark *et al.*, 2000, p. 6). According to this guideline, an intellectual property policy is pro-competitive when it integrates complementary technologies, reduces transaction costs, clears blocking positions, avoids costly infringement litigation and promotes the dissemination of knowledge. The pro-competitive affects are thus clearly related to their coordination function.

The same report states that the benefits of such a strategy are the elimination of problems caused by blocking patents, the increase in the disclosure of information between patent pool members, the reduction of licensing transaction costs and the distribution of risk: 'Like an insurance policy, a patent pool can provide incentive to further innovation by enabling its members to share the risks associated with research and development. The pooling of patents can increase the likelihood that a company will recover some, if not all, of its costs of research and development efforts' (see Clark *et al.*, 2000, p. 9). The latter argument also shows that the patent pooling strategy, which is gaining ground in new technology sectors (like biotechnology and ICT, in the latter case see Shapiro and Varian, 1998) is driven by the same profitability imperative that also explained the development of external means of forming 'knowledge capital'.

4.2. Patent pools and the construction of a hierarchy within an innovation network

Patent pooling is often studied in relation to its pro-competitive effects (cf. coordination function within the network of firms) but we would like to put forward that it also plays an important role in the definition of the position of the firm within its network. As a matter of fact, patent pooling, even in the case when complementary technologies are involved, supports the idea of a growing private and oligopolistic appropriation of the 'knowledge capital'. Even if the formation of "knowledge capital" depends on interdependent relations between increasing numbers of institutions (big firms, small concerns, research labs, etc.), only a few firms appropriate the return of their investment, thanks to the patents they own separately and/or collectively and that they license to each other. The other members of the innovation network (the users: clients, suppliers, subcontractors, etc.) are not the owners of the technology, have to pay a licence fee to use the technology and/or to produce the products and services that derive from this technology. This is true, even if they have participated in more or less easily observable ways (competencies, consulting, informal exchanges of information, etc.) in the constitution of the knowledge capital from which the licensed technology or set of technologies emerge. What is important here is that the practice of patent pooling, notably resulting from *ex-ante* cooperation processes, contributes towards defining the position of firms (their hierarchy) within the networks (see figure 2). The members of the patents pool – the ones that own the separate or shared patents – are the leaders of the networks. Thanks to the power conferred by the ownership of intellectual property rights, they build entry barriers protecting the highest level of networks (the leaders). These protected leaders can also keep their advance over competitors, by reinvesting the rents they receive from the commercialisation of licences in R&D processes meant to develop the next generation of technology (see Laperche, 2001). This strategy clearly shows the offensive role of intellectual property rights within innovation networks.

Figure 2: Patent pool and hierarchy within a network

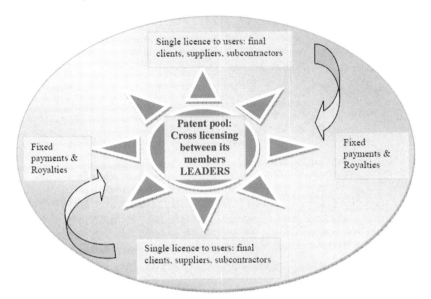

5. Conclusion

In this chapter we have developed the idea that in a networked enterprise that is focused on its double aim of being more innovative and improving the efficiency of its organisation, IPRs not only play their traditional defensive/incentive and offensive roles but also have an increasing coordination function. The networked firm is based more and more on ownership and intangible assets, compared to physical ones (in its organisation but also in the assessment of its value). Logically, we can say that in the networked enterprise, intellectual property rights tend to replace physical property rights in the coordination function (traditionally put forward in the contemporary theories of the firm). This coordination role is associated with the more traditional incentive/ defensive and offensive roles of IPRs (table 3). In this chapter, some examples illustrate the developed idea. However, applying this analysis empirically to some particular networked enterprises will be the next step of this work.

Table 3: The role of IPRs in the networked enterprise and in innovation networks

Role	Explanation
Coordination role	*Reduction of transaction costs within the networked enterprise *Reduction of transaction costs within the networks of firms (patent pools) *Solution to patent disputes (licences, patent pools) *Reputation within innovation networks *IPRs give a value to R&D investment (secure the shareholders)
Defensive/ incentive role	*Protection of the collectively built 'Knowledge capital' *Incentives to the diffusion of technology and to the investment in the constitution of the 'Knowledge capital'
Offensive role	*Definition of the position of the enterprise within the innovation network *Oligopolistic appropriation of knowledge capital and construction of barriers to competitors *Lead time

To conclude, we can say that the reasons for the evolution of laws on IPRs on an international level appear to be closely linked to the need for IPRs by firms. As firms are more and more open to their environment, constituting global networks at each step of the value chain, they need tools to improve their coordination and provide their own knowledge base with wider and stronger protection. The recent trend towards extending 'patentability' to new fields and closer to the scientific border can be regarded as an answer to this growing need for protection and coordination. Moreover, the scope of industrial property rights was widened at the end of the 1990s, with the Trade Related Industrial Property Rights (TRIPs) agreement. This agreement is managed by the WIPO and the WTO, and any infringement of this agreement can lead to commercial sanctions. The global protection given by the TRIPs agreement favours their appropriation strategies (see Gallini, 2002; Laperche, 2004). It also creates a favourable context for global diffusion – within the networked enterprise and/or within innovation networks – of patented technology (see Maskus, Reichman, 2004). All of these institutional changes provide evidence of a greater need for protection, as requested by firms themselves. These greater coordination and appropriation needs can be linked to what we have called the profitability imperative. Global corporations have to innovate in order to be competitive. The complexity and rapid pace of technological progress ('permanent innovation') lead to the increase in the cost, the complexity and hence the risk of the innovation process, which nonetheless has to be reduced if firms want to keep their precious investors. To reduce the cost, the risk and the length of the innovation process, firms rely on their own capabilities but also on the resources offered by their networks. However, being more open to their environment, they become more vulnerable; all the more so when 'appropriability' regimes are different in the countries in which they are active. That is why corporate lobbying is a major explanatory element of the evolution of laws on IPRs, as reported by J. Rifkin or S.K. Sell in the case of the TRIPs agreement (see Rifkin, 1998; Sell, 2003). This extension of intellectual property rights (application in new technological and geographic fields) may, however, reveal to be dangerous for the firms, as the assessment of their value is increasingly based on virtual rather than physical results. Moreover, the multiplication of IPRs may increase the cost of the innovation process and thus sterilise their incentive effects in terms of further investment. In this vein, a recent paper links the recent large development of IPRs with the current financial and economic crisis (see Pagano, Rossi, 2009). Did the firms dig their own graves?

Bibliography

Aglietta, M., Rébérioux, A., *Les dérives du capitalisme financier*, Albin Michel, Paris, 2004.

Alchian, A., Demsetz, H., "Production, information costs and economic organisation", in *American Economic Review*, 1972, 62, p. 777-795.

Antonelli, C., "Models of knowledge and systems of governance", in *Journal of Institutional Economics*, 2005, 1, p. 51-73.

Archibugi, D., Iammarino, S., "The globalisation of technological innovation: definition and evidence", in *Review of International Political Economy*, 2002, 9 (1), p. 98-122.

Barjot, D., "Lafarge, (1993-2004), Comment on devient firme mondiale", in *Revue économique*, 2007, 58 (1), p. 79-112.

Baudry, B., "La question des frontières de la firme, Incitation et coordination dans la firme réseau", in *Revue économique*, 2004, 55, p. 247-274.

Berger, S., *How we compete. What companies around the world are doing to make it in today's global economy?*, MIT Industrial Performance Center, Currency, 2005.

Bonneuil, C., Demeulenaere E., Thomas F., Joly P-B., Allaire G., Goldringer I., "Innover autrement? La recherche face à l'avènement d'un nouveau régime de production et de régulation des savoirs en génétique végétale", in P. Gasselin et O. Clément (eds.), *Quelles variétés et semences pour des agricultures paysannes durables?*, INRA, Paris, 2006, p. 29-51.

Castells, M., *The rise of the network society*, Blackwell Publishers, Oxford, 1996.

Chandler, A. D., *The visible hand: the managerial revolution in American business*, Harvard University Press, Cambridge MA, 1977.

Chandler, A. D., *Scale and scope: the dynamics of industrial capitalism*, MIT Press, Cambridge MA, 1990.

Chesnais, F., *La mondialisation du capital*, Syros, Paris, 1994.

Choi, J. P., "Patent Pools and Cross-Licensing in the Shadow of Patent Litigation", *Michigan State University*, 2003, http://www.msu.edu, accessed 13 July 2004.

Clark, J., Piccolo, J., Stanton, B., Tyson, K., "Patent Pools: a Solution to the Problem of Access in Biotech Patents?", USPTO, 2000, http://www.uspto.gov, accessed 13 July 2004.

Coase, R. H., "The problem of the social cost", in *Journal of Law and Economics*, 1960, 3, p. 1-44.

Coase, R. H., "The nature of the firm", in *Economica*, 1937, 16 (4), p. 386-405.

Cohen, W., Levinthal D., "Absorptive capacity: A new perspective on learning and innovation", in *Administrative Science Quarterly*, 1990, 35, p. 128-152.

Cohen, W. M., Nelson R. R., Walsh J. P., "Protecting their Intellectual Assets: Appropriability Conditions and why US Manufacturing Firms Patent (or Not)?", *National Bureau of Economic Research, Working Paper 7552*, 2000.

Cohendet, P., Kern, F., Mehmanpazir B., Munier F., "Knowledge coordination, competence creation and integrated networks in globalised firms", in *Cambridge Journal of Economics*, 1999, 23, p. 225-241.

Cohendet, P., Llerena, P., "A dual theory of the firm between transactions and competences: conceptual analysis and empirical considerations", in *Revue d'économie industrielle*, 2005, 110 (1), p. 175-198.

Dittrich, K., Dusters, G., de Man A. P., "Strategic repositioning by means of alliances networks: the case of IBM", in *Research Policy*, 2007, 36, p. 1496-1511.

Foray, D., "Exploitation des externalités de réseau versus évolution des normes", in *Revue d'économie industrielle*, 1990, 51, p. 113-140.

Fransman, M., "Information, knowledge, vision and theories of the firm", in *Industrial and Corporate Change*, 1994, 3, p. 713-757.

Gaffard, J. L., "Coordination, marché et organisation, Essai sur l'efficacité et la stabilité des économies de marché", in *Revue de l'OFCE*, 2003, 85, p. 235-270.

Gallini, N. T., "The economics of patents: lessons from recent US patent reform", in *Journal of Economic Perspectives*, 2002, 16, p. 131-154.

Gooroochurn, N., Hanley, A., "A tale of two literatures: transaction costs and property rights in innovation outsourcing", in *Research Policy*, 2007, 36, p. 1483-1495.

Hagedoorn, J., "Inter-firm R&D partnerships: An overview of major trends and patterns since 1960", in *Research Policy*, 2002, 31, p. 477-492.

Hamdouch, A., Laperche, B., Munier, F., "The collective innovation process and the need for dynamic coordination: general presentation", in *Journal of Innovation Economics*, 2008, 2, p. 3-13.

Hanel, P., "Intellectual property rights business management practices: a survey of literature", in *Technovation*, 2006, 26, p. 895-931.

Hart, O., Moore, J., "Property rights and the nature of the firm", in *Journal of Political Economy*, 1990, 98 (6), p. 1119-1158.

Jaffe, B., "The US patent system in transition: policy innovation and the innovation process", in *Research Policy*, 2000, 29, p. 531-557.

Jensen, M. C., Meckling, W.H., "Theory of the firm: managerial behaviour, agency costs and ownership structure", in *Journal of financial economics*, 1976, 3, p. 305-360.

Joly, P. B., Hervieu, B., "La marchandisation du vivant, Pour une mutualisation des recherches en génomique", in *Futuribles*, 2003, 292, p. 5-29.

Kapàs, J., "Industrial revolutions and the evolution of the firm's organisation: an historical perspective", in *Journal of Innovation Economics*, 2008, 2, p. 15-33.

Langlois, R. N., "Modularity in technology and organisation", in *Journal of Economic Behaviour & Organisation*, 2002, 49, p. 19-37.

Laperche, B., "Brevets et normes techniques, De l'incitation à l'invention au contrôle de l'innovation", in B. Laperche (ed.), *Propriété industrielle et innovation*, L'Harmattan, Paris, 2001, p. 81-98.

Laperche, B., "Patentability: Questions about the control of strategic technology", in C. A. Shoniregun, I. P. Chochliouros, B. Laperche, O. Logvynovskiy and A. Spiliopoulou-Chochliourou (eds.), *Questioning the Boundary Issues of Internet Security. E. Centre for Economics*, London, 2004, p. 117-140.

Laperche, B., "Large corporations and technostructures in competition", in B. Laperche, J. Galbraith, D. Uzunidis (eds.), *Innovation, evolution and economic change: New ideas in the tradition of Galbraith*, Edward Elgar Publishing, Cheltenham 2006, p. 142-161.

Laperche, B., "Knowledge capital' and innovation in multinational corporations", in *International Journal of Technology and Globalisation*, 2007, 3 (1), p. 24-41.

Lévêque, F., Menière, Y., *The Economics of Patents and Copyright, A Primer for Free*, Berkeley Electronic Press, 2004, http://www.cerna.ensmp.fr/PrimerForFree.htm. Accessed 15 June 2005.

Levin, R., Klevorick, R., Nelson, R., Winter, S., "Appropriating the returns from industrial research and development: a review of evidence", in *Papers on Economic Activity*, 1987.

Lung, Y., "Modèles de firme et forme du capitalisme: penser la diversité comme agenda de recherche pour la TR?", in *Revue de la régulation*, 2, 2008, http://regulation.revue.org. Accessed 22 January 2009.

Malerba, F., "Innovation and the evolution of industry", in *Journal of Evolutionary Economics*, 2006, 16, p. 3-23.

Mariotti, F., "Enterprise et gouvernement à l'épreuve des réseaux", in *Revue Française de Sociologie*, 2004, 45 (4), p. 711-737.

Maskus, K. E., Reichman, J. H., "The globalization of private knowledge goods and the privatization of global public goods", in *Journal of International Economic Law*, 2004, 7 (2), p. 279-320.

Michalet, C. A., "Dynamique des formes de délocalisation et gouvernance des firmes et des États", in *Revue française de gestion*, 2007, No. 177 (8), p. 141-148.

Michie, J. (ed.), *The handbook of globalisation*, Edward Elgar, Publishing, Cheltenham, 2003.

Milward, B., *Globalization? Internationalization and Monopoly Capitalism*, Edward Elgar Publishing, Cheltenham, 2003.

Mowery, D. C., Nelson, R., Sampat, B. N., Ziedonis, A., "The growth of patenting and licensing by US universities: an assessment of the effects of the Bayh Dole Act of 1980", in *Research Policy*, 2001, 30, p. 99-119.

O'Donoghue T., Scotchmer S., Thisse J. F., "Patent breadth, patent life and the pace of technological progress", in *Journal of Economics and Management Strategy*, 1998, 2 (1), p. 1-32.

OECD, *Science, Technology and Industry Scoreboard 2003*, OECD, Paris, 2003.

OECD, "Working paper on biotechnology, Task force on biotechnology for sustainable industrial development globalisation of industrial biotechnology R&D", DSTI/STP.BIO 13, Paris, 2008.

Pagano, U., Rossi, M. A., "The crash of the knowledge economy", in *Journal of Economics*, Cambridge, 2009, 33 (4), p. 665-683.

Plihon, D., *Le nouveau capitalisme*, Dominos, Flammarion, Paris, 2002.

Porter, M. E., *The Competitive Advantage of Nations*, Macmillan, London, 1990.

Rifkin, J., *The Biotech Century, Harnessing the Gene and Remaking the World*, Tarcher/Putman, New York, 1998.

Rosenberg, N., "Why do firms do basic research (with their own money)?", in *Research Policy*, 1990, 19, p. 165-174.

Schumpeter, J. A., *Capitalism, Socialism and Democracy*, Harper and Row, New York, 1942.

Schumpeter, J. A., *The Theory of Economic Development*, Transaction Publishers, New Brunswick and London, 1983, Harper and Row, New York, 1911.

Scotchmer, S., *Innovation and Incentives*, MIT Press, Cambridge, 2004.

Sell, S. K., *Private Power, Public Law, The Globalization of Intellectual Property Rights*, Cambridge University Press, Cambridge, 2003.

Serfati, C., "Financial dimensions of transnational corporations, global value chain and technological innovation", in *Journal of Innovation Economics*, 2008, 2, p. 35-61.

Shapiro, C., Varian, H., *Information Rules: a Strategic Guide to the Network Economy*, Harvard Business School Press, Boston Mass, 1998.

Shapiro, C., "Navigating the patent thicket: cross licensing patent pools, and standard setting", in E. Jaffe *et al.* (eds.), *Innovation Policy and the Economy*, 2001 (Vol. I), MIT Press, 119-150, Also available at http://haas.berkeley.edu/~shapiro/thicket.pdf, Accessed 1 June 2008.

Shapiro, C., "Antitrust limits to patent settlements", in *RAND Journal of Economics*, 2003, 34 (2), p. 391-411.

Sheehan, J., Martinez C., Guellec D., "Understanding business patenting and licensing: results of a survey in patents, innovation and economics performance" – Proceedings of an OECD Conference, OECD, Paris 2004.

Stigler, G. J., *The Theory of the Price*, Macmillan, New York, 1966.

Sturgeon, T., "Modular production networks: a new American model of industrial organisation", in *Industrial and Corporate Change*, 2002, 11 (3), p. 451-456.

Tidd, J., Bessant, J., Pavitt, K., *Managing Innovation, Integrating Technological, Market and Organizational Change*, J. Wiley and Sons Ltd, Chichester, 2005.

UNCTAD, *World Investment Report*, Transnational corporations and the internationalization of R&D, United Nations, New York and Geneva, 2005.

Uzunidis, D., Boutillier, S., Laperche, B., *Le travail bradé, Économie et Innovation*, L'Harmattan, Paris, 1997.

Uzunidis, D., *L'innovation et l'économie contemporaine*, De Boeck, Bruxelles, 2004.

Williamson, O. E., *Markets and Hierarchies: Analysis and Antitrust Implications*, Free Press, New York, 1975.

Williamson, O. E., *The Economic Institutions of Capitalism*, Free Press, New York, 1985.

CHAPTER III

Guanxi and the Business Environment in China

An Innovative Network
as a 'Process of a Knowledge-based Economy'

Francis MUNIER and Cao HUAN

1. Introduction

Guanxi is a specific management of Chinese firms. According to Bain (1994), guanxi is defined as the existence of a relationship between people who share a group status or are related to a common person. Guanxi is more focused on informal relations, non-normative agreements, which includes sometimes a form of corruption.

The role of guanxi is a good example of an entrenched cultural norm under pressure from international trends (see Dunfee *et al.*, 2001). Since China's entry into the WTO, the Chinese economy has also had to be close to international norms in order to develop trade, financial architecture and IDE, notably according to the OECD's norm of corporate governance. The main pressure consists of decreasing the corruption and developing a legal environment for business. In this way, an apparent contradiction appears between the openness of China and the strong cultural behaviour of Chinese managers, but we will see that this point could also be considered as a strength.

The aim of this article is precisely to show that guanxi is not so opposed to international constraints because it provides a support for knowledge creation, which is necessary in the context of a knowledge-based economy. In a certain way, guanxi also provides some security inside the network. It could be considered as a sort of substitute for a more formal legal environment (Xin, Pearce, 1996). Assimilated to a social network, it also provides a support for the interaction and sharing of knowledge. Chinese firms have to deal with both international pressures and cultural habits in order to keep this advantage.

In this article, we will not discuss the issue of corruption as this is not the subject and maybe western legal frameworks could change the nature of the practise, but maybe not so much the practise *per se*. Furthermore, Lovette *et al.* (1999) argue that guanxi could be ethical as any western system.

The originality of our work is to frame these questions in the context of recent concepts such as communities of practice (see Lave, Wenger, 1990; Brown, Duguit, 1991; Snyder, Wenger, 2000) and epistemic communities (see Cowan *et al.*, 2000). Based on these concepts, we will show that the firm can be analysed from a dual perspective: cognitive and organisational (see Munier, 1999). The first one belongs to the guanxi logic and the second one to the corporate governance logic.

In the first part, we present the dilemma between corporate governance and guanxi features. The second part explains that, despite the pressures of normative corporate governance as a best practise, guanxi also provides a system for exchange based on trust and appears as a support of knowledge creation and enhances the performance of the firm.

2. Features of Corporate Governance *vs.* Guanxi

2.1. Guanxi

Plenty of academic literature has been developed on the role of guanxi in the Chinese economy. The literature is related to the origin of success in business and also to more theoretical and more sociological analyses on the manifold sense of the term. Our aim here is not to give an exhaustive analysis of this concept (see Fan, 2002, for an analysis of the literature). We have focused on the essential elements of definitions to build the bases of the role of guanxi in the processes of creating new knowledge.

In the Chinese language, the first character of guanxi (guan) means "a pass" or "barrier", or "to close". The second character (xi) means "system", "tie up" or "link". Guanxi could therefore refer to many things (see Fan, 2002): (a) the existence of a relationship between people who share a group status or who are related to a common person, (b) actual connections with and frequent contact between people, and (c) a contact person with little direct interaction.

Technically, guanxi stands for any type of relationship. In the Chinese business world, however, it is also understood as the network of relationships among various parties that cooperate together and support one another (Davenport *et al.*, 1998). The Chinese businessman's mentality is very much one of "you scratch my back, I'll scratch yours." In essence, this boils down to exchanging favours, which are expected to be done regularly and voluntarily.

Guanxi can take on many forms. It does not have to be based only on money. It is completely legal in their culture. So, there is no need to feel uncomfortable about it. The trustworthiness of both the company and the individual is an important component. Following through on promises is a good indication of this. Treating someone with courtesy while others treat him or her unfairly is another aspect. Frequent contact fosters friendship as well. The Chinese feel obliged to do business with their friends first. There are risks with this system as well. When something goes wrong, the relationships are challenged, and friendships quickly disappear. More globally, as Fan (2002) pointed out, guanxi has been:

(1) identified as one of the most important key success factors in doing business in China; (2) regarded as a source of sustainable competitive advantage; (3) acclaimed as marketing's third paradigm, thus linking the concept with the school of relationship marketing; (4) extolled as the future direction for the western business practices in the 20th century.

People with guanxi are:

as though they carry special switches with them, and if you get involved with one person, you're suddenly involved with a whole network. Complex personal relationships, built of layer upon layer of interlocking connections, formed a dense net (see Liu, 1983; quoted by Fan, 2002).

This definition is important for our problematic. It shows that guanxi is a dynamic process that begins with two persons but involves more parties at later stages; at the end guanxi could be a social network. In most cases, the person may not have the solution and he has to search further connections for the solution. The role of the first person is a facilitator rather than a solution-provider.

We want to specify that the base of guanxi (two persons) does not correspond to the guanxi that requires more connections. The relations are then essentially informal, not contractual and based on trust. This point is determining and underlines the false dilemma between the western pressures and the Chinese principles of business. In other words, guanxi also creates a system upon which individuals can base themselves. In it, the problem of the main agent, on the basis of corporate governance, seems assured in Chinese traditional culture. Below, we suggest a reminder of the basic principles of these western pressures.

2.2. Corporate governance

An efficient corporate governance system is based on different points. Firstly, the residual claim and the control right should be matched as much as possible: whoever has claim to the residual and assumes risks should also have rights to control; conversely, whoever has rights to control should assume risks. Harris & Raviv (1989) argue that the residual claim should match the rights to control because otherwise "cheap vote rights" would lead to unqualified people being more likely to take over control of the firm. Dewatripont & Tirole (1994) argue that residual claim is an incentive for controlling parties to take appropriate courses of action. Of course, full matching between residual claim and control rights is impossible, otherwise there would be no agency problem at all.

Secondly, managerial compensation should be more closely linked to the performance of the firm, rather than fixed by contract and, thirdly, the authority of selecting and monitoring management should be assigned to capitalists. This argument can also be taken as a corollary of the first argument, since, by nature, capitalists are inevitably the eventual risk-bearers, and only they have adequate incentives to select good managers and dismiss bad managers, and to monitor managerial performance.

In order to mitigate the 'free-rider' problem of investors, concentration of ownership with large investors is preferred (see Aghion, Bolton, 1992). When control rights are concentrated in the hands of a small number of investors with a collectively large cash flow stake, concerted actions by investors are much easier than when control rights, such as votes, are split among many of them.

Has guanxi become the obstacle for the company? And should the phenomena be eliminated in China? In fact, in this chapter, we develop the idea that guanxi provides a support of knowledge creation, necessary in the context of a knowledge-based economy.

3. Guanxi as a Knowledge-based Process Support

3.1. Cognitive duality of the firm: the emergence of connections

The works of Nonaka have highlighted the crucial role of knowledge, and specifically of the interaction between tacit and explicit knowledge, for the emergence of organisational knowledge within the firm. The firm consists of pockets of tacit and codified knowledge and of data flows that sustain and permeate each other. The individuals within these firms possess skills that can be defined as an accumulation of knowledge and experience that can be directly used in action (see Spender, 1996). The emergence of cognitive communities enriches the traditional approach of governance structures (see Williamson, 1996) by identifying the places where knowledge and/or activities have been created for the organisation of the firm.

3.2 Epistemic communities and communities of practice

Epistemic communities and communities of practice are the places where knowledge is created. The main point is that epistemic communities are actually focused on creating new knowledge, whereas communities of practice are focused on the successful outcome of an activity. In this case, the creation of knowledge is an involuntary result.

Epistemic communities are defined as:

small working groups made up of agents working on a mutually recognised sub-set of problems linked to a particular type of knowledge, and who at the very least, accept a procedural authority that is also acknowledged by all of them, and which is deemed essential to the success of their cognitive activity (see Cowan *et al.*, 2000).

As such, they form a group of representatives sharing a common goal for the creation of knowledge, and a common structure that enables them all to understand it. Individuals belonging to epistemic communities focus mainly on the creation and codification of knowledge in order to establish a procedure for the resolution of problems. The process of the codification of knowledge suggests that there are codes that can be understood by the communicators. Moreover, a community is defined by the presence of a procedural authority that is either explicit or not. It has to mobilise the members of the community for the attainment of the cognitive objective. Consequently, it is the procedural authority that evaluates their membership.

People accumulate knowledge based on their own experience. The quality of this knowledge depends on two factors. The first is the variety of the individual experiences as they interact. The second factor is the "knowledge of experience". This corresponds to the notion of a rational evaluation of the feedback from experience that is validated by the procedural authority: it is the contribution by the members of the community to the cognitive objective that is assessed. And this assessment is based on criteria determined by the procedural authority.

Because of the heterogeneity of the representatives, the first task of epistemic communities is to create knowledge, which explains why it is necessary to create a codebook. From there, knowledge circulating within the epistemic communities becomes explicit but not codified, because it remains essentially internal to the community. The procedural authority validates the cognitive activity of a representative. This authority assesses the contribution of each person to the realisation of the chosen goal within the community.

The concept of a community of practice has been presented by Lave and Wenger (1990) who, by focusing on the practices of individuals, have identified groups of people involved in the same practices, who regularly communicate with each other in regard to their activities. The members of a community of practice seek first and foremost to develop their skill in the practice under consideration. Communities of practice can be seen as a means to develop individual skills. They focus on their own members (see Brown, Duguit, 1991). This goal is achieved by building, exchanging and sharing a common pool of resources (see Wenger, 1998).

Wenger (1998) and Brown and Duguid (1991) state that self-organisation is an essential characteristic of communities of practice. According to Lesourne (1991), self-organisation is the ability of a system to acquire new properties by organising itself or by modifying its own organisation. Self-organisation enables the system to evolve without the constraint of authority or any kind of determinism. The system is autonomous and creates a boundary between itself and the other functions of the company. This creates a kind of organisational frontier, according to the terminology used in the theory of self-organisation.

More precisely, the autonomy and identity of communities of practice, which are the key characteristics of self-organisation, provide for the collective acquisition and processing of environmental stimuli (see Dibiaggio, 1999). Identity and autonomy are essential elements that enable the agent to define himself in relation to his environment and allow the members of the community to behave collectively.

Identity can be seen in the mutual commitment of the community. It is based on the jointly understood and continuously negotiated activities of its members. One member of the community contributes his own experience to it and, in turn, relies on the knowledge accumulated by the community to bring his activity to a successful conclusion. This process takes the shape of "war stories" (see Brown, Duguit, 1991) that the members tell each other when they meet. In this way, they develop a jargon that is only understood by the members. It becomes a mutual commitment that binds the representatives within a social entity, and ensures the cohesion of the community and the recruitment of new members.

Wenger and Lave (1990) consider the practice of these communities as a vehicle for learning. On that basis, the community of practice assesses the individual. This assessment focuses on the values adopted by the individual and the progress made in his practice, both aspects being taken into account in the assessment.

Within communities of practice, knowledge is thus essentially "know-how" (see Brown, Duguit, 1991), which is tacit and socially localised. The type of knowledge depends on the aims and structure of the communities of practice. Consequently, the community has a tendency not to send any message to the outside world. Messages are usually only exchanged between the members of such a community. Lastly, they generate a common pool of resources (routines, sensitivities, artefacts, vocabulary, styles, etc.), which is mainly of a tacit nature, and the creation of knowledge is closely related to the "socialisation" type of knowledge conversion modes (see Nonaka, Takeuchi, 1995); distribution and conversion of tacit knowledge into tacit knowledge.

Communities of practice and epistemic communities suggest a cognitive division of the firm whereby the company resembles a seamless piece of material web (see Hughes, 1987) with much knowledge in common, differing as to the degree and the subject of the knowledge (fundamental knowledge, languages, rules, etc.). Cognitive duality goes beyond the organisation chart of the firm; it oversteps the internal and external boundaries of the firm. Nevertheless, this seamless cloth requires knowledge management.

This distinction based on membership in one of these communities, enables us to highlight a cognitive duality central to the process of creating and distributing new knowledge within the firm. In other words, this cognitive duality must be accompanied by an organisational duality that is necessary for the cohesion and performance of the company.

The creative friction between these different bodies of knowledge leads to a learning process by interaction, which in turn, leads to new knowledge. Epistemic communities are places where real interaction takes place between the communities of practice from which the members of the epistemic community originate (see Blackler, Mac Donnald, 2000). On a practical level, cognitive interrelations between communities of practice and epistemic communities can be deciphered by referring to the Nonaka and Takeuchi (1995) model of knowledge conversion.

The following table presupposes the existence of a spiral for the creation of knowledge in the sense used by Nonaka and the SECI model (see Nonaka, Konno, 1998).

**Table 1: The 'SECI' model and communities of practice –
Epistemic Communities**

	Community of practice	Epistemic community
Community of practice	*Socialisation*	*Externalisation*
Epistemic community	*Internalisation*	*Combination*

Knowledge conversion modes provide an explanation for the relations between the communities and the nature of the knowledge that is generated and diffused. *In fine*, a system is set up, whereby organisational knowledge is in the service of the entrepreneurial vision. Indeed, the expertise of the epistemic communities in their visionary quest, leads to the creation of new knowledge, which in turn give rise to predominant new beliefs in the firm (see Fransman, 1994). But for these beliefs to materialise, they must be spread throughout the organisation. The process of codification can then be set in motion with the help of a suitable medium (a detailed strategic plan, manuals, specifications for the suppliers, data sheets, etc.). The product generated by the epistemic community resembles certain formalised elements ("combination" conversion mode). At this point, the manager's task is to make the entrepreneurial vision operational. In order to do this, he relies directly on the same communities of practice that are partly responsible for the new beliefs, as well as on the standard governance structures ("internalisation" mode of conversion) The existing skills are then enriched with new beliefs that turn into new codified knowledge. This knowledge enriches both the quantity and quality of the knowledge base upon which the activity of communities of practice is founded. Members of communities of practice can then make use of codified knowledge, as well as their own know-how, as they pursue their goal of improving their practice. This process of enrichment through a particular repository of knowledge becomes a potential source of learning (see Cook, Brown, 1999).

3.3. The influence of guanxi on the communities

A firm can be understood as a form of duality where the dilemma of guanxi/corporate governance appears. Its role is not only to allocate resources according to the corporate governance vision and the accounting problems, but also to initiate and orientate the creation of new knowledge, to choose the learning process.

Thus, the dichotomy is as follows: firstly, the manager takes care of routine activities in the short term, and searches for profit and accounting activities. Secondly, the firm tries to mobilise a 'knowledge-based business', and find and develop sources of learning. The company is faced with several dilemmas to maintain a balance between its Chinese cultural and Western pressure: the dilemma between control and commitment and between change and stability.

Corporate governance is a source of coherence and order, but also a source of inertia if it seems too heavy. However, guanxi is a source of creativity, but it can also – when it is an extreme situation – involve the

disappearance of the organisational structure, thus destroying all references and codes. To enable the creation of skills in the firm, it must
consider both the advantages and disadvantages of each mode of governance.

In addition, guanxi provides greater flexibility in decision making;
corporate governance is more limited by weight constraints. The manager must strike a balance between the rapid emergences of problem-
solving, coupled with the development of a repertoire of responses
according to corporate governance. It should enable a variety of choices
while ensuring that the final choice meets the constraints of corporate
governance.

Guanxi is social capital, an important resource that a person can use
in order to find some best practises. Guanxi is a set of assets. Some
studies have drawn on resource-based theory by taking guanxi as a kind
of organisational resource and capability that not only affect the firm's
performance but could create competitive advantages (see Xin, Pearce,
1996).

Knowledge can be seen as a cultural product (see Bennett, 1999). It
is the networks of people who meet and work with each other that often
cause knowledge to migrate and be created. Technically, "guanxi"
stands for any type of relationship. In the Chinese business world,
however, it is also understood as the network of relationships among
various parties that cooperate together and support one another.

Bennett (1999) stresses the importance of culturally derived values in
the influence of organisational behaviour in China. In general, Chinese
societies are still based on traditional Confucian values which include
filial piety, industriousness, the saving of face and the networks of
personal relationships (see Bond, 1996). One of the key values of Con-
fucianism is its strong emphasis on inter-personal relationships and
conduct (see Ghauri, Fang, 2001).

The Chinese believe that duality and contradictions are inherent in
all aspects of life. Members of Confucian societies assume the interde-
pendence of events, and understand all social interactions within the
context of a long-term balance sheet; guanxi is maintained and rein-
forced through continuous, long-term association and interaction. In a
high-context culture such as China, trust or commitment to another is
secured by the potential damage to one's social position or reputation,
which may result from failing to honour exchange obligations. The
preservation of "face" and the accumulation of favours owed are the key
forces underlying the concept of guanxi (see Lo, Autis, 2003).

As many Chinese enterprises tend to be bureaucratic and rigid,
guanxi acts as a catalyst that enables a more flexible arrangement in the

transfer of resources and knowledge from the target company to the learning company (see Alston, 1989) By engaging in the networking activities through trust building and favour exchanging, the learning and source companies form a loosely structured network that is based mainly on guanxi (see Luo, 1997). Guanxi could also improve the quality of knowledge since information passed from a guanxi partner to the receiver could be assured of its reliability, richness and trustworthiness, thereby reducing the receiver's search cost, and allowing for a more informed decision (see Luo, 1997).

Guanxi can facilitate the transfer of tacit knowledge that is complex and difficult to be codified. Most of the knowledge in communities of practice is tacit, and difficult to be codified, and can be learned implicatively, through intimate interaction. And guanxi can build up the trust that is necessary for a person who wants to share his experience (see Levin, Cross, 2004). Moreover, the relationship-specific heuristics and specialised language that develop between strong ties are conducive to conveying complex chunks of knowledge (see Uzi, 1999).

4. Conclusion

We have shown that guanxi should not be opposed to Western values. It is important, in a globalised world where networks are essential, to understand the nature and strength of this cultural practice. It also seems important not to dwell on the scale of corruption as a value judgement.

Our analysis is based on the idea of a form of duality within the Chinese firm. Is this a sign of an advantage? It would obviously go beyond the analysis to answer this question.

Guanxi is not simply a key feature of Chinese culture, but the mother of all relationships. Despite the pressure of corporate governance, guanxi appears as a support of knowledge creation and enhances the performance of the firm. In the modern company in China, firms need the duality management both of guanxi and corporate governance.

Bibliography

Aghion, P., Bolton, P., "An Incomplete Contracts Approach to Financial Contracting", in *Review of Economic Studies*, 1992, vol. 59.

Alston, J. P., "Wa, Guanxi, and inhwa: managerial principles in Japan, China, and Korea", in *Business Horizons*, March-April, 1989.

Bain, Y., *Work and Inequality in Urban China*, Albany – SUNY Press, 1994.

Bennett, R. H., "The relative effects of situational practices and culturally influenced values/beliefs on work attitudes", in *International Journal of commerce & management*, 1999, 9 (1/2).

Blackler, F., McDonald, S., "Power, mastery and organizational learning", in *Journal of management studies*, 2000, 37 (6).

Bond, M. H., *The Handbook of Chinese Psychology*, Oxford University Press, Hong Kong, 1996.

Brown, J. S., Duguid, P., "Organizational learning and communities of practice: toward a unified view of working, learning and innovation", in *Organisation Science*, 1991, 2 (1).

Cook, S. D. N., Brown J. S., "Bridging epistemologies: the generative dance between organizational knowledge and organizational knowing", in *Organization science*, 1999, 10 (4).

Cowan, R., David, P. A., Foray, D., "The explicit economics of codification and tacitness", in *Industrial and corporate change*, 2000, 9 (2).

Davenport, T. H., DeLong, D. W., Beers, M. C., "Successful knowledge management project", in *Sloan Management Review*, Winter, 1998, p. 43-57.

Dewatripont, M., Tirole, J., "A Theory of Debt and Equity: Diversity of Securities and Manager-Shareholder Congruence", in *The Quarterly Journal of Economics*, 1994, Vol. CIX.

Dibiaggio, L., "Apprentissage, coordination et organisation de l'industrie: une perspective cognitive", in *Revue d'Économie Industrielle*, 1999, 88 (2).

Dunfee, T. W., Warren, A. E., "Is Guanxi Ethical: a normative analysis of doing business in China", in *Journal of business ethics*, 2001, 32.

Fan, Y., "Questioning guanxi: definition, classification and implications", in *International Business Review*, 2002, 11.

Fransman, M., "Information, knowledge, vision and theories of the firm", in *Industrial and corporate change*, 1994, 3 (3).

Ghauri, P., Fang, T., "Negotiating with Chinese: a socio-cultural analysis", in *Journal of world Business*, 2001, 36 (3).

Harris, M., Raviv, A., "The Design of Securities", in *Journal of Financial Economics*, 1989, 24 (2).

Hughes, T., "The evolution of large technical system", in W. E. Bijker, T. P. Hughes, T. Pinch (eds.), *The Social Construction of Technological Systems*, MIT Press, Cambridge Mass, 1987, p. 51-82.

Lave, J., Wenger, E., *Situated Learning: Legitimate Peripheral Participation*, Cambridge University Press, Cambridge, UK, 1990.

Lesourne, J., *Économie de l'ordre et du désordre*, Economica, Paris, 1991.

Levin, D., Cross, R., "The strength of weak ties you can trust: the mediating role of trust in effective knowledge transfer", in *Management Science*, 2004, Vol. 50.

Liu, B. (ed.), *People or Monsters? and Other Stories and Reportage from China after Mao*, Perry Link, IUP, 1983.

Lo, M.M., Otis, E.M., "Guanxi civility: processes, potentials, and contingencies", in *Politics and society*, 2003, 31 (1).

Lovett, S., Simmons, L.C., Kali, R., "Guanxi versus the market: ethics and efficiency", in *Journal of International Business Studies*, 1999, 30 (2), 231 (Summer).

Luo, Y., "Guanxi: principles, philosophies, and implications", in *Human system management*, 1997, 16 (1).

Munier, F., "Taille de la firme et innovation: une analyse fondée sur le concept de compétence pour innover", Thèse de Doctorat, Université Louis Pasteur, janvier 1999.

Nonaka, I., Konno, N., "The concept of Ba: building for knowledge creation", in *California Management Review*, 1998, 40 (3), Spring.

Nonaka, I., Takeuchi, H., *The knowledge creating company*, Oxford University Press, Oxford, 1995.

Snyder, W.M., Wenger, E.C., "Communities of practice: the organizational frontier", in *Harvard Business Review*, 2000, January-February.

Spender, J. C., "Making knowledge the basis of a dynamic theory of the firm", in *Strategic Management Journal*, 1996, 17, winter special issue.

Uzi, B., "Social relations and networks in the making of financial capital", in *American Sociological Review*, 1999, 64, p. 481-505.

Wenger, E., "Communities of practice; Learning as a social system", in *Systems Thinker*, June, 1998.

Williamson, O. E., *The Mechanism of Governance*, Oxford University Press, Oxford, 1996.

Xin, K. R., Pearce, J. L., "Guanxi: connections as substitutes for formal institutional support", in *Academy of Management Journal*, 1996, 39 (6), p. 1641-1659.

CHAPTER IV

The Dynamics between Plural and Network-based Entrepreneurship in Small High-Tech Firms

Thierry BURGER-HELMCHEN

1. Introduction

Forms of entrepreneurship in the academic literature are numerous and easy to find: academic entrepreneurship (see Bercovitz, Feldman, 2008); diffused entrepreneurship (see Minkes, Foxall, 1980); dispersed entrepreneurship (see Minkes, Foxall, 2003); distributed entrepreneurship (see Hsieh *et al.*, 2007); disintegrated entrepreneurship (see Royer, Stratmann, 2007); collaborative entrepreneurship (see Miles *et al.*, 2005); collective entrepreneurship (see Zito, 2001); community-based entrepreneurship (see Peredo, Chrisman, 2006, community in the social meaning of the term); corporate entrepreneurship (see Burgelman, 1984); intrapreneurship (see Carrier, 1996); knowledge-based entrepreneurship (see Witt, Zellner, 2007); managerial entrepreneurship (see Stevenson, Jarillo, 1990); modular entrepreneurship (see Brusoni, Sgalari, 2006); network entrepreneurship (see Harryson, 2008); open entrepreneurship (see Gruber, Henkel, 2006); plural entrepreneurship (see Burger-Helmchen, Llerena, 2008); and serial entrepreneurship (see Hyytinen, Ilmakunnas, 2007).

Not only are the forms of entrepreneurship (or entrepreneurial forms) numerous in the literature, but small firms in a high-tech industry rarely stick to only one of these forms. The type of entrepreneurial endeavour evolves over time. The dynamic leading from one entrepreneurial form to another depends on the structure of the environment and the position of the firm in that environment compared to the competitors, partners, users and suppliers (the network position of the firm) and the capabilities of the firm. In this work we try to clarify the cause and consequence relations between the network position, the firm's business model and innovation capabilities.

In the first section we briefly review some definitions of entrepreneurship and sort out the most relevant ones for the present case study. We especially develop the notions of plural entrepreneurship and network (or distributed) entrepreneurship. This presentation gives us some hints concerning the relationship between these two forms of entrepreneurship. The next section is a discussion of the case study methodology employed and a presentation of the originality of the firm studied. On the basis of the selected definitions we use a resource-based perspective, in order to capture the different dimensions of capability-building and the network position. This broad approach perfectly reflects the diversity of the problems that the entrepreneur encounters during the creation and development of the firm, and the diversity of resources that must be mobilised. The next section sums up and analyses the interview and archival data. A final section highlights the findings as well as the implications.

2. Forms of Entrepreneurship: Plural, Network or Distributed Entrepreneurship

Research on high-tech start-ups is a growing field of inquiry in economic and managerial literature. The major recession for many start-ups at the beginning of this century confirmed the need to understand their difficulties for surviving and the specificities of the knowledge-based entrepreneur behind those firms in comparison with regular entrepreneurs. The academic literature defines a high-tech start-up as a young firm (less than eight years old) launched by individuals for developing and exploiting (in various forms) an innovation (see Shan, 1990; Freeman, 1982). Regular entrepreneurship defines that innovation can be a product, a service, a process, a new commercial or organisational scheme. But researchers in strategic entrepreneurship management highlight one or several of these aspects, or add different approaches and thereby obtain many different definitions of entrepreneurship or forms of entrepreneurial firms. Many of these notions overlap, or are (simply speaking) synonyms. Figure 1 is a representation that we use to distinguish the different forms of entrepreneurship by plotting them along two axes. The two axes represent (i) the location of the entrepreneurial process, and (ii) the dimensions concerned by the entrepreneurial process.

Figure 1: Plural-entrepreneurship and other forms of entrepreneurship

		Entrepreneurship *Plural*	Entrepreneurship *Distributed/ Network*
Several		Entrepreneurship *Plural*	Entrepreneurship *Distributed/ Network*
One		Entrepreneurship *Classic*	Entrepreneurship *Dispersed/in community*

Dimension(s)

One Person/firm   Several Persons/firms

Localisation(s)

The horizontal axis selects the location of the entrepreneurial process – by location we mean how many firms/persons participate in the entrepreneurial process. Is it just one single entrepreneur, or are there several persons belonging to distinct firms?

The vertical axis corresponds to the dimensions along which the entrepreneurial process takes effect. Does it modify the product, the business model, the organisation, etc.? Are only one or several of these dimensions concerned?

The easiest situation corresponds to the case where there is one person performing an entrepreneurial act along one dimension. This case corresponds to the classic representation of entrepreneurship. The Schumpeterian entrepreneur, leading to the 'mark I innovation production', corresponds to this situation.

If we have several persons, eventually employed by several firms, we obtain a group of people involved in an entrepreneurial process. This corresponds to the notion of dispersed entrepreneurship or entrepreneurship in community. Dispersed entrepreneurship is a notion put forward by Simon (see Minkes, Foxall, 2003). In an engineering approach, he split the tasks necessary to create a new product into different sub-tasks. Each group of engineers had to resolve the problem corresponding to a specific part, or sub-task, of the project they were responsible for. More recently this approach has been developed in organisation studies together with the notions of communities (see Cohendet, Llerena, 2003). People can be working for different firms, but be involved in the same community. Because different persons/firms are linked by the same practice, and they can contribute to creating a new product, the community is entrepreneurial. A current example of this form of entrepreneurship is the open source community that creates new products by summing up the efforts of several persons dispersed around the world.

In this approach, there is only one dimension concerned: the product (or service) created by the entrepreneurial process. If several dimensions are concerned, and different firms are involved, meaning that some firms are in charge of creating a new product or service, some other firms develop a new business model/market strategy, and/or some firms organise themselves in an entrepreneurial manner around those activities, we obtain a situation of distributed or network-based entrepreneurship.

The links between the firms are essential to obtain the product, to create the appropriate market and to catch all the values created by the entrepreneurial process.

Finally, the last box in Figure 1, which we have not yet discussed, is the plural entrepreneurship situation. Plural means that one single firm or person must not only create a new product or new service, but also (if the product is really a novelty), find a new way of commercialising the product (a marketing/business model), and eventually develop an innovative organisation of their activities.

Figure 1 brings some order to the proliferating notions of entrepreneurship, but of course this is not the only representation possible to sort out the entrepreneurial forms. But Figure 1 raises intersecting issues that can potentially explain the difficulties of young high-tech firms to develop and survive. The first issue is: does a firm stick to one of these boxes during the whole life time or does it move from one box to another? Following the definitions we gave, the reader will agree with us that the entrepreneurial form can evolve during the firm's lifetime and that this evolution can even occur in a brief period after the firm has been created. It would not be surprising that a young start-up created for developing a new product discovers shortly after its creation that the market does not understand the product qualities and must therefore also innovate in the business model and be entrepreneurial in the marketing techniques. By doing this, the firm evolves from a classic entrepreneurship to a plural entrepreneurship form. Imagine now that this young firm searches for help in achieving one of these entrepreneurial dimensions by concluding a partnership with another start-up. This time we would move from plural entrepreneurship form to distributed/network entrepreneurship form in Figure 1.

If the answer to the question of whether the entrepreneurial form is fixed or evolves is obvious, other questions are less easy to answer. For example, is the starting form always classic entrepreneurship? Is there an evolution path more probable than another (clockwise rotation, or counter clockwise rotation)? Is the evolution path dependent on the maturity of the industry or/and the maturity of the firm? Does a path create more value than another, or create more future options than another? We do not further investigate these questions concerning the polymorphic form of entrepreneurship in this work, but rather we concentrate on the dynamics between the two most frequent forms of entrepreneurship in high-tech industries: plural and network-based entrepreneurship. We would like to identify some of the possible causes of the evolution from one form to another by discussing the relation between the business model, innovation capability building and the network position of the firms.

Our model is based on the following statement: the firm's performance is dependent on how the business model, innovation capabilities and network position interact. Thereby we follow the idea that the internal activities and intergenerational relationships are complements. The firm's network, as well as the firm's internal resources and competences, can be the source of inimitable and non-substitutable value. Also, when the resources linked to the network position become of a predominant importance, by definition it is in a network form of entrepreneurship. Conversely, when the resources linked to the network are of minor importance in comparison with internal resources then it is a plural-entrepreneurship form.

Our thesis is that the entrepreneurial form and the evolution from one form to another are not just dependent on the network position of the firm, but that the business model and innovation capabilities are also dependent on the network position and that those elements co-evolve.

Research framework and firm presentation

We saw in the previous section that plural-entrepreneurship is characterised by the fact that a new start-up must be entrepreneurial/innovative on several dimensions simultaneously. Also, the business model and innovation capabilities are measured following several dimensions. For assessing the firm's ability to master all these dimensions we use a longitudinal case study in which we first evaluate the resources of the firm and the evolution of these resources over several years. This approach is completed by several interviews of the founders and employees to confront our results, the actual position of the firm and their views. In this section we present the information we collected from the firm and how we link them to our plural-entrepreneurship framework. Then we describe the firm studied. But, before that, we mention the methodological position of this research.

Following on from Edmonson and McManus (2007), this work follows the methodology of intermediate theory research. This type of study draws from prior works, often from separate bodies of literature with different maturities, to propose new constructs or to search for new relationships. This is clearly the case here. We use a mature body of literature on network strategy in which we try to merge new forms of entrepreneurship. For Edmonson and McManus (2007) the methodology that best fits this type of endeavour is a field research merging qualitative case studies with reference to previous quantitative findings coming from the mature body of literature. The goal of the study is then to obtain preliminary or exploratory testing of new propositions and/or new constructs. Our aim, and therefore methodology, strictly follows their recommendations.

2.1. Evaluating capabilities

To test our framework we consider two dimensions: the technological dimension, where innovation leads to the product/service the firm offers to the consumers, and the business model/marketing dimension, where innovation allows the firm to create a market for its products and services. Each of these dimensions is estimated by a specific combination of resources possessed by the firm. We create the specific combination of indicators by following the literature on innovative small firms and the resource-based approach of the firm and dynamic capabilities (see Capaldo *et al.*, 2003; Barney *et al.*, 2001; Teece, 2007).

We create two constructs:

- Technological/product innovation capability (*TPIC*), corresponding to the firm's capability to increase its technological know-how and expertise leading to a product or service innovation.

- Business model/market innovation capability (*BMIC*), corresponding to the firm's capability to enhance its business model and understand the consumers' needs, leading to an innovation in the marketing strategy or to the creation of a new market.

Each of these constructs corresponds to a specific combination of resources between four main categories: (C1) entrepreneurial resources, (C2) human resources, (C3) resources linked to external network, and (C4) economic resources. Table 1 presents a list of all the different items we observed, and indicates how we combined the different items to obtain an estimation of the two constructs.

**Table 1: Resources employed to evaluate
the business model/market innovation capability (*BMIC*)
and the technological/product innovation capability (*TPIC*)**

Resources observed	linked to	
	BMIC	*TPIC*
C1: Entrepreneurial resources		
C1.1: Number of persons forming the entrepreneurial group	√	√
C1.2: Entrepreneurs' know-how		
C1.2.1: Percentage of entrepreneurs with technical knowledge		√
C1.2.2: Percentage of entrepreneurs with market knowledge	√	
C1.2.3: Percentage of entrepreneurs with business and management experience	√	
C1.3: Involvement of entrepreneurs in technical activities	√	√
C1.4: Involvement of entrepreneurs in marketing activities	√	
C2: Resources linked to human resources		
C2.1: Total number of employees	√	√
C2.2: Percentage of technical/product developers	√	√
C2.3: Percentage of internal developers having a graduate degree		√
C2.4: Job rotation	√	√
C2.5: Training		
C2.5.1: Marketing and management training	√	
C2.5.2: Technical Training		√
C2.6: Percentage of internal persons involved in marketing activities	√	
C3: Resources linked to external network		
C3.1: Use of non proprietary tool or external development		√
C3.2: Intensity of technical collaboration with other firms		√
C3.3: Intensity of commercial collaboration with other firms	√	
C3.4: Implication of users		
C3.4.1: Users are involved in technical problem detection phase		√
C3.4.2: Users are involved in innovation / creativity phase		√
C3.4.3: Users are involved in diffusion / commercialisation phase	√	
C4: Economic resources / indicators		
C4.1: Total profit deriving from firm's technology/product	√	√
C4.2: Total profit due to non proprietary technology and product	√	
C4.3: Total profit coming from other activities	√	

Source: Capaldo *et al.*, 2003; Morh *et al.*, 2008; Burger and Guittard, 2008.

(C1) The entrepreneurial resources combination contains indicators related to the entrepreneurs at the origin of the firm. We account for the numbers of entrepreneurs (C1.1). The more there are, the more they can distribute the different entrepreneurial activities among themselves; therefore, we found this item relevant for both concepts studied. We also distinguish their domains of expertise (C1.2), between market knowledge involved in the business model, technical knowledge necessary for product innovation, and management experience necessary for organisational innovations. The more entrepreneurs with previous knowledge in one of these dimensions, the more probable it is that they will succeed in making it more innovative. We consider these items as mutually exclusive with regard to the two constructs. As in this case study we do not search for organisational innovation, we add the management experience item to the *BMIC* indicator, following the hypothesis that this kind of experience upgrades the business model formation capabilities of the entrepreneurs. Finally, we search for the involvement of the entrepreneurs in one of the dimensions, to see if the entrepreneurs are distributed equally in all the dimensions, or if they are predominant in one of them (C1.3 and C1.4).

(C2) The human resources combination contains indicators related to the type and quantity of human resources available in the firm. We consider the total number of employees and the percentage involved in technology/product development, and those involved in marketing activities (C2.1, C2.2 and C2.6). We expect that a higher number of employees and a larger percentage involved in one of these activities lead to a higher innovation rate and a better success probability. We also take into account the diploma of the developers and the training of the developers and other employees during their stays at the firm (C2.3 and C2.5). We also expect that job rotation influences the probability of innovation in one of the dimensions.

(C3) The resources linked to external network combinations contain indicators related to the contact the firm is able to create and to maintain with other firms and with consumers/users. We look for the existence of non-proprietary technology as a factor explaining exchanges with other firms (C3.1) and if there is collaboration, whether the collaboration is of a technical nature (C3.2) or a commercial nature (C3.3). The relations with other firms are not the only important ones, relations with users can be of critical importance for firms. Following on from Burger-Helmchen and Guittard (2008), we distinguish between the involvement of users for technical problem detection, creativity and innovation, and commercialisation/distribution of the product (C3.4).

(C4) The economic resource clusters summarise different profit indicators. We distinguish three sources of profit: profit coming from the firm's own technology/product (C4.1), profit coming from non-proprietary technology and directly linked to the main product of the firm (C4.2), and profit coming from other activities but that are not dependent on the core technology of the firm (C4.3).

To appreciate the evolution of the firm and of these resource combinations, we obtained documents aimed at investors, at different phases of the firm, where the aims, products and market of the firm are presented. To understand these documents and sometimes the real motivation behind them – this does not always show through in factual data – we conducted several semi-direct interviews with the entrepreneur and the management team.

We also had access to an amount of information coming, among others, from reports, press releases, advertising articles, etc. Because this data can have different origins (internal or external to the firm), we verified their mutual coherence. In the following text, we describe the firm as F.

2.2. The firm selection

The firm studied – to be considered as a plural entrepreneurial attempt at evolving back and forth to distributed entrepreneurship – had to be a high tech start-up with at least one innovative product and one additional dimension (marketing, organisation, etc.). To select such a firm we used a firm established in the context of the research project 'Keins' on knowledge-based entrepreneurship (see Burger-Helmchen, Llerena, 2008 for explanation on that project). We sought a firm founded by people whose main reason for starting the venture was the willingness to develop their own business conception independently of the business conception of their previous employer. We also looked for a firm that had relations with different networks and who gave importance to the knowledge they had obtained from their previous work on customers' needs, the technology, the suppliers, competitors and institutions (by looking at the financial help they obtained). Finally, to be relevant in terms of the plural-entrepreneurial scheme, the founders of the firm had to believe that their specific technological knowledge and marketing/organisational entrepreneurial activity was of critical importance. Also, to be relevant to the distributed/network form, a significant amount of resources of the firm had to be linked to an external network. Firm F, met all of the criteria.

Firm F was created in August, 2000, by entrepreneurs A and B. Both are owners of the patents at the origin of the firm. Entrepreneur A is now CEO of the firm and supervises the international development of the firm. Previously he was employed as an international brand manager for a major phone company, in charge of the system convergence between different phone operators, among other duties Before that he worked as IT consultant for McKinsey. He holds a master's degree in IT engineering. Entrepreneur B is now CSO of the firm. He was previously employed as a project leader for developing new products by a major telephone operator. Before that he worked in the field of technical development for another major phone manufacturer in California. He holds an engineering degree. Both entrepreneurs have an MBA from a major international business school.

Firm F is active in the field of multi-country mobile telecommunications, providing initially its services in France, Luxembourg, Belgium and the Netherlands. In 2007 the firm entered the UK market and in 2008 expanded its operation to Germany, Switzerland and two non-European countries. The firm offers services addressing two different target groups. Firstly, it serves the end-user segment, providing a multi-country contract solution which allows frequent travellers to reduce roaming costs significantly. Secondly, to other enterprises that want to create their own brand of phone services, firm F offers them a share of its spectrum of license agreements and its know-how. Thanks to its unique, patented, technology, firm F allows the customer to avoid expensive roaming fees.

Roaming is a general term in wireless telecommunications that refers to the expansion of connection services in a geographical location that is different to the original home location where the service was registered. Roaming occurs when a wireless service subscriber uses the facilities of another wireless service provider and not the one he subscribed to. This second provider has no direct pre-existing financial or service agreement with this subscriber to send or receive information. The typical example of "roaming" is in the use of cellular phoning when a phone is in a location where its wireless service provider does not provide coverage (for example, another country). Roaming fees are traditionally charged on a per-minute basis and they are typically determined by the service provider's pricing plan.

The business idea is based on several patents which allow them to have numerous regional numbers, e.g. a French and a Belgian one, on the same SIM phone card. The user has to choose one "active" line; logically depending on his location. The other lines, in "inactive" mode, can receive calls which are forwarded to the active line. For example, if the user is located in France, his French line is active. He can call on local rates (ranging from 14 to 22 cents per minute for domestic calls), and receive calls to his French number at no cost and calls to his Belgian number for a forwarding cost of 18 cents per minute. Compared to an average roaming price of 85 cents per minute, possible cost reductions for firm F's customers are obvious. Furthermore, the consultation of voicemail from the subscribed country is free. In addition, thanks to a unified message service, customers can access and manage their messages (voicemail, fax and emails) not only from their mobile phones but also from the internet or any other phone. Roaming outside the subscribed countries is charged at the average industry price.

Firm F is a Mobil Virtual Network Operator (MVNO). An MVNO is defined as a company that provides mobile subscription services under its own brand name without having a spectrum licence (the firm does not have its own mobile phone network). They target a market niche which is not well served by the incumbents by settling an agreement with major national phone operators, buying a package of phone minutes and reselling them to individuals and firms adding specific services.

Firm F has agreements with major national phone operators in different countries where the firm provides its services. Firm F does not only target the retail business. Its agreements include the right to resell its interconnection rights to other MNVOs, which makes the company a Mobil Virtual Network Enabler (MVNE). An MVNE provides infrastructure and services to enable MVNOs to offer services to end-user customers.

In January, 2002, the company also launched a mobile service under its own brand targeting international frequent travellers and bringing 30% to 100% price reductions on GSM mobile roaming charges, plus improved seamless services.

3. Results

3.1. General results

As mentioned earlier, the purpose of this research is to understand the evolution of the different entrepreneurial resources activities, looking especially at the differences between the initial and the current situation.

The development of firm F has been relatively smooth when we look at the variation of the resources and the results obtained. The distinct feature of firm F is that it constantly acted in such a way as to exploit her patented technological base. Unfortunately, but not surprisingly for the founders, the quest for profitability took several years. Launched in 2000, firm F reached profitability for the first time in 2004. Meanwhile, the firm had to raise 5.3 million euros at different steps of development between 2000 and 2006, and had to manage the financial crisis of the IT sector between 2001 and 2003. Since its launch in 2000, Firm F has almost doubled its turnover each year, reaching 6.2 million euros in 2005. Employment has grown fast since the launching of the MNVE activity, amounting today to more than 60 persons, which represents three times the recruitment at the beginning of 2005.

The founding team made a realistic and suitable analysis of the market and conceived appropriate technology. This is probably due to their previous experience in neighbouring industries and commercial training. It is also worth noticing that market entry was eased by some major national players with whom the entrepreneurs had contacts before the launch of the firm.

As in every case study carried out after the start of the firm, it is difficult to reconstruct the original ambition and to draw the mindset of the entrepreneurs at that time on the basis of documents and interviews. Also, we cannot tell whether the evolution of the firm and of its capital corresponded to the real intended plan. However, the initial plan seems to us to be coherent and the final outcomes are close to the initial mindset we deduced. The major source of variation is related to the time horizon. This variation can work against the firm (time to be profitable) but can also be favourable (time to develop other activities around the initial project). In the following text, we link these to the evolution of the resources of the firm.

3.2. Plural or network entrepreneurial activity oriented results

In this study we identified two types of entrepreneurial activity that enabled the firm to overcome the problems a start-up faces in its early days: a technological science-based entrepreneurship (patenting activity); a business model/marketing entrepreneurship (to communicate about a new type of product); and, depending on the amount of resources linked to the network position, we can classify the firm in a specific entrepreneurship type.

Tables 2 and 3 show our initial estimation and evolution of the resources linked to the technological/product innovation capability and the resources linked to the business model/market innovation capability

**Table 2: Resources linked to
the technological/product innovation capability**

Resources observed	*Initial evaluation*	*evolution*
C1: Entrepreneurial resources		
C1.1: Number of persons forming the entrepreneurial group	2	=
C1.2.1: Percentage of entrepreneurs with technical knowledge	100%	=
C1.3: Involvement of entrepreneurs in technical activities	Average	=
C2: Resources linked to human resources		
C2.1: Total number of employees	2	60
C2.2: Percentage of technical/product developers	80%	–
C2.3: Percentage of internal developers having a graduate degree	100%	=
C2.4: Job rotation	Slow	=
C2.5.2: Technical Training	Seldom	+
C3: Resources linked to external network		
C3.1: Use of non proprietary tool or external development	Yes	=
C3.2: Intensity of technical collaboration with other firms	High	+
C3.4.1: Users are involved in technical problem detection phase	No	Yes
C3.4.2: Users are involved in innovation / creativity phase	No	No
C4: Economic resources / indicators		
C4.1: Total profit deriving from firm's technology/product	High	–

The resources linked to the technological/product innovation capability

One of the founders of the firm took on the technological entrepreneurial activity. Therefore he himself is the main resource of this category. At the launch of the start-up, the main technology was created, and only a few practical problems still had to be resolved. The most urgent critical task was to obtain the patent (which is not entrepreneurial). Despite the fact that both entrepreneurs had a technology background (100% in item C1.2.1, Table 2) only one of them was involved in the technical activities on a daily basis (average on C1.3). The total number of employees has grown strongly since the launch of the firm. As both entrepreneurs had a technological background when the firm was launched, subsequent hiring of employees logically decreases this percentage. Over the past two years the major part of the hiring was linked to the sale and adaptation of the products to the needs of the consumers or administrative tasks (C2). For facilitating the implementation of Firm F's products and services some non-proprietary features were added. Therefore the firm has frequent relations with the major phone companies (C3.1 and C3.2). The firm's geographical expansion leads to a growing quantity of relations with these kinds of phone opera-tors. From the launch of the firm to today, the main part of the total profit of the firm is derived from the firm's technology and its main product/service. But expansion of other activities naturally implies a decline in this proportion. Therefore from the resources linked to the technological/product innovation capability the firm seems to be a distributed/network type of entrepreneurial firm. Following the specific nature of the product, the development of the firm would simply not be possible without relations with the major phone companies.

Table 3: Resources linked to
the business model/market innovation capability

Resources observed	*Initial evaluation*	*evolution*
C1: Entrepreneurial resources		
C1.1: Number of persons forming the entrepreneurial group	2	=
C1.2.2: Percentage of entrepreneurs with market knowledge	100%	=
C1.2.3: Percentage of entrepreneurs with business and manage-ment experience	50%	+
C1.4: Involvement of entrepreneurs in marketing activities	Average	=
C2: Resources linked to human resources		
C2.1: Total number of employees	4	60
C2.2: Percentage of technical/product developers	80%	–
C2.4: Job rotation	Slow	=
C2.5.1: Marketing and management training	Seldom	=
C2.6: Percentage of internal persons involved in marketing activities	20%	+
C3: Resources linked to external network		
C3.3: Intensity of commercial collaboration with other firms	Very High	=
C3.4.3: Users are involved in diffusion / commercialisation phase	No	Yes
C4: Economic resources / indicators		
C4.1: Total profit deriving from firm's technology/product	High	–
C4.2: Total profit due to non proprietary technology and product	Low	=
C4.3: Total profit coming from other activities	Low	+

The resources linked to the business model/market innovation capability

When starting their firm, the entrepreneurs had to choose between a wide range of possible business models, each entailing advantages but also technical, legal and managerial challenges. They chose to focus on one type of activity at the beginning of the start-up, and deliberately ignore some other forms of activities they could have performed with the patented technology. The resources dedicated to the implementation of the business model and adaptation of the product to the different markets were those that grew fastest in the firm (C2.6). The contribution of users to the diffusion of the product was very limited in the beginning. Later, the firm engaged in some viral-advertising and proposed several sponsorship actions to the consumers (C3.4.3). All of those activities are carried out by the firm as a stand-alone, corresponding therefore to a plural-entrepreneurship form.

The evolution between plural-entrepreneurship and network entrepreneurship

This part of the study explored the configurations, evolution and organisation of the firm. This approach enhances research on entrepreneurial networks and dispersed forms of entrepreneurial activities (see Minkes, Foxall, 2003). Such an approach certainly extends our understanding of organisational inertia and adaptability capacities, and helps to explain the dynamics of start-up firms. Let us say some words about the effects of the plural-entrepreneurial configuration on the performance of the firm.

We identified two main entrepreneurial activities, but they did not receive the same amount of resources and time from the founders. Resource allocation between the plural-entrepreneurial activities is certainly a source of performance (and survival) of the firm. As we expected, the technologically oriented entrepreneurial activity and marketing entrepreneurship were important in the early stages of the firm. It already had a technology product at the beginning (yet to be patented) but still had to develop the technology and overcome many minor practical problems. Another task appeared to be crucial: the coordination of all the elements of novelty to obtain coherence in the activities and cohesion between the employees. The need for coherence and cohesion was also significant in terms of relations with the partners (a limited number at the beginning).

This configuration of plural-entrepreneurial activity proved advantageous for the performance of the firm because it gave it the capacity to be connected with a diverse set of external partners in a broad range of important firms and to integrate all the information internally.

In the beginning the focus allowed the firm to avoid being overloaded with tasks and problems. The overload occurs when too many tasks must be coordinated by a small number of individuals. Secondly, the founders focused on a business model that was new, but close enough to their previous activities in major phone companies. Therefore they could use their former network of contacts and build on it to obtain new focused relations. At the same time, the entrepreneurs could feel assured by one of the major financers who approved their business model strongly so that the two founders could focus on their main entrepreneurial activities: science-based entrepreneurship and marketing entrepreneurship. We can see that, even when the initial form of entrepreneurship was plural (or even classic) it quickly evolved into network-based entrepreneurship. The network-based entrepreneurship existed because there where resources in the firm and outside of the firm that needed to be coupled.

Discussions with the founders in the summer of 2007 also showed that during the period when only one of the entrepreneurial activities was followed, the firm did not do well. The firm had to manage to align the entrepreneurial activities, but each activity needed to be focused on one task and needed specific resources and training. It thus seems important for both theory and practice to be concerned about the factors that constrain and enable a firm to identify and adapt the entrepreneurial activities with changing knowledge, environment and resources.

This also suggests that it can be fruitful for researchers to consider the interplay between different forms of entrepreneurship. Plural-entrepreneurship is generated and maintained by individuals. As our study tries to show, strong and cohesive ties at the individual level have a positive effect on the firm's performance. We believe that the more heterogeneous the entrepreneurial tasks, the more important the cohesion between the individuals.

4. Conclusions and Implications

Some issues emerge from the analysis of firm F. There is a clear need to adapt the commercial behaviour of the firm to its technological innovation (see Mohr *et al.*, 2008). The emphasis on the marketing and organisation setting as an entrepreneurial activity was necessarily contemporaneous with the technological entrepreneurial task.

One of the major problems when the firm began was the anticipation of the pace of the adoption of services provided for the customers. In contrast, the organisation that had to be implemented was relatively well anticipated. This rather smooth development probably comes from the fact that the major patent and the major technological development were obtained shortly after the foundation of the firm.

The objective was to deepen our understanding of the dynamics of entrepreneurial forms. The high-tech start-up we analysed showed that actually it is true that the evolution of firm F was mainly a plural-entrepreneurial attempt at the beginning and that it turned out to be more a network-based form of organisation. This represents a significant evolution, and so we observe a strong modification of the firm between its infancy and today's development phase (still too early to speak about a maturity phase). Again we emphasise the importance of the 'triplet' of technology, product and market, the related entrepreneurial tasks and the more standardised activity of financing.

It is clear that a failure in terms of one of the above elements would have been a hard blow for the firm, hindering its development and profitability. Therefore the strategy behind the firm's decisions and their influence on the dynamics between plural- and network-based entrepreneurship must be conducted in a coherent way. We observed a modification of the form of entrepreneurship organisation when the firm needed resources that it did not have. The sequence we observed was the following: a lack of product innovation capability created the need to find external resources. The resources position could only be achieved by simultaneously modifying the business model, which caused the expected creation of innovative capabilities.

As a single case study, this cause/consequence scheme – and the passage from plural to network-based entrepreneurship that is behind it – cannot not be generalised. More studies are needed to find out whether this pattern is a general evolution or not. But, already, some similarities exist between this work and an empirical study on software firms' business strategy made by Venkatraman *et al.* 2008. These authors, starting from a thesis close to ours, and using firms that had characteristics and network positions that co-evolved with time, showed that the time sequence interaction between the business model and the network position was the following: first the business model evolves, then the network position is modified. But they admit that this result may be particular to the packaged software sector they studied. For them, and for us, more systematic thinking and analysis is needed to develop plausible alternative time-sequenced models with a nuanced typology of linkage for products from different types of sectors.

We would also like to mention that it is not only the business model that has to evolve: when the entrepreneurial form is modified, the governance should also probably evolve – or rather, it should precede the evolution to prevent any problems.

Finally, as mentioned by Vekatraman *et al.* (2008), we need robust evaluation criteria that fit empirical data sets for econometrics, instead of qualitative measure as we used in this longitudinal case study. Such measures (or stable sets of measures) should be employable in all forms of entrepreneurship to allow a comparison between the performances of different firms, whether they be creative stand-alone firms or ones that operate in networks.

Bibliography

Barney, J., Wright, M., Ketchen, D., "Resource-based theories of competitive advantage: A ten-year retrospective on the resource-based view", in *Journal of Management*, 2001, 27, p. 625-641.

Brusoni, S., Sgalari, G., "New combinations in old industries", in *Journal of Evolutionary Economics*, 2006, 16, p. 25-43.

Burgelman, R., "Designs for corporate entrepreneurship", in *California Management Review*, 1984, 26, p. 21-42.

Burger-Helmchen, T., Guittard, C., "Are users the next entrepreneurs? A case study on the video game industry", in *International Journal of Entrepreneurship Education*, 2008, 6, p. 57-74.

Burger-Helmchen, T., Llerena, P., "A Case study of a creative start-up: Governance, communities and knowledge management", in *Journal of Innovation Economics*, 2008, 2, p. 127-148.

Capaldo, G., Iandoli, L., Raffa, M., Zollo, G., "The evaluation of innovation capabilities in small software firms: A methodological approach", in *Small Business Economics*, 2003, 21, p. 343-354.

Carrier, C., "Intrapreneurship in small businesses: An exploratory study", in *Entrepreneurship: Theory & Practice*, 1996, 21, p. 5-20.

Cohendet, P., Llerena, P., "Routines and communities in the theory of the firm", in *Industrial and Corporate Change*, 2003, 12, p. 271-297.

Edmonson, A. C., Mcmanus, S. E., "Methodological fit in management field research", in *Academy of Management Review*, 2007, 32, 4, p. 1155-1179.

Freeman, C., *The Economics of Industrial Innovation*, Frances Pinter, 1982.

Gruber, M., Henkel, J., "New ventures based on open innovation – an empirical analysis of start-up firms in embedded Linux", in *International Journal of Technology Management*, 2006, 33, p. 356-372.

Harryson, S. J., "Entrepreneurship through relationships – navigating from creativity to commercialisation", in *R&D Management*, 2008, 38, p. 290-310.

Hsieh, C., Nickerson, J.A., Zenger, T.R., "Opportunity discovery, problem solving and a theory of the entrepreneurial firm", in *Journal of Management Studies*, 2007, 44, p. 1255-1277.

Hyytinen, A., Ilmakunnas, P., "What distinguishes a serial entrepreneur?", in *Industrial and Corporate Change*, 2007, 16, p. 793-821.

Kodama, M., "Innovation through dialectical leadership – case studies of Japanese high-tech companies", in *Journal of High Technology Management Research*, 2005, 16, p. 137-156.

Maurer, I., Ebers, M., "Dynamics of social capital and their performance implications: Lessons from Biotechnology start-ups", in *Administrative Science Quarterly*, 2006, 51, p. 262-292.

Miles, R. E., Miles, G., Snow, C. C., *Collaborative Entrepreneurship: How Groups of Networked Firms Use Continuous Innovation to Create Economic Wealth*, Stanford University Press, Stanford CA, 2005.

Minkes, A. L., Foxall, G. R., "Herbert Simon and the concept of dispersed entrepreneurship", in *Journal of Economic Psychology*, 2003, 24, p. 221-228.

Minkes, A. L., Foxall, G. R., "Entrepreneurship, strategy, and organisation: Individual and organisation in the behaviour of the firm", in *Strategic Management Journal*, 1980, 1, p. 295-301.

Mohr, J., Sengupta, S., Slater, S., *Marketing of High-technology Products and Innovations*, Prentice Hall, Englewood Cliffs, N.J., 3rd edition, 2008.

Penrose, E., *The Theory of the Growth of the Firm*, Oxford University Press, 1959.

Peredo, A. M., Chrisman, J., "Toward a theory of community-based enterprise", in *Academy of Management Review*, 2006, 31, p. 309-328.

Royer, S., Stratmann, U., "Independent entrepreneurs as an obsolete model? Considerations for the European automotive repair and service markets", in *International Journal of Globalisation and Small Business*, 2007, 2, p. 47-65.

Shan, W., "An empirical analysis of organizational strategies by entrepreneurial high-technology firms", in *Strategic Management Journal*, 1990, 11, p. 129-139.

Stevenson, H., Jarillo, J. C., "A paradigm of entrepreneurship: entrepreneurial management", in *Strategic Management Journal*, 1990, p. 7-27.

Teece, D., "Explicating dynamic capabilities: the nature and micro-foundations of (sustainable) enterprise performance", in *Strategic Management Journal*, 2007, 28, p. 1319-1350.

Venkatraman, N., Lee, C. H., Iyer, B., "Interconnect to win: the joint effects of business strategy and network positions on the performance of software firms", in J. Baum, and T. Rowlet (eds.), *Network Strategy, Advances in Strategic Management*, 2008, 25, p. 391-424.

Witt, U., Zellner, C., "Knowledge-based entrepreneurship: The organizational side of technology commercialization", in F. Malerba, S. Brusoni (eds.), *Perspectives on Innovation*, Cambridge University Press, 2007, p. 352-371.

Zellner, C., "The Economic Effects of Basic Research: Evidence for Embodied Knowledge Transfer via Scientists' Migration", in *Research Policy*, 2003, 32, p. 1881-1895.

Zito, A. R., "Epistemic communities, collective entrepreneurship and European integration", in *Journal of European Public Policy*, 2001, 8, p. 585-603.

SECOND PART

KNOWLEDGE POOL AND CLUSTERING INNOVATION

CHAPTER V

The Local Basis of Innovation and Growth Processes

Maryann P. FELDMAN

1. Introduction

Modern economic growth is a complex phenomenon that is increasingly dependent on innovation – the ability to create economic value through the application of knowledge. Innovation has a decidedly local focus, as certain locations provide an advantage for creative activity. Just as firms are one of the means towards organising economic activity, geography provides a platform to organise resources and relationships for economic gain. Beyond the natural advantages of resource endowments, proximity to markets, or climate, certain places have internal dynamics that increase the productivity of investments and result in higher innovation and creativity. These internal dynamics are socially constructed and involve a wide variety of actors. Most importantly, since it is difficult to predict future technological change and market evolution, the greater the number of individuals who are able to participate in creative endeavours, the higher the probability that a place – be it a city, region or nation – is able to capture the resulting benefits. Education, as an investment in human capital, creates the potential for innovation and prosperity.

This chapter applies an appreciation of the benefits that accrue to innovation in certain locations to the discussion of education for innovation and economic growth. There is currently an active debate in academic literature about whether the world is flat or spiky – that is to say whether opportunities are uniformly distributed or if there are certain places at certain times that offer greater. The premise of my work is that the world is spiky: innovation exhibits a pronounced tendency to cluster both spatially and temporally (see Feldman, 1994). This chapter provides a review of the literature that supports the proposition that innovation and economic growth are local phenomena. After offering a set of concepts that economists use to discuss innovation, this chapter considers that what matters most for future economic growth is creating engaged places with internal dynamics that promote creativity, experimentation and, subsequently, innovation.

While outsourcing allows firms to lower production costs, technologically sophisticated firms compete on the basis of differentiated performance and innovation. While firms are the entities that take ideas to the market and realise value from innovation, even the largest multinationals are embedded in ecosystems that support and sustain their activity. These systems are globally connected but are typically focused in certain locations or industry clusters: collections of firms within one specialised industry or technology, concentrated within the same local geographical area (see Bathelt, Malmberg, Maskell, 2004). These clusters typically include an infrastructure of related and supporting industries, the presence of specialised skilled labour and proximity to a strong research base (see Krugman, 1991; Porter, 1990). The profitability of firms reflects strategy, and location is one dimension. However, the most profitable locations are themselves the result of entrepreneurial efforts to build the resources that provide an advantage for an industry (see Feldman, 2001; Feldman, Francis, 2004). The most productive locations develop a coherent place-specific activity set that is not easily transferred or replicated. This ecosystem forms the basis for sustainable advantage for both firms and industries (see Feldman, Martin, 2005a). Thus, the economic fortunes of firms and places are intricately interwoven. Despite advances in telecommunication, innovative activity remains concentrated (see Feldman, 2001), due in large part to the unique characteristics of knowledge and its relationship to economic activity.

2. The Terms of the Debate

When an issue is significant the popular discussion may easily become muddled. Terms are used interchangeably and without precision and, as a result, debate becomes superficial. As we accept that we live in a knowledge economy, there is a need for clarity and an appreciation of the nuances that make knowledge and innovation different from tangible goods and routine production activities. This chapter begins with a series of definitions that economists use to discriminate between the components of innovation (see Feldman, Link, Siegel, 2004; Link, Siegel, 2007 for additional background). The intention is to advance the discussion and enrich the choice of policy options.

The most decisive input for innovation is knowledge. While information is the flow of data, knowledge is a stock of information that is organised into a conceptual schema. Innovation is the ability to blend and weave different types of knowledge into something new, different and unprecedented, which has economic value. Similar to art, innovation is a creative expression. However, unlike art, the measure of innovation is not in the eye of the beholder, but in acceptance within the marketplace, which brings commercial rewards to the innovating entities and returns to society in terms of economic well being, prosperity and growth.

Knowledge is arguably the most important asset in the modern economy. Of course, knowledge is an ethereal concept that is perhaps best considered as embodied in human capital, which is individuals who have received the benefit of education and who are able to appreciate, integrate, augment knowledge, and innovate. Skilled human capital requires investment in higher education institutions dedicated to advanced learning, sophisticated research, and public service important to the functioning of the modern economy. There is a debate in the literature about the primacy of human capital or institutions in creating and sustaining economic growth (see Glaeser *et al.*, 2004). In large part, universities and other educational and research institutions are arguably critical, as they span both sides of this debate, providing skilled human capital in the context of enduring structure and mechanisms of resource allocation, collaboration and governance.

Knowledge has characteristics such as being non-rival and non-excludable, which classify it as a public good. Once knowledge is created, it is similar to a sunset in that it is possible for many to appreciate the beauty and enjoy the benefits. *Non-rival*, in the economists' terminology, indicates that one person's use of knowledge does not impede another's use of it. Consider the example of a mathematical formula. Knowledge is created when the formula is first derived and formal proofs are demonstrated. The result is most likely a scholarly publication which would codify the knowledge, rendering it easy to diffuse and put into practice. The author would receive credit from the academic community for the publication. Once the formula is codified and put into the public domain, others may use it and freely build upon the discovery, expanding knowledge and advancing the communities' appreciation of the results. The fact that one scientist uses the formula does not diminish its usefulness or utility to other scientists. In fact, the value of the formula will actually increase as a result of its greater use and augmentation. Thus, knowledge, once created, is non-rival in that many economic actors may enjoy it simultaneously. *Non-excludability* refers to the fact that once knowledge is discovered it is difficult to contain or to prevent others from using it and benefiting from it. Continuing with the example of the mathematical formula, once the discovery is known it can be replicated at what is known as zero marginal cost.

The burden of discovery rests with the individual who created the formula, but once they have made the discovery and codified the knowledge others will benefit simply by using the formula. As a result of these two conditions, the social value of knowledge is greater than the value that the creator may be able to capture, a classic case of an externality or spillover. As a result, private decision-makers, either individuals or firms, are likely to under-invest in knowledge production since the returns to the firm are smaller than the returns to society. This is the traditional economic justification for government funding for research (see Feldman, Kogler, 2007). As knowledge become more important to economic activity, there are attempts to privatise knowledge, to be able to more fully capture or appropriate the resulting returns. Yet this may result in inefficiencies that limit the further development of knowledge, impede the accumulation of innovative capacity and diminish the overall functioning of the economy.

Knowledge is unlike other types of commodities and manufactured products. One of the most interesting characteristics is the *tacitness* of knowledge. Tacitness refers to something that you can not quite codify and easily write down. We can conceptualise knowledge on a continuum for the most concrete and codified, like a mathematical formula, to the most ethereal and hard-to-pin-down meaning of work in progress. This was brought back to me in an interview when I asked about the importance of being located in close proximity to other scientists who were working on the same topic. The scientists, capturing the nature of tacit knowledge, noted: "I can say more than I can write, but I know more than I can say." By coming together in a conference, such as the event behind this volume, individuals form a temporary spatial agglomeration. Rather than simply read codified material, spatial proximity allows face to face inquiry and the observation of subtle queues that reveal meaning. This is true for academics but also holds for other professions. Despite the internet and the ease of costless communications, the convention and conference business is booming, suggesting that these activities are complements rather than substitutes. Predictions that computers would result in a paperless office have not come true and predictions about the death of distance are also exaggerated (see Cairncross, 1997). The evidence seems to point to the fact that once someone knows what they are looking for, and have identified a specific piece of information, it is easy to search the Internet, find the information, or find a person who might know, and email or otherwise communicate with them. However, when new knowledge is being developed in a specialised context, and under great uncertainty, then being at the locus of where high opportunity creative activity is concentrated offers an advantage (see Audretsch, Feldman, 1996b). This is especially true for scientific activity.

Science, in a broad sense, is the unfettered search for knowledge for the sake of understanding. This search is based on observed facts that may be replicated through experimentation or theory. Thus, science searches for some unknown results to address fundamental questions related to hypotheses. The process of investigation is known broadly as *research*, and research may be *basic*, with the intention of advancing science, or *applied*, with the orientation towards some practical end. In general, the more basic the science involved in a research project, the more difficult it is to appropriate the resulting returns. For this reason, science is typically conducted by universities, while more applied R&D is typically conducted by private firms. These are two ends of a continuum of problem-solving, as basic research suggests avenues of inquiry that are advanced by applied research. In turn, research is enriched, as applied work creates the need for more theoretical work and suggests new avenues for further basic research. In contrast to the logic of specialisation, there are benefits in science from cross fertilisation and collaboration (see Jones, 2006). In addition, while science is classified by disciplines that define traditions of inquiry, applied problem-solving frequently creates the need for multidisciplinary teams, or even creates new disciplines to colonise the frontiers of knowledge. Examples would be the rapidly evolving fields of biochemistry and biomedical engineering, or the emerging fields of nanotechnology, genomics, or proteomics.

A distinction also exists with regards to the definition of *education* and *training*. While training is task oriented, education has a broader goal of developing innate abilities, enabling human creativity and perpetuating civil society. Training relies on taking an educated individual and imparting specific vocational skills that are useful to a function in the economy. Of course, these two concepts are complementary: we train someone to memorise multiplication tables, while reinforcing with education the use of the technique to solve problems, interpret results and make inferences. Education, like research, seeks to advance understanding of the world in contrast to the focused orientation of training that is often context specific. For example, law schools train students to work within a legal framework, and these skills are not easily translated to other places or even other sub-fields of law. In general, it is easier for an individual to capture the benefits of training. The broader benefits of education have similar 'public good' characteristics: knowledge becomes embodied in individuals and all of society benefits.

Education may be viewed through either a microeconomic or macroeconomic lens. Individuals invest in education in order to increase their earnings, job security and job satisfaction. As such, attending school and seeking additional training is an investment in human capital that is expected to pay off in terms of higher lifetime wages and upward social mobility. In addition, educated individuals are better citizens, friends and parents, so that there is a gain to society that is larger than the gain to the individual. Viewed through a macroeconomic lens, high aggregate levels of human capital – an economist's way of saying that the average individual in a country has benefited from education – is associated with higher rates of economic growth. The economies of countries also undergo structural transformations, notably moving to higher value-added activities, as cost advantages shift and innovation changes their competitive advantage. Lesser-developed economies have concentrations of employment in agriculture, while more-developed countries have greater shares of employment in knowledge-intensive manufacturing and services. Of course, the macroeconomic performance of the economy is dependent on individuals' decisions, just as those individual decisions are a response to incentives and opportunities in the larger economy. When these two spheres of influence are congruent and reinforcing, the economies of countries grow the fastest.

Spiky World

Location matters to economic activity, especially innovative, creative and non-routine activity (see Feldman, 2001; Audretsch, Feldman, 2004 for a review). Most recently, we observe pronounced spatial clustering in places like the Silicon Valley in the US and Bangalore, India. However, this is not a modern phenomenon. The tendency of innovation to cluster both spatially and temporally is a regular occurrence. Think about Florence under the Medici's, Vienna during Mozart's career, Manchester during the Industrial Revolution, or Paris in the 1920s, all places where creative activity flourished. Multinational firms like to perceive the world as flat because they benefit by exploiting wage differentials. Small and medium-sized firms, lacking the resources of their larger counterparts, are more tied to specific locations.

Alfred Marshall wrote about the spatial cluster of industries in 1890 (reprinted in 1929), noting that easy access to pools of skilled workers, specialised suppliers, localised competition, and the ability to benefit from knowledge externalities, provided an advantage to local firms. This is a well-known finding due to the prominence of modern technology-based clusters (see Braunerhjelm, Feldman, 2006).

New technologies and new industries, while offering potential for economic growth, do not emerge fully developed, but begin rather humbly as scientific discoveries, often made in academic laboratories. At the time of discovery, the commercial potential is unknown and only a few experts may appreciate its significance. Translating the discovery into commercial activity and realising its economic potential entails a process that involves building an appreciation of what is possible among potential investors, customers and employees. Moreover, realising the commercial potential of a piece of technology requires taking it out of the lab, into a community and building companies. Increasingly, there is recognition that what matters for place-specific industrial development is not necessarily resources or initial conditions but the social dynamics that occur within a place, and that define a community of common interest around a nascent technology or emerging industry (see Feldman, Romanelli, 2007). Community building – as opposed to insular scientific dialogue – can be essential to regional industrial development by constructing a shared understanding and appreciation of the emerging technology (see Lowe, Feldman, 2008).

Geography and place-specific interactions shape industries. If you enjoy coffee or fine wine, then you know that there is something about the soil, the climate, the angle of the sun, the age of the trees, and the growing and harvesting traditions that create something very unique. Even the best vineyards experience different vintages, reflecting the myriad of variations that determine quality. While quality winemaking is spreading around the world – with products now exported from Chile, Argentina, Australia, New Zealand, and South Africa – wines have become more complex and differentiated rather than homogenous. Connoisseurs talk about *terroir*, a French term used to denote the special characteristics that geography bestows. The term can be translated literally as "dirt" but more poetically as a "sense of place". The term captures the total effect that the local environment has on the product, when the total effect is more than the sum of its parts.

In my field, we view location as a geographic platform that provides a means to organise the human activity and that is essential to the creation of innovation and the production of knowledge. Firms are one well-known way of organising productive activity, epistemic communities of scholars are certainly another. Geography, spatial proximity and collocation are a third. As technology allows greater communication over long distances, we experiment with distant collaboration and knowledge sharing. But sometimes there is simply no substitute for just being there – being at the place where exciting work is taking place, where high-content, unstructured conversations take place, and where the unexpected may be explored and spark something new (see Gertler, 1995).

Constructing Jurisdictional Advantage

In a series of papers, Roger Martin and I introduce the concept of jurisdictional advantage with the intention of adapting concepts from business strategy to advance economic development theory (see

Feldman, Martin, 2005b). We demonstrate how places might strategically position themselves to gain economic advantage through the creation of a coherent, reinforcing activity set. The term jurisdiction is used to define the set of actors that have a common interest in a spatially-bound community and stands in stark contrast to the concepts of place or region. Jurisdictions are entities with a legitimate political ability to influence social and economic outcomes within their political boundaries. A successful jurisdictional strategy produces relatively high and rising wages for the workers and increasing real estate values for property owners. If wage levels are higher than other comparable jurisdictions, then the jurisdiction is translating its human, physical and other capital into higher economic output per worker than its counterparts. If wages are rising, then the jurisdiction is likely to be increasing its relative effectiveness rather than losing ground and regressing towards the mean. Similarly, if real estate values are increasing, current owners of real estate are rewarded with appreciation of the value of their property in the jurisdiction. The best jurisdictional strategy will maintain high and rising wages and property values in the long run.

Jurisdictional advantage is the result of specific unique capabilities that are built up over time to form a coherent place-specific activity set that is not easily transferred or replicated (see Feldman, Martin, 2005a). This requires a vision for the industry sector that often advances because of new business models, new ways of combing expertise and then carrying this vision forward to the market. Bangalore is a good example of a complex self-organising cluster. Twenty years ago Bangalore was known as a retirement community, but it did have an aerospace industry and prominent educational institutions. Over time, the software industry and an outsourcing business model developed. Notably, government played a perverse role as restriction on manufacturing computer equipment favoured programming. Entrepreneurs, who were highly trained engineers, developed their companies but also worked together to create opportunity. This is very similar to the story of Silicon Valley and other successful places – entrepreneurs build clusters while they build their companies (see Feldman *et al.*, 2005).

When entrepreneurs confront new technological opportunities, they fashion solutions that adapt what they have on hand from what is easily accessible. The solutions they adopt are more likely to come from local sources – either through tapping networks of people working on similar things or through serendipitous encounters. Most importantly, entrepreneurs use local ingredients in creative and adaptive ways. Solutions that appeared to work are repeated and fine-tuned, gradually evolving into accepted routines and operating procedures – the industrial recipes for the region. These recipes are adopted by institutions to define common practices and a common vision of the industry. This encourages further experimentation and adaptation. Knowledge of what does not work, what approaches have previously been tried, and led to dead ends, are part of this local knowledge.

Many view universities as engines that are able to drive innovation and economic growth. This is a rather exaggerated view of what universities can accomplish. In contrast to commercial firms with a relatively simple profit motive, universities have complex objective functions that involve a variety of educational and societal objectives, as well as the interests of faculty members and the larger scientific community. Comprehensive case studies of Silicon Valley and Route 128 highlight the supportive role of local universities, however; the literature concludes that research universities are a necessary, but not sufficient, condition for economic development (Rothaermel, Agung, and Jiang 2007). What matters is a healthy ecology of actors and institutions that come together to think about how to adapt a new piece of technology or realise a new opportunity.

When considering the development of industrial clusters, there are two diametrically opposing models. One model, practised in China, relies on government dictating the growth of designated science cities. This is a very top-down approach to economic development that has been successful in Singapore and Taiwan: the central government dictates that a specific location will have a concentration of R&D and accomplishes this in a relatively short period of time. The verdict is still out as to whether these locations will be successful at creating a sustained competitive advantage, given that innovation is more complex than simply conducting R&D.

The other model occurs in the US and other market economies, and relies on self-organisation and local initiative. In market economies, the central government cannot dictate the actions of private companies but may only offer incentives to encourage firm location decisions and investments in R&D. The closest we have to government-induced clusters is Research Triangle Park (RTP) in North Carolina, which was the result of state and local government actions. RTP was a very long undertaking that began in the 1920s, and is now the largest research park in the world (see Link, 1995). While there are many other examples of government trying to build clusters in market economies, the results typically look very different from what was originally intended (see Leslie, Kargon, 1997).

While economic development officials and government planners want to define long term strategies, it is difficult, if not impossible, to predict scientific discoveries, new technologies and new opportunities.

IBM, an industry leader, underestimated the potential of the computer industry, creating an opportunity for new firms to create personal computers. Few people predicted the potential of the Internet and how it would change the way we access information and communicate. Moreover, successful entrepreneurs make their own luck, adjusting and adapting to survive. Instead of wisely-considered, far-sighted solutions, entrepreneurial activity is by necessity messy, adaptive and unpredictable. Economic development strategies need to be equally adaptive. The biggest problem is that it is impossible to predict which technologies are going to yield any pay-off. By the time a new industry, for example, biotech or nanotechnology, has a defined name and is on its way to becoming a household name, it is probably too late for other places to decide that they will participate as major centres. Creating a cluster in a market economy is a messy social process. Designing an effective economic development strategy may be the ultimate local innovation.

Ready to Innovate

Given that it is difficult to anticipate new technologies and create clusters, the only thing that can be done is to have the necessary resources available and the incentives right. When we think about different kinds of production, education is the ultimate craft industry. Baumol and Bowen (1966) put forward a paradox in the literature when they asked how many musicians it takes to produce a Beethoven string quartet. Well, for a string quartet the answer seemingly must be four. Well, when Beethoven composed the music in the 1800s, how many people did it take? The answer is four again. Just imagine that with the entire range of technological change over 200 years. There is no productivity gain; it still takes four musicians. Similarly you can think about the gestation of a human being. It still takes nine months, even with all of the advances in reproductive technology. Nine women cannot produce a baby in one month. There are limits to what is possible even with the best technology. I think it is instructive to think about that metaphor for education. I would like to recall the dichotomy of education *vs.* training and between codified *vs.* tacit knowledge. When we think about training, we are really thinking about things that you can codify, or put forward as formulas or lists. It is easy to train people to do codified tasks. However, these are the occupations that are most easily deskilled – once you can codify a skill, you can then start to programme a computer to do it.

Education in the US looks more and more like standardised mass production and not craft production. Students' performance is slipping dangerously behind other countries. The US has been the beneficiary of the migration of scholars who have augmented our declining indigenous enrolments in science, engineering and mathematics. This is starting to change as India and China offer not only educational opportunities but also comparable employment opportunities.

Universities are under great pressure to transfer technology to private companies and there is great experimentation around the world to find the most efficient means. The challenge is to maintain the integrity of the academic enterprise while transferring technology. Yet this is a slippery slope: if there is too much emphasis on profitability then universities lose their unique focus, moving toward more near-term projects, educating students narrowly and potentially competing with private enterprise. Trying to increase the relevance of universities may have the perverse effect of diminishing their contributions to society.

The best economic development strategy is to have a well-educated population who are able to innovate and be creative. Pasteur is noted to have said: *Fortune favours the prepared mind.* Certainly, fortune favours those who are able to understand and act upon serendipitous discoveries and chance occurrences. Fortune, most certainly, will favour the prepared place.

Bibliography

Audretsch, D. B., Feldman, M. P., "The geography of innovation and spillovers", in V. Henderson and J. F. Thisse (eds.), *Handbook of Regional and Urban Economics: Cities and Geography, Volume 4*, North-Holland and Elsevier Science Publisher, 2004, p. 2713-2739.

Audretsch, D. B., Feldman, M. P., "Innovative clusters and the industry life-cycle", in *The Review of Industrial Organization*, 1996a, 11, p. 253-273.

Audretsch, D. B., Feldman, M. P., "R&D spillovers and the geography of innovation and production", in *American Economic Review*, 1996b, 86, p. 630-640.

Bathelt, H., Malmberg, A., Maskell, P., "Clusters and knowledge: local buzz, global pipelines and the process of knowledge creation", in *Progress in Human Geography*, 2004, 28, p. 31-56.

Baumol, W. J. and W. G. Bowen., *Performing Arts: The Economic Dilemma*, 20th Century Fund, New York, 1966.

Braunerhjelm, P., Feldman, M. P. (eds.), *Cluster Genesis: The Origins and Emergence of Technology-based Economic Development*, Oxford University Press, Oxford, 2006.

Cairncross, F., *The Death of Distance: How the Communications Revolution Is Changing Our Lives*, Harvard Business School Press, Cambridge Mass, 1997.

Feldman, M. P., Kogler D. F., "Chapter 12, The contribution of public entities to technological change and innovation", in S. Scott (ed.), *Blackwell Handbook on Technology and Innovation Management*, 2007.

Feldman, M. P., Romanelli, E., "Organization legacy and the internal dynamics of clusters: the US human Bio-Therapeutics industry", *Working Paper*, 2007.

Feldman, M. P., Link A.N., Siegel D. S., *The Economics of Science and Technology*, Kluwer Academic Publishers, Boston, 2002.

Feldman, M. P., "The internet revolution and the geography of innovation", in *International Social Science Journal*, 2001, 54, p. 47-56.

Feldman, M. P., Martin, R., "Jurisdictional advantage", in A. B. Jaffe, *et al.* (eds.), *Innovation Policy and the Economy*, Vol. 5, MIT Press, Cambridge, 2005a, p. 57-85.

Feldman, M. P., Martin R., "Constructing jurisdictional advantage", in *Research Policy*, 2005b, 34, p. 1235-1249.

Feldman, M. P., Francis, J., "Homegrown solutions: fostering cluster formation", in *Economic Development Quarterly*, 2004, 18, p. 127-137.

Feldman, M. P., *The Geography of Innovation*, Kluwer Academic Publishers, Boston, 1994.

Feldman, M. P., Francis, J., Bercovitz, J. E. L., "Creating a cluster while building a firm: entrepreneurs and the formation of innovative clusters", in *Regional Studies*, 2005, p. 129-142.

Gaspar, J., Glaeser, E. L., "Information technology and the future of cities", in *Journal of Urban Economics*, 1998, 43, p. 136-156.

Gertler, M., "Being there: proximity, organization, and culture in the development and adoption of advanced manufacturing technologies", in *Economic Geography*, 1995, 71, p. 1-26.

Glaeser, E. L., La Porta, R., Lopez-de-Silanes, F., Shleifer, A., "Do institutions cause growth?", in *Journal of Economic Growth*, 2004, 9, p. 271-303.

Jones, B. F., "The burden of knowledge and the'death of the renaissance man': is innovation getting harder?", *NBER*, Working Paper, 2006.

Krugman, P., *Geography and Trade*, MIT press, Cambridge MA, 1991.

Leslie, S., Kargon, R., "Recreating Silicon Valley", in *Business History Review*, 1997.

Link, A. N., *A Generosity of Spirit: The Early History of the Research Triangle Park*, Research Triangle Park, The Research Triangle Foundation of North Carolina, 1995.

Link, A. N., Siegel, D. S., *Innovation, Entrepreneurship, and Technological Change*, Oxford University Press, Oxford, UK, 2007.

Lowe, N., Feldman M.P., "Constructing entrepreneurial advantage: consensus building, technological uncertainty and emerging industries", in *Cambridge Journal of Regions, Economy and Society*, 2008, 1 (2), p. 265-284.

Marshall, A., *Principles of Economics*, Macmillan, London, 1929.

Porter, M. E., *The Competitive Advantage of Nations*, Free Press, New York, 1990.

Rosenthal, S. S., Strange, W. C., "Geography, industrial organization, and agglomeration", in *The Review of Economics and Statistics*, 2003, 85 (2), p. 377-393.

Rothaermel, F. T., Agung, S. D., Jiang, L., University entrepreneurship: a taxonomy of the literature, Industrial and Corporate Change, 2007, 16 (4), p. 691-791.

CHAPTER VI

The Innovative Milieu
as the Driving Force of Entrepreneurship

Sophie BOUTILLIER and Dimitri UZUNIDIS

1. Introduction

The geographical proximity between science, technology, industry and finance contributes to the emergence of innovations. Interactions are organised through the interplay between private actors and political institutions. Today, economists (see for example: Storper, 1992; Audretsch, Feldman, 1996; Torre, Gilly, 2000; White, 2002; Julien, 2007, Acs, 2001; Bellet, L'Harmet, 1998; Den Hertog, Bergman, Remoe, 2001; Feldman, Francis, Bercovitz, 2005; Florida, 2003) consider the regional economy as a geographical and economic platform for the organisation of production and, as a consequence, as an opportunity to create new activities, goods and services, new jobs and sources of income. For almost four decades, the innovative approach based on proximity and, in particular, on the concept of the "innovative milieu" has demonstrated its pertinence as a form of modelling of decentralised economic growth, but also as a source of entrepreneurship.

An analysis starting from the innovative milieu makes it possible to study the entrepreneur's economic role and function, and its contribution to the innovation process. The systemic nature of the relationships that characterise an economic and social milieu (see Cooke, 2001; Hamdouch, 2008) makes it possible to identify what contributes (or not) to the innovative act. Innovation and entrepreneurship (as a product of the milieu) depend on inter-personal exchanges. Are they only the result of a specific organisation of economic relations? Our argument is that the systemic nature of the milieu does not exclusively relate to economic interactions but, more precisely, also takes into consideration the social structures that are at the origin of innovative behaviours. Moreover, institutions (states, local communities) play an important role in the organisation and development of socio-economic structures. In its turn, the innovative milieu – thanks to the relations of proximity – contributes to the entrepreneurial innovative performance through the supply of scientific, technological and financial resources.

In the first part of this chapter we will examine the role of synergic (spatial, organisational and cognitive) relations – named proximity – in the innovation and entrepreneurial process. The density of these relations reinforces the capability of a local economy to generate small independent enterprises (essentially start-up). But in contemporary capitalism, the entrepreneur, as the owner and the manager of a small enterprise, has a specific function (second part). He is not a hero (as Schumpeter noted it), but a socialised entrepreneur. The former is at the origin of the development of big industries and new areas of activities; the latter is the result of the financial strategies and industrial policies of the major actors of the economy (big firms, financial institutions, central and local public administrations, etc.). In the third part we will analyse the "resource potential" of the entrepreneur as a necessary condition to business creation. This potential, composed of capital, knowledge and social relations, can give value to the entrepreneur's function. In this case, the relations of proximity, applied on the territorial level of analysis, must be characterised by the logic of collaboration, confidence and reciprocity.

Several studies on the territorial economy, based on the network analysis and the systemic relations, are developed along this line of thinking. The entrepreneur is not considered as a mere actor of the economic system. He is studied as a systemic relation in the network or as the result of the functioning of this network (see Ehlinger, Perret, Chabaud, 2007; Grossetti, Barthe, 2008; Nicolaou, Birley, 2003). We thus point forward how the entrepreneur builds his potential of resources in a local economy, and how he uses his resources (knowledge, financial resources, social relations) to develop new relations and new economic activities.

2. Proximity and the Innovative Milieu

2.1. Economic proximity and social relations

The concept of proximity is now widely used in both industrial economics and innovation studies (see notably Isard, 1956; Rallet, Torre, 1995; Boschma, 2005). *A priori*, proximity seems to be related to the existence of localised externalities, generating phenomena of spatial concentration and regional dynamics. From this perspective, we propose a three-dimensional approach to proximity: spatial proximity, organisational and cognitive proximity. In this approach, the issue of location is coupled with the organisational and informational/cognitive capacity of firms.

A local economy (or a local production system) may be defined as a geographical area consisting of a set of systemic relationships among enterprises and also between enterprises, public authorities (the State) and local communities; these systemic relationships characterise the area localised for a given type of activity or final production. That economy is observed and studied as a mode of productive relations that contributes to regional and local development (see Uzunidis, 2008).

Alfred Marshall (1919) demonstrated that the regional efficiency of such an organisational mode resides in what we call today economies in transaction costs. The concentration in a single geographical location of the main actors of the same productive system (mainly producers on one side and users on the other) not only facilitates transactions, but the mutual relations of knowledge and confidence between different partners (spatial proximity). The development and accumulation of expertise will therefore create what Marshall called the 'industrial atmosphere' facilitating the functioning of the local labour market. This phenomenon is related both to the workers' qualifications and experience, and to the location of several enterprises in the same locality. In the meaning attributed by Marshall to the 'industrial district', this environment includes a specific density of population with proven qualifications, a set of actors constituting the different links of a single production system, as well as a degree of know-how strongly resulting from acquired experience.

Before Marshall, Von Thünen (2009) in the 19th century underlined that the free market mechanisms are not an abstraction, but they take place in a particular territory. In this approach, the territory is defined geographically, but it is also the place where relations of proximity between individuals are developed. Von Thünen's analysis shows that the question on territory and its role for economic dynamics is not a new phenomenon. On the other hand, Braudel (1975) had argued in the Mediterranean case that the commercial activities are developed thanks to networks of merchant entrepreneurs.

The main characteristic is that the local organisation of production is not linked to a hierarchical principle regulating an enterprise, but is rather based on a principle of collaboration and cooperation between different production units. Therefore, the concept of solidarity between economic actors is of considerable importance. The local production system is mainly characterised by the proximity between productive units (individual firms, service suppliers, research centres, training institutions, etc.). The relations between these units have a variable intensity and may take on highly differentiated forms: formal or informal relations, market or non-market, etc. Alliances mainly relate to the flow of materials, services, labour, technologies and knowledge. The specific nature of the activities involved in the production of new knowledge and the interactions associated with them have led economists to introduce the concept of cognitive proximity in addition to spatial-temporal proximity and organisational proximity. Cognitive proximity and knowledge exchange means the more or less formalised sharing of experiences, codes, languages, models resulting from and facilitating the communication of information inside – and between – organisations (see Nooteboom, 2002; De la Mothe, Foray, 2001; Foray, 2003).

Proximity contributes to the coordination of the innovation process. This one, both flexible and evolutionary, imposes on the firm or on the entrepreneur the pressing need to be provided with the different types of technological and intellectual means to acquire and combine uninterrupted flows of material and immaterial resources. The "knowledge theory" applied to the company states: the ability to adapt and the efficiency of the company depends on its cognitive categories, on the interpretation codes of the information itself, on the tacit skills and its procedures in solving the problems it encounters (see Dosi, Nelson, Winter, 1999). The scientific, technical and industrial information as a system of knowledge (knowledge-capital), which is articulated, formalised and likely to be communicated or transferred, is a means of production and identifiable as such (see Laperche, 2001, 2007). Its use provides innovation for the economic process and the accumulation of capital. The task of the manager or the entrepreneur consists, therefore, of finding the balance between managing the partnerships and developing the internal instruments of organisation (see Laperche, Galbraith, Uzunidis, 2006). To survive or grow, a company is forced to acquire new knowledge to create new competences (see Penrose, 1959).

Piore and Sabel (1984) integrated the proximity in a flexible system of production founded on multidirectional and horizontal relations. The dynamics of the evolution of the structures and the organisation of the local system of production highlights the importance of the small enterprises. Those that are more flexible and more adaptable are committed to renew the local system of production and to create new jobs, since flexibility facilitates the adaptation to the new economic context. Moreover, the proximity between the large companies and the small enterprises contributes to the emergence of the innovative milieu.

Table 1 identifies the main parameters characterising the different categories of proximity as well as the operating field and the types of stakes related to them. It is worth noting that interactions are generally multi-dimensional: they represent a combination of different dimensions from which a major dimension emerges. In our case, this core dimension relates to space and time.

Table 1: The three categories of proximity

Proximity	Parameters	Operating field and stake
Spatial	Distance/speed	Displacement: Flows, time
Organisational (intra and inter-organisational)	Hierarchy/market Intra-firm/extra-firm Vertical/horizontal Instruction/Contract	Co-ordination Strategy, actions, routines
Cognitive	Code/content Context/ understanding (awareness and interpretation)	Communication Concept, ideas, knowledge

2.2. An innovative milieu

Our central theoretical assumption concerning the concept of the innovative milieu – the social and economic environment of a region developed over the course of history ('path dependence') – is that all innovative milieus are the product of interactions between firms, institutions and labour. Such interactions are exclusively the result of mutual synergies (networks, partnerships, etc.) between different local agents (public or private) participating in economic and industrial development. For example, we may refer to the different forms of cooperation between enterprises and research labs. It is firstly the surrounding socio-economic industrial and scientific environment that contributes to the creation of new activities (in particular through entrepreneurship and spin-off) and to the genesis of innovations (see also Konstadakopoulos, 2003; Camagni and Capello, 2009). In addition, this can only develop in a 'natural' form if some preconditions are respected, including: existence at the regional level of a community of actors (enterprises, research and training centres, public administrations, professional qualifications, etc.); presence of material, human, financial, technological and information resources in the immediate geographical neighbourhood; existence of specific know-how leading to high-quality productive activity; existence of relational capital favourable to the creation of local, national or international networks; and the existence of norms, rules and values promoting positive behaviour among economic actors.

The concept of the innovative milieu generally relates to the capacity of a local economy to generate innovations through, for example, the emergence of new enterprises. The local economy is therefore represented in the form of a spatial system valuing all kinds of capital and merchant exchange. This spatial, economic and social system must reduce the risks related to the uncertainty of a given investment; it triggers an innovation process that includes the creation of enterprises and the incorporation of already-existing technological enterprises. International competitiveness of a territory is due to the richness of its innovative capacity (see Porter, 1998, 2003).

The organisation of the innovative milieu is ensured by two logics: the first is related to the interaction between local actors, and the second to the dynamics of collective learning (see Lundvall, Johnson, 1994). Interactions contribute towards the organising of a regional economy. They make it possible to bring together local actors within a production process. The dynamics of the collective learning appears in a process where the milieu initially mobilises resources and thereafter uses them to adapt to the change that comes from outside. The capacities of innovation are the result of the cooperation between the local actors and the use of specific resources of the milieu (raw materials, capital, technology, knowledge, competencies, etc.). By the installation of the mechanisms of coordination, the milieu is able to ensure the balance of the cooperative relations between the local actors and internal and external competition.

Spatial, organisational and cognitive relations of proximity form an innovative milieu. The regional anchorage of the enterprise enables it to avail itself of a pool of resources (and sometimes a market) in order to amortise the costs inherent in its investments, in an economy undergoing constant change. However, this regional anchorage depends on the quality of the 'pool' mentioned above, compared to the entrepreneur's expectations with regards to innovation, business start-up and consolidation. Hence arises the necessity for governments and local authorities to create a system and organise the resources with a view to generating multiple innovation processes, taking into account the competition-cooperation behaviours between the same actors, in an open economy (see in particular Amable, Barré, Boyer, 1997; Pitelis, Sugden, Wilson, 2005). This system is a supplier of those productive resources that are capable of generating innovative entrepreneurship but also attracting other enterprises with confirmed performances in the innovation field (see Madeuf *et al.*, 2005; Uzunidis, 2004).

3. The Entrepreneur's Function in the Current Stage of Capitalism

3.1. The end of the heroic entrepreneur

At the core of an innovation milieu, specific attention can be paid to the creation of small enterprises. In the present economic uncertainty, and following the trend towards decentralisation, the establishment of enterprises is supposed to solve many problems linked to the rigidities resulting from institutional interventionism. Its flexible structures enable much easier reaction to consumers' expectations. Moreover, the possible bankruptcy of an enterprise does not threaten the financial and industrial fabric of the country, region or place. Establishing a considerable number of small firms is considered as a privileged instrument of industrial policy and national planning; financing and marketing activities seek to organise the markets and the development of technologies through alliances, mergers, agreements and political interventions; and the hope for economic renewal is concentrated on small enterprises that are in full harmony with economic needs. A small enterprise is also a formidable machine able to enrich or destroy capital. It presents itself as a sort of carrier of values to the extent that it creates bridges for the transfer of productive resources (financial capital technologies, labour force with different qualifications and competencies) to activities, markets and large companies able to make profits.

Entrepreneurs have been at the centre of economists' concerns and public policies since the beginning of the 1980s in capitalist economies (see Boutillier, 2008). This fact is relatively new. Since the end of the Second World War, the paradigm of the big enterprise has prevailed. The years of growth that followed the Second World War were marked by phenomena of industrial vertical concentration and the evolution of managerial capitalism. Economy was directed by a "techno-structure" (see Galbraith, 1968) and, in particular, by managers being salaried workers (see Chandler, 1977). Entrepreneurs, as founders-owners-managers of firms, seemed to belong to an age that had gone, to the heroic period to which J. A. Schumpeter often refers. The big company imposed itself, together with mass production and salaried employment. W. J. Baumol (1968) wrote in a famous paper that the entrepreneur had disappeared from the economic literature. For many economists, the main economic actor is not the entrepreneur, but the enterprise.

In Schumpeter's *Theory of Economic Development* (see Schumpeter, 1934), the entrepreneur is the economic agent achieving new combinations of production factors. He is the hero of capitalism (see Freeman, 1982). Five combinations must be taken into account:

1. The introduction of a new good – that is one with which consumers are not yet familiar – or a new quality of a good.

2. The introduction of a new methof of production that is almost unknown in the specific industrial branch; it is not imperative that it is based on a new scientific discovery and it may also be found in the new commercial process applied to a commodity.

3. The opening of a new market, that is a market into which the particular branch of manufacture of the country in question has not previously entered, whether or not this market has existed before.

4. The conquest of a new source of supply of raw materials or half-manufactured goods, again irrespective of whether this source already exists or whether it has first to be created.

5. The formation of a new organisation, for example the creation of a monopolistic situation or sudden emergence of a monopoly: the heroic entrepreneur who creates a new industry, similar to what happened at the end of the 19th century (movies or electricity) or at the end of the 20th century (electronics, computer).

In his ultimate book entitled *Capitalism, Socialism and Democracy*, published in 1942, Schumpeter was largely pessimistic about the future of capitalism. It was because the development of capitalism led, according to him, to the disappearance of competition. Companies were becoming bigger and bigger. In addition, these were powerful organisations, bureaucratic enterprises. Schumpeter insisted on the idea that the entrepreneur is being replaced by an organisation. Entrepreneurs are no longer responsible for innovative activities, which are now performed by teams composed of expert members who have no direct link with the market or the consumer.

The vanishing of the Schumpeter entrepreneur is a metaphor used to analyse the development of managerial capitalism, the evolution of big enterprises. In the 1960s, J. K. Galbraith (1968) pursued Schumpeter's analysis of managerial capitalism and demonstrated that the economy of capitalist industrialised countries did not fit with the paradigm of pure and perfect competition. Six distinctive elements emerged:

1. The domination of a handful of big enterprises, whose ownership is split between a myriad of shareholders, and a plethora of small owners of enterprises.

2. The presence of a considerable number of very small firms, although rather marginal with regards to the creation of wealth.

3. The disappearance of the entrepreneur replaced by a division between the owners of capital (shareholders) and capital management (managers): the "techno-structure".

4. The development of planning tools in order to minimise the uncertainty resulting from the functioning of the market.

5. The presence of a plethora of small entrepreneurs who do not operate in a market characterised by pure and perfect competition, but in markets dominated by big firms.

6. The expansion of a huge bureaucracy, related to technological and not political considerations.

3.2. The socialised form of entrepreneurship

But since the 1980s, the entrepreneur, as a concept, is reappearing in economics because of the positive factors that contribute towards the creation of a propitious environment for the creation of enterprises. We hold the idea according to which the economic, social and political environment facilitates the development of specific economic behaviours – for example, entrepreneurial behaviour (see Boutillier, Uzunidis, 1995; 1999; 2006; Julien, 2007). According to the OECD (2005), the emergence of entrepreneurship is related to the rank it holds on the scale of values and to the intensity of incentives and support it receives. However, the beginning of the 1980s was marked by a whole set of major economic and social changes that consecrate a sort of rupture from the previous period:

1. A policy of liberalisation of the economy (contestable markets theory) and the development of the financial markets: the privatisation of the economy releases capital in huge quantities: new investment opportunities emerge; the development of investment funds and pension funds; the ageing of the population and the withdrawal of the social state from the financing of pensions stimulated their development (see Aglietta, Rebérioux, 2004). The major problem was to identify new investment opportunities in a context of slow economic growth (see Galbraith, 1968). Capital becomes impatient (see Harrison, Blustone, 1990).

2. The development of information and communication technologies and biotechnologies (see Castells, 1990) generated new investment opportunities.

3. The "garage mythology" and "the legend of the entrepreneur" prevailed (see Boutillier, Uzunidis, 1999). As in the early days of capitalism, an idea that was already considered outdated was revived and propagated: the heroic entrepreneur. However, one tends to forget that the knowledge the new, innovative entrepreneurs use to succeed is the result of institutional and networking (military or civilian) scientific research.

4. The crisis of the welfare state: G. Gilder (1985) argued that the welfare state generates poverty because it encourages too many people to rely on social services instead of looking for a job (since the 1970s, the Public Choice School and the Theory of Bureaucracy have strongly criticised Keynesianism). According to Gilder, only the entrepreneur is capable of fighting poverty and unemployment (see Esping-Anderson, 1990).

5. The increase of mass unemployment and growing insecurity of salaried employees (development of part-time employment and multi-employment, etc.): the "end of work" (see Rifkin, 1995) or the beginning of the "entrepreneurial society" (see Audretsch, 2007)?

6. New public policy: The main question is to help unemployed workers to create their enterprises (their means of existence, their job), thanks to the emergence of an institutional environment (reduction of taxation, of administrative barriers, flexibility of the labour market, etc.). For Keynesian economists in the 1960s-1970s, the fundamental role of the state was to sustain demand and create markets. In fact, the main objective of J. M. Keynes was social peace and political stability. In the 1980s the economists of endogenous growth theories (see Aghion, Harris, Howitt, Vickers, 2001) explain that the state has a major role to play in order to sustain supply and support enterprises to innovate. In this way, innovation generates wealth and employment. Through an appropriate public policy, the state tries to facilitate the transition from the situation of worker to that of entrepreneur, or from wage-earner to entrepreneur: to introduce more flexibility in the labour market (see Boutillier, 2006; 2007).

7. The big managerial enterprise with its pyramidal architecture (see Sennet, 2006) is no longer adapted and is compelled to change: the structure of the network enterprise is flexible and decentralised (to benefit from new information and communication technologies).

8. With regards to the number of salaried workers/employees, the size of enterprises has also been reduced.

9. Since the beginning of the 1990s, entrepreneurship has become an academic discipline taught in universities. Awareness programmes that target the youth are also elaborated upon (see Audet, 2001; Gasse, Tremblay, 2002; Riverin, Jean, 2006).

Thus, we have a definition of new capitalism: a socio-economy organisation based on private property and a free market. The characteristics of managerial capitalism were the same. The fundamental differences between new capitalism and managerial capitalism are: (1) the organisation of industrial production is decentralised (network enterprise and enterprise networks), assisted and coordinated by the ICTs and finance, (2) development of the financial markets (which generate capital funds for investment), (3) flexibility of the labour market, (4) the new role of the state, which is to build an institutional environment to create enterprises and jobs.

In the first decade of the 21st century the economy of industrialised countries is undergoing major transformations at the scientific, technological and productive levels. The financial crisis of 2008 is also the beginning of major changes in the productive systems. If one refers to Schumpeter's theory about entrepreneurship, this situation lays fertile ground for innovation and for business creation (see Langlois, 1987; Perroux, 1965; 1970; Kirzner, 1973; 1985; Shane, 2003; Heerjte, 2006), a process that fuels the ascending phase of an economic cycle.

In this context, the entrepreneur is no longer heroic, but rather socialised (see Boutillier, Laperche, Uzunidis, 2008). He is stuck between three logics: that of the big enterprise that structures and outsources all or a part of its activities; that of the state striving to promote the creation of new businesses – on the one hand, to fight against unemployment and, on the other, to foster the development of innovations seen in the Schumpeterian meaning of the term (product, process, organisation); and that of relations of proximity on a local (spatial) but also on an inter-institutional (networks) level. The concept of the socialised entrepreneur must be distinguished from the collective entrepreneur – or even from the entrepreneurial corporation (see Hagedoorn, 1996) that characterises the managerial enterprise. In fact, the socialised entrepreneur may be defined in the first place by his macroeconomic function (job creation, innovation, the outsourcing of production and service activities of big companies, localisation).

In the new capitalism, the socialised entrepreneurs take their place in the networks. They are entrepreneurs sitting at the interface between two logics:

1. The logic of the big industrial and financial enterprise that seeks to stimulate the creation of enterprises in order to test new markets.

2. The logic of the state that seeks by these means to fight against unemployment and promote innovation.

Indeed, faced with the complexity of the innovation process, M. Castells (1998) went as far as to maintain, quite cleverly, that the fundamental unit of the economic system is no longer the entrepreneur, the family, the firm or the state, but the network composed of different organisations. Thus, this network gives birth to the new entrepreneur.

Table 2: Big enterprises and entrepreneurs
since the second half of the 20ᵗʰ century

	Since the end of the Second World War	Since the 1980s
Place of the big enterprises	Development of managerial enterprises	Reorganisation of big enterprises (networks)
Organisation of labour and production	Assembly chain Fordism Taylorism Rigid organisation	ITCs Robotisation and production and services Flexible organisation
Place and role of the entrepreneur	Entrepreneur = employer = authority	Entrepreneur = innovator = creator
Form of recruitment	Mass wage earning Mass employment	Increasing Precariousness of salaried employment Term contract
Financing of the economy	Indebtedness (important role of banks) Public financing	Development of financial markets
Role of the state	Welfare state	Privatisation / deregulation Public policies to promote entrepreneurship and free market

4. The Entrepreneur's 'Resource Potential' and the Innovative Milieu

4.1. The 'resource potential' and the entrepreneur's function

The entrepreneur's individual qualities and personality undoubtedly play a major role in the decision to create or buy out a small firm. Nevertheless, the action of starting up that initiative is determined by the macro-systemic dynamics of accumulation and profit. These dynamics generate barriers as well as personal enrichment opportunities that encourage an individual to become an entrepreneur who will ultimately succeed or fail. The fact is that nobody is born an entrepreneur but may become one through the mobilisation of a potential of resources composed of capital, knowledge and relations (see Boutillier, Uzunidis 2001; 2006). Support involves capital for investments and operations, knowledge for choices and decisions, and relations for the financing, association and selling of products.

We define the entrepreneur as the founder, manager and owner of at least a part of the enterprise. In such conditions, he may also be an innovator (Say or Schumpeter analysis); however, unemployment may also be at the origin of his decision (see Casson, 1991). Nevertheless, he always remains the economic agent who bears the risk (see Cantillon, 1755; Knight, 1921) since he is in every case, the main financial backer of his enterprise, together with his relatives. On the other hand, the entrepreneur may be defined as a set of resources. By using the concept of the potential of resources of the entrepreneur, we relocate the entrepreneur and his enterprise in the general logic of the capitalist system. The potential of resources is split up in the following way:

1. A set of financial resources including all the effective financial resources (own spending, family assets, heritage) or potential (access to credit, subsidies, various public aid, etc.).

2. A set of knowledge including all entrepreneurs' knowledge whether they are certified by a diploma or the result of professional experience: technological, organisational, economic knowledge, etc.

3. A set of social relations: personal, family or professional relations that the entrepreneur may mobilise in order to fulfill his project. Two social relation networks may be distinguished: on the one hand, a network of institutional relations (relations with public institutions, enterprises, banks, etc.), and on the other, a network of informal relations with relatives, family, friends, neighbours, working relations, etc. (see Granovetter, 1973). In our example, these two networks develop interdependently. Thus, it is through the information given by a friend that we learn about the existence of a specific type of financing. However, the individual's social background plays a fundamental role because it largely determines the network of friendly or family relations (see Bourdieu, 1985; Coleman, 1988; Putman, 1995).

The three components of the entrepreneur's resource potential are determined by the place he holds in the social organisation chart – in spite of the increasing socialisation of the economy (see Durkheim, 2007). The elements assume a fundamental role. The family gives a taste to start a business; at the same time, it is a source of financing. We observe this phenomenon in France, in the United States, but also in Russia where business regulation is very new. Many entrepreneurs had a member of their family involved in business activity. In the Russian case for example, we note also that many entrepreneurs have a member of their family in the communist party. It means that the communist party is a means to develop social relations. With the support of the family, the functions exerted by the entrepreneur draw their logic from public policies targeted at the dampening of the consequences of the crisis (employment of innovation policies) and from strategies aimed at the productive and financial reorganisation of big enterprises.

Table 3: Resource potential of the entrepreneur

Resource potential	Major characteristics
Knowledge	Tacit and various types of knowledge acquired in the family context Scientific and technological knowledge acquired at school Knowledge acquired during our relations with third parties (family, professional activity, etc.)
Financial resources	Own spending Affective inputs: parents, relatives Bank credit Institutional financial aid (e.g. direct assistance from the state) Financial inputs brought in by another entrepreneur
Social relations	Informal relations (family, friends, neighbours, colleagues, etc.) Formal relations (stat, banks, other enterprises, research centres, etc.)

Source: Boutillier S., 2008, p. 8.

4.2. How the relations of proximity increase the resource potential of the entrepreneur

The ability of the entrepreneur results from the variety and richness of the resource potential he has himself constituted. In its turn, the composition of that resource potential depends on factors that are external to the enterprise and entrepreneur. In particular, public policies of assistance for the creation of businesses (to stimulate innovation and/or to fight against unemployment) will largely determine the financial resources to which the entrepreneur will be authorised to have access in order to create his enterprise and ensure its survival. The economic and social organisation has several dimensions and therefore several effects. The general level of development of knowledge and technology in society will have an impact both on the knowledge acquired and assembled by the entrepreneur (on the basis of his education and the competences of the members of his team; activities related to economic and information watch) and the technological level of his activity. The nature of the financial system (e.g. ease or difficulty of going public, bankers' degree of "conservatism", level of development of venture capital, etc.) influences both the capacity of an individual to become an entrepreneur and the capacity of an enterprise to more or less accelerate its development.

The degree of concentration in the market – for example, the presence of big enterprises – also plays a considerable role in the dynamics of creating small enterprises and in their type of activity (in particular subcontracting). Finally, it is necessary to underline the policy led by enterprises with a view to innovate, either by their own means (R&D budget) or by implementing different types of partnership, including the injection of venture capital. In conclusion, the presence and nature of the links between the "POBE" factors – Public Policy, Economic organisation, Big enterprises, Entrepreneur's resource potential – lead us to relocate the entrepreneur in his economic social, political, technological and spatial context. This organic square provides a way to analyse the creation of enterprises on the scale of a specific – local – economy (Figure 1).

**Figure 1: The socialised entrepreneur,
the core of the organic square of business activity**

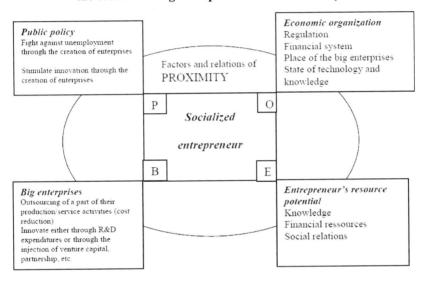

The emergence of a 'successful' region results from the fact that it is able to manage its own capacity to develop new products, new techniques and new organisations. Thus, innovative milieu is the combination of a given geographical space of enterprises, training centres and public or private research units involved in a partnership approach, with the purpose of identifying synergies around common projects of an innovative nature. It combines attractiveness (agglomeration effects: Isnar, 1956), diffusion (dispersion effects) and externalities. These three factors are essential for the generation and propagation of innovations. Externalities can be defined (see Marshall, 1891) as having positive or negative effects, which involve an activity of an economic agent outside this activity or that the agent is subjected to from outside. The most attractive for a company is to achieve, in a setting favourable to investment, substantial external savings, without having to bear the slightest cost that its activity creates for the community as a whole (pollution or various nuisances) (see Krugman, 1991). It is therefore important to underline that the creation of the enterprise will have various effects on the local community, but, in return, the entrepreneur will expect from the community the means and opportunities to enlarge its property (assets) or where necessary, to defend it.

What is favourable to an innovative entrepreneurship, offering the possibility to support 'network economies', is the existence of an area created, in economic and social terms, by the relations of proximity: infrastructures of transport, communication, telecommunications, education, engineering, etc.; contractual and cognitive interactions; confidence and cooperation; the sharing of the same codes and business competencies; a dense network of enterprises; fiscal and financial supports and aids, etc. Figure 2 presents the links between the relations of proximity, the resource potential of the entrepreneur and the realisation of socialised entrepreneurship through the insertion in networks and risk reduction.

Figure 2: Proximity and entrepreneurship

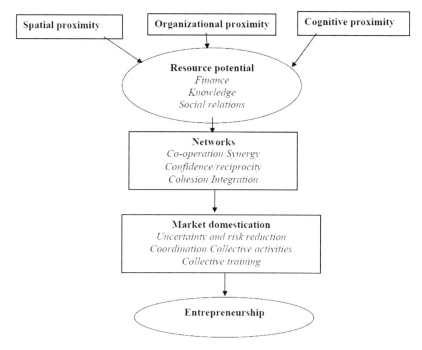

Relations of proximity enrich the resource potential of an entrepreneur, create synergies and a large range of confidence and reciprocity links. As a consequence, there is also a reduction of the risks related to the uncertainty of a given investment (market domestication).

The entrepreneurial activities take place in a particular spatial milieu. It is in this milieu that the entrepreneur builds his potential of resources (knowledge, financial resources and social relations). The entrepreneur develops his social relations in a particular territory, even if his objective is to develop more large scale (and international) activities. The territory becomes a special innovative milieu by the density and the intensity of the three dimensions of the proximity: spatial, organisational and cognitive. Enterprises (big or small) can be located in a territory for different reasons (costs reduction, demand access) and if public policy plays a non-neglect role to new business development and attractiveness, the entrepreneur, as a social agent, benefits principally from his relations to create his business. These different social relations (family, socialisation, education, etc.) are also the engine of the future development of his enterprise (see Ehlinger, Perret, Chabaud, 2007; Grossetti, Barthe, 2008; Nicolaou, Birley, 2003). So, economic activities are embedding (according the Polanyi's concept redefined by Granovetter) in a particular territory (see White, 1992).

5. Conclusion

Since the 1980s, the entrepreneur has made his comeback at the forefront of the economic and political scene. In an approach combining economics and sociology, in this chapter, we tried to go deeper into the analysis of the origin of the entrepreneur's function, studying the construction of what we call his "resource potential":. the set of knowledge, social relations and financial resources gathered together by the entrepreneur in his environment. This resource potential is not stable and may be increased or reduced, in different economic, political and social contexts. According to the approach by the innovative milieu, relations of proximity reinforce the entrepreneur's potential. Business start-ups become easier. The first meaning of physical proximity was soon supplemented by other interpretations (listed by Sierra, 1997) in which the operating field of proximity (space, organisation or institution) is intertwined with the contents of the proximity relationship (information, training, knowledge, technology, etc.). The three types of proximity that we retained have made it possible to better examine the process of business creation. The systemic links between an individual and his socio-economic environment create investment and profit opportunities. If this environment is oriented towards innovation, these opportunities will be more numerous. Thus, we studied the innovative milieu as a major source of entrepreneurship in the current stage of the market economy.

An innovative milieu, as an innovation system, describes the relationships (scientific, technological, industrial, commercial, financial, political) between private and public institutions (enterprises, research and engineering labs, administrations etc.). In general, the relationships consist of financial and information flows and the movement of persons. The purpose of that system is to produce innovations (new organisations, new goods and processes, new resources, new combinations of productive resources). This system facilitates business creation on the local level and contributes to define the socialised entrepreneur. This new entrepreneur is a socialised entrepreneur because he develops his activity in a particular economic environment which is structured by the business networks and by the financial, tax and legal incentives of central or local public authorities.

In a network economy, local economies are now seeking to develop by relying on private initiatives, coupled with targeted public and individual action. Investment attractiveness, the capacity to create enterprises and the creation of jobs determine the performance of an innovative milieu. The milieu is integrated in a context resulting from the development of complex interactions between its actors. These actors and interactions constitute a system that is defined both by its objectives and its composition. The analysis of the innovative milieu as a complex system leads us to study all of the local actors (enterprises, authorities, public services, etc.) in relation to outside factors. Inside this system, the innovation plays a central role. The integration of the actors within the milieu contributes to the emergence of new enterprises by offering the future entrepreneur the essential financial, relational and cognitive resources.

Bibliography

Acs, Z., *Regional Innovation, Knowledge and Global Change*, Continuum, London, 2001.

Aghion, P., Harris, C., Howitt, P., Vickers, J., "Competition, Imitation and Growth with Step-by-step Innovation", in *Review of Economic Studies*, 2001, 28, p. 467-492.

Aglietta, M., Rebérioux, A., *Dérives du capitalisme financier*, Albin Michel, Paris, 2004.

Amable, B., Barre, R., Boyer, R., *Les systèmes nationaux d'innovation à l'ère de la globalisation*, Economica, Paris, 1997.

Audet, J., "Une étude des aspirations entrepreneuriales d'étudiants universitaires québécois: seront-ils des entrepreneurs demain?", Document de travail,

Institut de recherche sur les PME, Université du Québec à Trois-Rivières, 2001.

Audretsch, D., *The Entrepreneurial Society*, Oxford University Press, Oxford, 2007.

Audretsch, D. B., Feldman, M. P., "RD Spillovers and Geography of Innovation", in Henderson J.-V., Thisse J.-F. (eds.), *Handbook of Regional and Urban Economics*, Elsevier, Amsterdam, 1996, 4, p. 2713-2739.

Baumol, W., "Entrepreneurship in economic theory", in *The American Economic Review*, 1968, 58 (2), p. 64-71.

Bellet, M., L'Harmet, C. (eds.), *Industry, Space and Competition*, Edward Elgar, Cheltenham, 1998.

Boschma, R., "Proximity and Innovation: A Critical Assessment", in *Regional Studies*, 2005, 39 (1), p. 61-74.

Bourdieu, P., "The forms of capital", in J. G. Richardson (ed.), *Handbook of theory and research for the sociology of education*, Greewood, New York, 1985, p. 241-258.

Boutillier, S., "Finance, State and Entrepreneurship in Contemporary Economy", in Laperche B., Uzunidis D. (eds.), *Powerful Finance and Innovation Trends in High-risk Economy*, Plagrave Macmillan, London, 2008.

Boutillier, S., "Marché et création d'entreprises. L'entrepreneur « deus ex machina » du capitalisme?", in Rasselet G. (ed.), *Dynamisme et transformation du capitalisme*, L'Harmattan, Paris, 2007.

Boutillier, S., "Finance, State and Entrepreneurship in the Contemporary Economy", in B. Laperche, D. Uzunidis (eds.), *Powerful Finance and Innovation Trends in a High-risk Economy*, Palgrave Macmillan, London, 2008a.

Boutillier S., Uzunidis D., *L'entrepreneur. Une analyse socioéconomique*, Economica, Paris, 1995.

Boutillier S., Uzunidis D., *La légende de l'entrepreneur*, Syros-Alternatives économiques, Paris, 1999.

Boutillier S., Uzunidis D., *L'aventure des entrepreneurs*, Studyrama, Paris, 2006.

Boutillier S., Uzunidis D., "L'utilité marginale de l'entrepreneur", in *Innovations, Cahiers d'économie de l'innovation*, 2001, 30, p. 17-42.

Boutillier, S., Laperche B., Uzunidis D., "The entrepreneur's 'resource potential', innovation and networks", in B. Laperche, D. Uzunidis and N. von Tunzelmann (eds.), *Genesis of Innovation, Systemic Linkages between Knowledge and Market*, Edward Elgar, Cheltenham, 2008, p. 208-228.

Braudel, F., *Mediterranean and the Mediterranean World in the Age of Philip II*, Fontana, 1975.

Camagni, R., Capello, R., "Knowledge-Based economy and knowledge creation: the role of space", in U. Fratesi and L. Senn (eds.), *Growth and Innovation of Competitive Regions, The Role of Internal and External Connections*, Springer, Berlin, 2009, p. 145-165.

Cantillon, R., *Essai sur la nature du commerce en général*, Institut National d'Études Démographiques, Paris, 1952, 1755.

Casson, M., *L'entrepreneur*, Economica, Paris, 1991.

Castells, M., *La société en réseaux*, Fayard, Paris, 1998.

Chandler, A. D., "The visible hand. The Managerial Revolution", in *American Business*, The Belknap Press of Harvard University Press, Cambridge, 1977.

Coleman, J. S., "Social capital in the creation of human capital", in *American of Sociology*, 1988, 94, p. 95-120.

Cooke, P., "Regional Innovation Systems, Clusters, and the Knowledge Economy", in *Industrial and Corporate Change*, 2001, 10 (4), p. 945-974.

De La Mothe, J., Foray, D. (eds.), *Knowledge Management in the Innovation Process*, Kluwer, Boston, 2001.

Den Hertog, P., Bergman, E., Remoe, S., *Innovative Clusters: Drivers of National Innovation Systems (Enterprise, Industry and Services)*, OECD, Paris, 2001.

Dosi, G., Nelson, R. R., Winter, S. G., *The Nature and Organizational Capabilities*, 2000, Oxford University Press.

Durkheim, E., *De la division du travail social*, PUF, Paris, 2007 (1re édition 1893).

Ehlinger, S., Perret, V., Chabaud, D., "Quelle gouvernance pour les réseaux territorialisés d'organisations?", in *Revue française de gestion*, 2007, 170, p. 155-171.

Esping-Anderson, G., *The Three Worlds of Welfare Capitalism*, University Press, Princeton, 1990.

Feldman, M., Francis, J., Bercovitz, J., "Creating a Cluster While Building a Firm: Entrepreneurs and the Formation of Industrial Clusters", in *Regional Studies*, 2005, 39 (1), p. 129-141.

Florida, R., "Entrepreneurship, creativity and regional economic growth", in D. M. Hart, *The Emergence of Entrepreneurship Policy*, Cambridge UP, 2003, p. 39-60.

Foray, D., *The Economics of Knowledge*, MIT Press, Cambridge, 2003.

Freeman, C., *The Economics of Industrial Innovation*, MIT Press, Cambridge, 2nd edition, 1982.

Galbraith, J. K., *The New Industrial State*, Houghton Mifflin, Boston, 1968.

Galbraith, J. K., *A Short History of Financial Euphoria*, Penguin Book Ltd, 1994.

Gasse, Y., Tremblay, M., "L'entrepreneuriat à l'université Laval: intérêts, intention, prévalence et besoins des étudiants", Rapport d'analyse, *Centre d'entrepreneuriat et de PME*, Université Laval, 2002.

Gilder, G., *L'esprit d'entreprise*, Fayard, Paris, 1985.

Granovetter, M., "The Strength of Weak Ties", in *American Journal of Sociology*, 1973, 78, p. 1360-1380.

Granovetter, M., "Economic action and social structure: the problem of embeddedness", in *American Journal of Sociology*, 1985, 91, p. 481-510.

Grossetti, M., Barthe, J.-F., "Dynamiques des réseaux interpersonnels et des organisations dans les créations d'entreprises", in *Revue française de sociologie*, 2008, 49 (3), p. 582-612.

Hagedoorn, J., "Innovation and entrepreneurship: schumpeter revisited", in *Industrial and Corporate Change*, 1996, 5 (3), p. 883-896.

Hamdouch, A., "Conceptualizing innovation clusters and networks, working paper", in *Research Network of Innovation*, 2008, No. 6. http://rrifr.univ-littoral.fr/wp-content/uploads/2008/06/doc-3.pdf, 31 p.

Harrisson, B., Blustone, B., *The Great U-Turn, Corporate Restructuring and the Polarizing of America*, Basic Books, 1990.

Heertje, A., *Schumpeter on the Economics of Innovation and the Development of Capitalism*, Edward Elgar, Cheltenham, 2006.

Isard, W., *Location and Space-Economy*, MIT Press, Cambridge, 1956.

Julien, P.-A., *A Theory of Local Entrepreneurship in Knowledge Economy*, Edward Elgar, Cheltenham, 2007.

Kirzner, I., *Discovery and the Capitalist Process*, University of Chicago Press, Chicago, 1973.

Kirzner, I., "Entrepreneurial discovery and the competitive market process: an Austrian approach", in *The Journal of Economic Literature*, 1985, 35, p. 60-85.

Knight, F., *Risk, Uncertainty and Profit*, Chicago University Press, Chicago, 1921.

Konstadakopoulos, D., "Milieux innovateurs et apprentissage dans le Sud-Ouest de l'Angleterre", in *Innovations, Cahiers d'économie de l'innovation*, 2000, 11, p. 139-154.

Krugman, P., "Increasing returns and economic geography", in *Journal of Political Economy*, 1991, 99 (3), p. 483-499.

Langlois, R. N., "Schumpeter and the Obsolescence of the Entrepreneur", The History of Economics Society, annual meeting, Boston, 1987, WP 91-1503.

Laperche, B., "'Knowledge capital' and innovation in multinational corporations", in *International Journal of Technology and Globalisation*, 2007, 3 (1), p. 24-41.

Laperche, B., Galbraith, J. K., Uzunidis, D. (eds.), *Innovation, Evolution And Economic Change. New Ideas in the Tradition of Galbraith*, Edward Elgar, Cheltenham, 2006.

Laperche, B., "Potentiel d'innovation des grandes entreprises et État, argumentation évolutionniste sur l'appropriation des informations scientifiques et techniques", in *Innovations, Cahiers d'économie de l'innovation*, 2001, 13 (1), p. 61-85.

Lundvall, B. A., "Johnson, B., The Learning Economy", in *Journal of Industry Studies*, 1994, 1 (2), p. 23-42.

Madeuf, B., Carre, G., Lefebvre, G., Milelli, C., "TIC et économie de la proximité: organisation et localisation de la R&D au sein des entreprises globales", in *Innovations, Cahiers d'économie de l'innovation*, 2005, 21 (1), p. 243-272.

Marshall, A., *Industry and Trade*, MacMillan, London, 1919.

Marshall, A., *Principles of Economics*, MacMillan, London, 1891.

Nicolaou, N., Birley, S., "Social networks in organizational emergence: the university spinout phenomena", in *Management Science*, 2003, 49 (12), p. 1702-1725.

Nooteboom, B., "A cognitive theory of the firm", *Paper for ESNIE workshop Alternative Theories of the Firm*, November, Paris, 2002.

OCDE, *Perspectives de l'OCDE sur les PME et l'entrepreneuriat*, Paris, 2005.

Penrose, E., *The theory of the growth of the firm*, Basil Blackwell, Oxford, 1959 (5th ed. 1972).

Perroux, F., *La pensée économique de J. Schumpeter*, Presses de Savoie, 1965.

Perroux, F., "Note on the concept of "growth poles"", in McKee, Dean, Leahy (eds.), *Regional economics, Theory and practice*, The Free Press, New York, 1970, p. 93-106.

Piore, M., Sabel, C., *The Second Industrial Divide, Possibilities for Prosperity*, Basic Books, New York, 1984.

Pitelis, C., Sugden, R., Wilson, J. R., *Clusters and Globalisation*, Edward Elgar, Cheltenham, 2005.

Porter, M. E., "The Economic Performance of Regions", in *Regional Studies*, 2003, 37 (6-7), p. 549-578.

Porter, M. E., "Clusters and the New Economics of Competition", in *Harvard Business Review*, 1998, 76 (6), p. 77-90.

Putman, R. D., "Bowling alone: America's declining social capital", in *Journal of democracy*, 1995, 6 (1), p. 65-78.

Rallet, A., Torre, A., *Économie industrielle et économie spatiale*, Economica, Paris, 1995.

Rifkin, J., *La fin du travail*, La découverte, Paris, 1995.

Riverin, N., Jean, N., "L'entrepreneuriat chez les jeunes du Québec, état de la situation (2004)", Chaire d'entrepreneuriat Rogers J. A. Bombardier, HEC, Montréal, 2006.

Schumpeter, J. A., *The theory of Economic Development*, Transaction publishers, New Brunswick and London, 2005, 1934.

Schumpeter, J. A., *Capitalism, Socialism and Democracy*, Harper Perennial, New York, 1976, 1942.

Sennett, R., *La culture du nouveau capitalisme*, Albin Michel, Paris, 2006.

Shane, S., *A General Theory of Entrepreneurship, The individual-opportunity Nexus*, Edward Elgar, Cheltenham, 2003.

Sierra, C., "Proximité(s), interactions technologiques et territoriales", in *Revue d'économie industrielle*, 1997, 82, p. 7-38.

Storper, M., "The limits to globalization: technology districts and international trade", in *Economic Geography*, 1992, 68, p. 60-93.

Torre, A., Gilly, J.-P., "On the analytical dimension of proximity dynamics", in *Regional Studies*, 2000, 34, p. 169-180.

Uzunidis, D. (ed.), *L'innovation et l'économie contemporaine*, De Boeck, Bruxelles, 2004.

Uzunidis, D., "The logic of the innovative milieu", in B. Laperche, D. Uzunidis and N. von Tunzelmann (eds.), *Genesis of Innovation. Systemic Linkages between Knowledge and Market*, Edward Elgar, Cheltenham, 2008, p. 187-207.

Von Thünen, J. H., *The isolated state in relation to agriculture and political economy*, Palgrave Macmillan, London, 2009, 1826, 1850 and 1867.

White, H. C., *Identity and Control, A Structural Theory of Social Action*, Princeton University Press, Princeton, 1992.

White, H. C., *Market From Networks, Socioeconomic Models of Production*, Princeton University Press, Princeton, 2002.

CHAPTER VII

Biotechnology and Nanotechnology Innovation Networks in Canadian Clusters

Catherine BEAUDRY and Andrea SCHIFFAUEROVA

1. Introduction

Over the last decade there has been a widespread resurgence of interest in the economics of industrial location and particularly in the issue of geographical clusters.[1] Following successful cases in the United States (e.g. Silicon Valley) as well as in Europe (e.g. Baden-Württemberg), governments of the industrialised countries have launched a large number of programmes with the aim of supporting regional innovation policies. To encourage innovative activities and promote competition, the government's Innovation Strategy for Canada has decided to create at least ten internationally renowned technology clusters by 2010.

The attractiveness of a cluster depends on many factors that have direct and indirect impacts on its innovation production rate. Marshall (1920), who pioneered the original theories about the emergence of clusters, and later Krugman (1991), identified three factors facilitating the agglomeration of enterprises: a pool of skilled labour, a specialised intermediate goods industry and knowledge spillovers. These elements represent the supply-side benefits of clustering, because they refer to the production process of a firm. Baptista and Swann (1998), who surveyed the factors that enhance and cause clusters, identified four additional benefits on the demand-side: strong demand, market share gain, lower search costs and customer feedback.

The most discussed and controversial of these factors are localised knowledge spillovers.[2] Localised knowledge spillovers are frequently

---

[1] A cluster is defined by Porter (1998) as a geographic concentration of interconnected companies, specialised suppliers, service providers, firms in related industries, and associated institutions (for example, universities, standards agencies, and trade associations) in particular fields that compete but also cooperate.

[2] Localised knowledge spillovers are defined as knowledge externalities bounded in space that allow companies operating nearby key knowledge sources to introduce

claimed to be a key explanatory factor for the geographical concentration of innovative activity (see Dahl, Pedersen, 2004). This phenomenon is explained by Jaffe (1989), Acs *et al.* (1992, 1994), who suggest that investments in R&D by private corporations and universities spill over for third party firms to exploit. Since it is presumed that the transmission of knowledge is distance sensitive, the ability to receive knowledge spillovers is influenced by the distance from the knowledge source, which was also empirically confirmed by Jaffe *et al.* (1993), who proposed that knowledge spills over locally and takes time to diffuse across geographical distance. Hence in industries where new knowledge plays a crucial role, innovative activity tends to cluster in locations where key knowledge inputs are available (see Audretsch, Feldman, 1996).

Canada has a small population dispersed over a great geographical area and its private sector is dominated by small-sized and medium-sized companies. Therefore, in order for the innovation system to work effectively, research and development concentrate in geographical agglomerations and clusters. The main focus of this chapter is on the collaboration within these clusters, specifically on the knowledge diffusion and hence the transmission of knowledge spillovers through the innovation networks in the clusters. The network of innovators is an inter-personal network of individual innovators, who collaborate and exchange information in order to produce innovations and scientific knowledge. Social network analysis[3] (via co-inventorship or citation networks for instance) has been used to analyse the way these innovators are interconnected. Within the research community investigating innovation networks, it is widely presumed that two innovators, who have worked together on at least one patent or one scientific article, will keep in touch afterwards in order to exchange information and to share knowledge assets. The patent documents and bibliometric data could thus be exploited to map the complex web of social ties among innovators and to construct the innovation networks.

The network of scientists, whose links are established by their co-authorship of scientific articles, may be the largest social network ever studied (see Newman, 2001a). To our knowledge, Newman was the first to construct networks of collaboration between scientists in physics, biomedical research and computer science using four computer databases of scientific papers and to study a variety of the statistical properties of these networks to describe the network structure. In his subsequent papers (see Newman, 2001b, 2001d), Newman pursued his research on

---

innovations at a faster rate than rival firms located elsewhere (see Breschi, Lissoni, 2001).

[3] The essence of social network analysis is described in the following section.

the scientific networks, exploring a variety of non-local network properties and measures. Newman (2001c) then examined empirically the time
evolution of scientific collaboration networks in physics and biology.
Breschi and Lissoni (2003 and 2004) and later Balconi *et al.* (2004)
constructed the network of collaborative relationships linking Italian
inventors using data on co-inventorship of patents from the European
Patent Office (EPO). They built a bipartite graph of applicants, patents
and inventors. Using this graph, they derived various measures of social
proximity between cited and citing patents. Beaucage and Beaudry
(2006) constructed a network of Canadian biotechnology inventors
based on a similar methodology as Balconi *et al.* (2004). Cantner and
Graf (2006) proposed to build the networks of innovators based on
technological overlap, which is a measure of closeness of the technological field of two scientists. They also describe the evolution of the
innovator network of Jena, Germany, using the information on scientific
mobility. Singh (2005) inferred collaborative links among individuals
using a social proximity graph, which he also constructed from patent
collaboration data. Many other researchers[4] adopted the co-inventorship
of patents as an appropriate device to derive maps of social relationships
between inventors and to build their networks. Based on interviews with
inventors, Fleming *et al.* (2006), however, warned that patent co-
inventorship links differ significantly in their strength and information
transfer capacity. Also, since their decay rates vary greatly, a substantial
number of old ties remain viable even if the relation does not exist
anymore.

The findings from the aforementioned research studies reveal some
interesting properties of innovation networks. Most importantly, apparent differences in collaboration patterns, according to the nature of
subjects under study, are observed. The characteristics of the network
structures differ, depending on whether they contain purely industrial or
also academic researchers. Balconi *et al.* (2004) observed that networks
of inventors within industrial research are usually highly fragmented. In
contrast, the networks constructed by Newman (2001a) are very clustered, but since they are issued from scientific co-authorship we assume
that these were mainly academic networks. Newman (2001b) also
observed that for most scientific authors, the majority of the paths
between them and other scientists in the network go through just one or
two of their collaborators. This is in agreement with Balconi *et al.*
(2004) who found that academic inventors that enter industrial research
networks are, on average, more central than non-academic inventors –

---

[4]   For instance Mariani (2000), Ejermo and Karlsson (2006); Gauvin (1995) and
Fleming *et al.* (2006).

they exchange information with more people, across more organisations, and therefore play a key role in connecting individuals and network components. Academics also have a tendency to work within larger teams and for a larger number of applicants than non-academic inventors (see Balconi *et al.*, 2004).

Newman (2001c) showed that the probability of a pair of scientists collaborating increases with the number of other collaborators they have in common, and that the probability of a particular scientist acquiring new collaborators increases with the number of his or her past collaborators. Cantner and Graf (2006) did not, however, find any relation between previous and present cooperation with the same partners, suggesting that collaborations in the studied region are not persistent. Former collaborations are also found to be determinant of the future success. Cowan *et al.* (2007) claimed that previous collaborations increase the probability of a successful collaboration and Fleming *et al.* (2006) argued that an inventor's past collaboration network will strongly influence subsequent productivity.

Some of the researchers who adopted the network approach have also included geographical aspects into their models. Gittelman (2006) argues that the geography of the research collaborations has distinct impacts on firms' scientific contribution and their inventive productivity. The work of the co-located research teams results in scientifically more valuable knowledge, whereas the more dispersed research groups are more likely to produce commercially valuable technologies. Beaucage and Beaudry (2006) also characterised three major Canadian biotechnology clusters in terms of their innovation network structures and collaborative patterns.

Another line of research related to innovation networks involves theoretical simulation studies, in which researchers build innovation network models to simulate knowledge diffusion through the network. Cowan and Jonard (2003) develop a model of knowledge diffusion and study the relationship between the network structure across which knowledge diffuses and the distribution power of the innovation system. Cowan *et al.* (2004) pursue with the simulation study of knowledge flows and compare the mean knowledge growth under different network architectures (ranging from the highly clustered to the one that has no spatial structure). In order to capture the observed practice of informal knowledge trading, Cowan and Jonard (2004) model knowledge diffusion as a barter process in which agents exchange different types of knowledge, only if it is mutually profitable. They examine the relationship between network architecture (characterised by different levels of path length and cliquishness) and diffusion performance. Morone and

Taylor (2004) identify the limitations of Cowan and Jonard's model (2004) and improve it by introducing a network structure that changes as a consequence of interactions. They investigate the dynamics of knowledge diffusion and network formation. Finally, Cowan *et al.* (2007) model the formation of innovation networks as they emerge from bilateral decisions. They develop a model of alliance formation and examine the nature of the networks that emerge under different knowledge and information structures. One of the most important conclusions of these studies is that the existence of network structure can significantly increase long-run knowledge growth rates. The finding that the architecture of the network over which innovators interact influences the extent of diffusion and thus the innovative potential of the whole network is also the main theme of our research.

This chapter brings together the research on clusters and innovation networks, and is aimed at understanding the role of collaboration networks in the creation of innovation in high technology clusters. Our research will examine the diffusion of knowledge through the network of Canadian biotechnology and nanotechnology inventors constructed from patent co-inventorship data. The construction of the network will allow us to derive the collaborative behaviour of the inventors within and among clusters. The special focus is on the local network architecture, its role in the knowledge generation and thus in the growth of high technology clusters in Canada. We aim to compare biotechnology and nanotechnology networks in Canada and to examine how their structures differ. As nanotechnology is much more recent in Canada, we would expect the networks to be more fragmented and scattered throughout the country, rather than as organised as biotechnology.

The chapter is organised as follows: section 2 introduces the methodology and data used in this study; section 3 examines the evolution of the biotechnology and nanotechnology fields in Canada and presents the basic characteristics of the Canadian biotechnology and nanotechnology clusters; section 4 investigates the collaboration patterns among the inventors; section 5 presents the results of the network analyses related to the local collaboration within the clusters; and, finally, section 6 concludes.

2. Data and Methodology

The patent database used for the empirical analysis regarding the biotechnology clusters is the United States Patents and Trademarks Office (USPTO) database. This is the only patent database which provides the geographical location of the residence for each inventor (unlike the Canadian Intellectual Property Office database (CIPO) or the

European Patent Office (EPO)). The use of the USPTO database instead of the CIPO may introduce a bias in the data, but we consider it minimal, since Canadian inventors usually patent both in Canada and in the US. For example, in 1998 and 1999 out of all the patent applications submitted worldwide by Canadian biotechnology firms, the majority (36%) was sent to the USPTO, followed by 28% to the CIPO, 21% to the EPO and the balance (16%) to other offices[5] (Statistics Canada, 2001). The population of Canada is relatively small and as a consequence, building a viable industry based on domestic sales alone may prove difficult. In addition, because of the long development cycles for biotechnology products (typically 10 years for a single product), access to large markets is needed to ensure an adequate return on investment (see Strachan, 1995). As a result, Canadian biotechnology firms prefer to protect their intellectual property in the USA. The much larger and easily accessible US biotechnology and nanotechnology markets offer great potential to Canadian firms. An analysis of the Canadian patents registered at the USPTO should provide a realistic picture of Canadian biotechnology innovation.

Biotechnology encompasses several different research technologies and several fields of application. A Statistics Canada study (see Rose, 2000) has shown that different interpretations of the meaning of biotechnology can result in differences in the results of biotechnology surveys. One of the initial tasks for us was therefore to select a clear and practical definition of biotechnology. We have opted to base our USPTO search strategy on the OECD definition of biotechnology, which is based on the group of carefully selected International Patent Codes (IPC).[6] The OECD has carried out an extensive consultation, including the work conducted by Statistics Canada, which shares similar definitions of biotechnology (Munn-Venn and Mitchell, 2005), to develop the definitions of biotechnology techniques, and the validation showed that the definition appears to capture a significant proportion of biotechnology patents. It might not be complete and may include some patents with non-biotechnology techniques. However, errors are likely to be small (OECD, 2005).

---

[5]   Note that firms may have submitted patents regarding the same invention to a number of patent offices at the same time. For instance, some patents are registered at the USPTO, CIPO and EPO.

[6]   The OECD definition of biotechnology patents covers the following IPC classes: A01H1/00, A01H4/00, A61K38/00, A61K39/00, A61K48/00, C02F3/34, C07G(11/00, 13/00, 15/00), C07K(4/00, 14/00, 16/00, 17/00, 19/00), C12M, C12N, C12P, C12Q, C12S, G01N27/327, G01N33/(53*, 54*, 55*, 57*, 68, 74, 76, 78, 88, 92).

An automated extraction programme was used to collect the required information[7] from the biotechnology patents. All the biotechnology patents registered before March 31, 2007, were included. According to the above definition, there are around 100,000 biotechnology patents registered at the USPTO. We have thus created a patent database, which contains all the patents in which at least one inventor resides in Canada and which comprises 3550 patents. The total number of Canadian patents registered at the USPTO each year found by the aforementioned search strategy largely correspond with what other authors have found: for example, the results of Statistics Canada (2001) or the study of Rasmussen (2004). We have nevertheless noticed substantial differences in the findings of other researchers. These were usually caused by the choice of different search strategies such as keywords in the patents' names and abstracts (as in Niosi, Bas, 2001) or by the decision to use a rather narrow biotechnology definition (as in Beaucage, Beaudry, 2006).

In order to build the network of Canadian nanotechnology inventors we used the patent co-inventorship data contained in the Nanobank database. Nanobank is a public digital library comprising data on nanotechnology articles, patents and federal grants, as well as firms engaged in using nanotechnology commercially. The Nanobank patent database is based on data from the United States Patents and Trademarks Office (USPTO) database as well. From the Nanobank database we have selected the patents in which at least one inventor resides in Canada (5067 patents). We have employed additional filters, which enabled us to select only the patents that are strictly related to nanotechnology[8] and created a Canadian nanotechnology patent database, which comprises 1443 patents.

From these two databases, biotechnology and nanotechnology innovation networks were created by following the precepts of Social Network Analysis. A social network consists of a finite set of actors and the relations defined on them (see Wasserman, Faust, 1994). The nodes in the network represent the inventors, whereas the links show knowledge relationships between them. Collaboration on or co-invention of a patent is considered to be such a relationship and the inventors whose names appear on the same patents are connected by the direct links in our innovation networks. It is supposed that each collaboration involves an active interchange of information and sharing of knowledge assets, with an aim to produce innovations and scientific knowledge. Social network

---

[7] Extracted information necessary for the research leading to this chapter includes the patent number and the inventors' names and their addresses.

[8] For the exact description of our selection methodology see Schiffauerova and Beaudry (2008).

analysis is used to analyse the way these inventors are interconnected and to evaluate the impact of the network structures on the knowledge creation and diffusion. The social network analysis programme PAJEK was used to build the networks from the patent data. An analysis of these collaborative networks enabled us to describe their structural properties and to understand the collaborative behaviour of the inventors inside or outside Canadian biotechnology clusters. Since the obtained patent data in both databases span over a period of around 30 years (biotechnology: 1976-2007 and nanotechnology: 1976-2005), we have assumed that once inventors collaborate on one patent they continue to be in contact afterwards and are able to exchange knowledge acquired long after the patent has been granted. This allows us to disregard the time of collaboration and consider all links among inventors in the network as simultaneously active.

3. Canadian Biotechnology and Nanotechnology Clusters

In 2002, biotechnology was considered to be one of the most dynamic and fastest growing sectors in Canada. According to Statistics Canada (2003), biotechnology companies have more than quadrupled their revenues in 1997-2003. By 2002, Canada was the second most active country in the world in biotechnology in terms of new firms, venture capital and patents – after the US and ahead of the UK (see Niosi, 2005). Metrics such as R&D spending, market capitalisation, as well as the total number of firms and revenues, all showed strong growth over the five years preceding 2002 (see Ernst & Young, 2002). Nevertheless, the recent survey of Statistics Canada (2005) found that the number of innovative biotechnology firms increased only by 9% in the period 2003-2005, whereas it increased by 31% between 2001 and 2003. Niosi (2006) noted that in recent years (particularly since 2000), Canadian biotechnology companies have experienced financing problems and even some of the well-financed firms have abandoned the sector altogether. He suggests that the new trend of Canadian biotechnology is directed towards concentration of activity into a small number of dedicated biotechnology companies.

Figure 1 shows the growth of biotechnology and nanotechnology patents (filed at the USPTO) with at least one named Canadian inventor based on the year of granting. It illustrates a phenomenal growth, with a sharp increase in the annual number of patents in those years. It is also evident that after the peak in 2001-2002, the number of biotechnology patents invented or co-invented by Canadians has been decreasing.

Figure 1: Biotechnology and nanotechnology patents of Canadian inventors by the year of granting

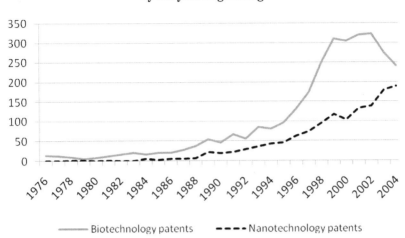

Nanotechnology research was rather sporadic before 1987 when patent production started to accelerate. Apart from a short period of decline in 2000, the number of nanotechnology patents granted per year has been steadily increasing, and during the last 15 years it has in fact increased ten-fold. Moreover, in 2004, the annual production of nanotechnology patents was almost reaching that of biotechnology patents.

Most of these patents are owned by a single assignee (see Table 1).[9] This implies that innovation teams usually work for only one organisation, suggesting that there is little cooperation amongst organisations. There seem to be a slightly higher proportion of patents assigned to a single entity in nanotechnology. This is probably due to the fact that around 30% of all nanotechnology patents invented or co-invented by Canadian residents are assigned to a single American company – Xerox Corporation. Very few biotechnology and nanotechnology patents are assigned to more than two assignees.

Assignees who are the full or partial owners of more than 20 biotechnology and 10 nanotechnology patents at the USPTO are listed in Table 2. The data confirms that biotechnology innovation is strongly based on publicly-funded research. Out of the first 30 assignees with the highest number of biotechnology patents, 13 are universities, five are government institutions and two are hospitals. The most important

---

[9]   Patent assignee is an entity (original or legal company, organisation or person) that is registered as proprietor of the patent or patent application.

producers of patents are universities with McGill University (123 patents) heading the league table. The contribution of government institutions to biotechnology research and development is also substantial: among the five highest ranking patent holders is the National Research Council of Canada (95 patents), the Government of Canada's premier agency for research and development and Her Majesty the Queen in right of Canada (92 patents) usually representing various federal ministries (agriculture, health, national defence). The Hospital for Sick Children (71 patents) and the Mount Sinai Hospital (31 patents), which are both affiliated to the University of Toronto, lead the patent league among hospitals. Finally, a number of private companies are also the owners of a considerable number of biotechnology patents.[10]

Table 1: Biotechnology and nanotechnology patents by the number of assignees in a patent

	Biotechnology		Nanotechnology	
	Patents	*%*	*Patents*	*%*
single assignee	2932	83%	1252	87%
multiple assignees	306	9%	105	7%
non-assigned	312	9%	86	6%
	Σ 3550	100%	Σ 1443	100%

The results differ in nanotechnology, where the marketplace seems to be more concentrated. As mentioned above, almost one third of all nanotechnology patents invented or co-invented by Canadian residents is owned by the American Xerox Corporation (444 patents). Publicly-funded research is less represented in nanotechnology than in biotechnology; indeed, half of the first 18 assignees with the highest number of patents are private companies (Northern Telecom with 42 patents, Hydro-Quebec with 31 patents, D-Wave Systems with 29 patents and Adherex Technologies with 20 patents). However, the single most important Canadian producer of the nanotechnology patents is a government institution – the National Research Council of Canada (57 patents). In biotechnology, McGill University (32 patents) and the University of British Colombia (26 patents) are the most active Canadian universities in nanotechnology patenting as well.

---

[10] For a more detailed analysis of patent-owning organisations and the role of publicly funded research in Canadian biotechnology see Schiffauerova and Beaudry (2009).

Table 2: Assignees with more than 20 biotechnology or nanotechnology patents filed with the USPTO

Biotechnology

Assignee	Nb. of patents	Cluster	Prov.	Type
McGill University	123	Montreal	QC	Univ.
Connaught Laboratories Ltd	118	Toronto	ON	Firm
University of British Columbia	114	Vancouver	BC	Univ.
National Research Council of Canada	95	Ottawa	ON	Inst.
Her Majesty the Queen of Canada	92	Ottawa	ON	Inst.
University of Saskatchewan	78	Saskatoon	SK	Univ.
Pioneer Hi-Bred International Inc.	75	-	USA	Firm
Hospital for Sick Children	71	Toronto	ON	Hosp.
Aventis Pasteur Ltd	63	Toronto	ON	Firm
Queen's University	61	Kingston	ON	Univ.
University of Calgary	59	Calgary	AB	Univ.
University of Alberta	57	Edmonton	AB	Univ.
Allelix Biopharmaceutical	52	Toronto	ON	Firm
Merck Frosst Canada Inc.	42	Montreal	QC	Firm
Visible Genetics Inc	40	Toronto	ON	Firm
University of Guelph	35	Toronto	ON	Univ.
Alberta Research Council	34	Edmonton	AB	Inst.
Université de Montréal	32	Montreal	QC	Univ.
Université Laval	32	Quebec	QC	Univ.
Syn X Pharma	32	Toronto	ON	Firm
Mount Sinai Hospital	31	Toronto	ON	Hosp.
University of Toronto	28	Toronto	ON	Univ.
University of Ottawa	26	Ottawa	ON	Univ.
Canadian Patents and Development	26	Ottawa	ON	Inst.
Boehringer Ingelheim Canada Ltd	26	Montreal	QC	Firm
Adherex	25	Ottawa	ON	Firm
University of Manitoba	22	Winnipeg	MB	Univ.
NPS Allelix Corp.	22	Toronto	ON	Firm
Spectral Diagnostics Inc.	21	Toronto	ON	Firm
Ontario Cancer Institute	21	Toronto	ON	Hosp.

Nanotechnology

Assignee	Nb. of patents	Cluster	Prov.	Type
Xerox Corporation	444	-	USA	Firm
National Research Council of Canada	57	Ottawa	ON	Inst.
Northern Telecom Limited	42	Montreal	QC	Firm
McGill University	32	Montreal	QC	Univ.
Hydro-Quebec	31	Montreal	QC	Firm
D-Wave Systems Inc.	29	Vancouver	BC	Firm
University of British Columbia	26	Vancouver	BC	Univ.
Adherex Technologies Inc.	20	Ottawa	ON	Firm
Centre National de la Recherche Scientifique	19	-	FRA	Inst.
University of Calgary	18	Calgary	CA	Univ.
Hospital for Sick Children	16	Toronto	CA	Hosp
Westaim Technologies, Inc.	16	Edmonton	CA	Firm
Connaught Laboratories, Inc.	14	-	USA	Firm
University of Toronto	14	Toronto	CA	Univ.
Université de Montréal	14	Montreal	CA	Univ.
Zenon Environmental Inc.	12	Toronto	CA	Firm
University of Alberta	12	Edmonton	CA	Univ.
Angiotech Pharmaceuticals Inc.	11	Vancouver	CA	Firm

The production of both biotechnology and nanotechnology patents is not uniform throughout Canada. Most of the Canadian biotechnology or nanotechnology innovation is concentrated in a few regions. Based on the residences of inventors, we have identified twelve Canadian biotechnology clusters and eight Canadian nanotechnology clusters.[11] For biotechnology, 20% of inventors reside in the Toronto cluster (34% of all patents), 15% in the Montreal cluster (19% of all patents) and 9% in the Vancouver cluster (10% of all patents). Only a small portion of biotech inventors (4%) residing in Canada lives outside the defined clusters (2% of patents) and around 29% of the innovators in our sample reside outside the Canadian borders (21% of all patents are assigned solely to foreigners).[12]

The situation is quite different in nanotechnology. The greatest part of all the patents (47%) invented or co-invented by Canadian scientists is assigned to foreign entities, most of which reside in the US; 69% of the patents owned by non-Canadian subjects is assigned to a single American company – Xerox Corporation. Only 28% of the inventors whose patents were assigned to foreign subjects are foreigners as well, most of them (62%) reside in the Toronto cluster. The consequence is a low number of assignees compared to a disproportionally high number of inventors residing in Toronto (see Figure 3). Regarding the number of inventors residing in each of the eight identified Canadian nanotechnology clusters, Toronto is leading (25% of inventors), followed by Montreal and Ottawa (9% of inventors in each cluster).

Table 3 shows the respective situations of the 12 biotechnology and 8 nanotechnology clusters, as described by the measures of the number of the patents in the cluster and the number of inventors. Table 3 also shows that most of the Canadian biotechnology and nanotechnology activities take place within clusters, usually the few main ones. Only 2% (biotechnology) or 4% (nanotechnology) of the patents are owned by assignees with residences in Canada but outside the predefined clusters. In both sectors there are only a very few patents with co-assignees from multiple Canadian clusters. The lack of common inter-cluster ownership of patents suggests that there is not much cooperation at the assignee level between clusters, and if there is, ownership of patents is not shared.

---

[11] A cluster is defined in this study as a geographically continuous region active in biotechnology and nanotechnology (as measured by the patent production).

[12] For a detailed analysis of the inventors and other characteristics of the Canadian biotechnology clusters see Schiffauerova and Beaudry (2009).

Figure 2: Patents and inventors claims in each biotechnology cluster based on the location of patent's assignees and the residences of inventors

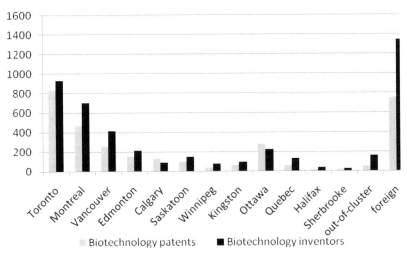

Figure 3: Patents and inventors claims in each nanotechnology cluster based on the location of patent's assignees and the residences of inventors

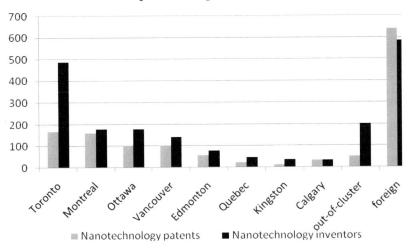

Table 3: Summary of the results for biotechnology and nanotechnology clusters

High technology cluster	Biotechnology			Nanotechnology			
	Number of patents[a]	Number of inventors[b]	Patents per inventor[c]	Number of patents[a]	Number of inventors[b]	Patents per inventor[c]	Patents per inventor[d]
Toronto	834	927	1.44	169	487	1.52	0.35
Montreal	466	698	1.05	162	180	1.16	0.90
Vancouver	255	411	0.95	103	142	0.95	0.73
Ottawa	279	224	1.26	103	179	0.92	0.58
Edmonton	153	210	1.21	57	79	0.94	0.72
Calgary	127	91	2.19	34	33	1.30	1.03
Quebec	57	127	0.97	23	47	0.79	0.49
Kingston	63	94	1.01	14	35	1.05	0.40
Saskatoon	98	147	1.04	-	-	-	-
Winnipeg	33	77	0.91	-	-	-	-
Halifax	20	33	1.06	-	-	-	-
Sherbrooke	16	26	1.07	-	-	-	-
out-of -cluster	84	159	1.16	52	201	0.87	0.26
foreign residence	753	1345	-	640	585	-	-
non-assigned[e]	312	-	-	86	-	-	-
Canada	Σ 3550	Σ 4569	1.21	Σ 1443	Σ 1968	1.03	0.69

a Based on the residence of the assignees (the patents with multiple residences were allocated to only one cluster.

b Based on the residence of the inventors (the inventors who patented while living in several clusters were assigned to only one cluster.

c Counted as the number of patents co-invented by at least one inventor from the cluster divided by the number of inventors who at least once patented while living in that cluster.

d Counted as the number of patents allocated to the clusters by assignees' residences divided by the number of inventors allocated to that cluster based on their most frequent residence.

e The inventor still has not decided who will own the patenting rights.

The third column of table 3 shows the numbers of patents per inventor produced in various biotechnology clusters (counted as the number of patents co-invented by at least one inventor from the cluster divided by the number of inventors who at least once patented while living in that cluster) and gives a certain indication about the productivity of the inventors in each cluster. The highest biotechnology productivity is in the Calgary cluster (2.19 patents per inventor), followed by Toronto (1.44 patents per inventor).

Regarding nanotechnology clusters (see the sixth column), this number is again highest for the Toronto cluster (1.52 patents per inventor). In the seventh column we have computed an alternative indicator based on the nanotechnology assignee's residence (counted as the number of patents allocated to the clusters by assignees' residences divided by the number of inventors allocated to that cluster based on their most frequent residence). It is extremely low for the Toronto cluster (0.35 patents per inventor), to which only very few patents are assigned, even though it has many inventors. This suggests that many nanotechnology inventors residing in Toronto work for companies headquartered in the US. As we have already mentioned above, 62% of inventors whose patents were assigned to foreign subjects reside in the Toronto cluster.

4. Collaboration Patterns in Canadian Biotechnology and Nanotechnology

The following two sections explore the collaboration characteristics and the structure of innovation networks formed by the inventors in the clusters. The network of Canadian biotechnology inventors that we created includes 4569 vertices (representing inventors) and 9731 edges (representing collaborative relations[13]), whereas the network of Canadian nanotechnology inventors involves only 1968 vertices and 4920 edges. Our main concern consists in the study of knowledge flows and information exchange among the researchers, i.e. in the characterisation of the links between them. For instance, we have found that 36% (biotechnology) or 34% (nanotechnology) of all collaborative relations between pairs of inventors involve repetitive instances of collaboration.[14] Most of the relationships between a pair of inventors are, how-

---

[13] Each collaborative relation (also called a tie or a link) represents a connection between a pair of inventors, which involves one or more instances of co-invention of a biotechnology patent.

[14] An instance of collaboration (or simply collaboration) is a connection between a pair of inventors for the purpose of co-invention of one biotechnology patent. Each col-

ever, single collaboration instances (i.e. they resulted in only one patent).

An inventor in a Canadian biotechnology network has on average 4.26 collaboration partners[15] (five partners in the nanotechnology network), but some of them have a considerably higher number of relationship ties, the highest one amounting to 66 co-inventors (54 co-inventors for nanotechnology). Canadian inventors most commonly have one collaborator (16% of biotech inventors and 12% of nanotech inventors), two collaborators (20% of biotech and 19% of nanotech) or three collaborators (17% of biotech and 16% of nanotech). Only a small number of inventors (4% in both networks) do not collaborate with anybody else on their patent(s) (single inventors or isolates), and only a few (6% of biotech and 8% of nanotech inventors) have more than 10 co-inventors. The average number of collaborating partners per inventor and per patent in each cluster is presented in Table 4. While in biotechnology these numbers seem quite comparable for each cluster, in nanotechnology the average number of collaborators in the Toronto cluster clearly stands out (it is almost double compared to other clusters). This suggests that the Toronto nanotechnology inventors collaborate more intensively and exchange information with more inventors than researchers in other clusters.

Our general results (4.26 or five collaborators per inventor) are comparable with the average number of collaborators per inventor found by Beaucage and Beaudry (2006) who observed 5.12 collaboration partners per Canadian biotechnology inventor. Even though their figures are slightly higher, they roughly correspond to ours in terms of the average collaboration partners in each biotechnology cluster. Out of the three main biotechnology clusters they studied, the average Montreal inventor has the highest number of collaborators, while the Toronto inventor the lowest (which can be observed in our results for biotechnology in Table 4 as well). We calculated the average number of collaborators per inventor for the networks of Balconi *et al.* (2004, calculated from p. 139, Table 5) in order to compare its value with our network. Our calculation shows that the networks of Balconi *et al.* (2004) have on average 2.09 collaborators per inventor, considerably less than the 4.26 collaborators (biotechnology) or five collaborators (nanotechnology) observed in our networks. The difference can be explained by the distinct samples of patents selected for the analysis: contrary to our nar-

---

laborative relation may thus involve one or more instances of collaboration (collaborations).

[15] Collaboration partner (or collaborator) is here defined as a co-inventor of at least one biotechnology or nanotechnology patent registered at the USPTO.

rowly focused patent sample (only biotechnology or nanotechnology), in the study of Balconi *et al.*, the industry range is quite broad. Newman's findings (2001a) differ even more from our results. He observed a much larger number of collaborators in his innovation networks; especially for the scientists in experimental disciplines (for instance, an average high-energy physics scientist had 173 collaborators during a five-year period). The scientific papers have, however, traditionally more numerous co-authors than the patents (the largest number of authors on a single paper found by Newman was 1681!), since joint article authorship was found to reflect a variety of phenomena other than the exchange of information and research collaboration.[16] Even though the legal requirements for article co-authorship and patent co-inventorship are officially very similar, the number of article co-authors is on average much higher than the number of co-inventors of the patent, which reflects exactly the same discovery or invention. Ducor (2000) found that the number of article co-authors is on average more than three times higher than the number of inventors on the corresponding patent.

Table 4 also shows the results of some basic statistics regarding collaborators and collaborations in clusters. The results in the second and the fifth columns (co-inventors per patent) would at first glance suggest that the average team size is similar in all the clusters; however, ANOVA tests (see Appendix A for biotechnology and Appendix B for nanotechnology) showed that the population means are in fact different and the team sizes within both Canadian biotechnology and nanotechnology research thus differ across the country. Balconi *et al.* (2004) proposed that the differences in team sizes may be explained by the affiliations of the inventors – the researchers affiliated to academic institutions work in larger teams and for a larger number of applicants than industrial researchers do. This research does not yet distinguish between academic and industrial researchers, but it is our intention to do so in future.

---

[16] Cockburn and Henderson (1998) suggest that: article co-authorship may be offered as a quid pro quo for supplying information or resources; it can serve as a means of resolving disputes about priority; it may also be an acknowledgement of an intellectual debt; it may just be a listing of laboratory directors or other project leaders as authors; or it may reflect an effort to gain legitimacy, or admission to networks of other researchers.

**Table 4: Statistics regarding collaborators or collaborations
for each cluster**

High technology cluster	Biotechnology			Nanotechnology		
	Collabora-tors per inventor	Co-inventors in one patent	Collabora-tions per inventor	Collabora-tors per inventor	Co-inventors in one patent	Collabora-tions per inventor
Toronto	3.49	2.91	8.88	7.02	2.88	14.13
Montreal	4.04	3.23	7.57	3.97	3.07	7.48
Vancouver	3.67	3.05	5.95	3.65	2.89	5.22
Ottawa	4.55	2.96	9.28	3.69	2.88	5.34
Edmonton	4.83	3.28	8.49	4.10	3.23	6.35
Calgary	3.93	2.59	10.13	3.88	3.41	8.55
Quebec	3.31	2.83	4.78	3.49	3.78	4.81
Kingston	2.86	2.68	4.52	3.71	3.43	6.63
Saskatoon	4.54	3.29	8.10	-	-	-
Winnipeg	2.53	2.11	3.08	-	-	-
Halifax	2.09	2.25	3.24	-	-	-
Sherbrooke	2.50	2.44	3.23	-	-	-
out-of cluster	2.85	2.96	4.05	2.93	2.62	3.61
Average in Canada	4.26	3.09	7.46	5.00	3.00	8.60

The third and the sixth columns in Table 4 show a number of collaborative instances per inventor in each cluster. To sum up, Table 4 suggests that in order to generate innovations, biotechnology researchers in the clusters of Saskatoon, Ottawa, Edmonton and Montreal collaborate slightly more intensively and exchange information with more inventors than researchers in other clusters. In nanotechnology, it is mainly the inventors from the Toronto cluster that show substantially higher collaborative intensity.

To investigate the geographical aspects of collaboration, we first classified all these instances of collaboration according to their location into *intra-cluster collaborations* (both inventors in a collaborating pair are from the same cluster), *inter-cluster collaborations* (one inventor in a pair resides in a different cluster or elsewhere in Canada) and *international collaborations* (one inventor in a pair resides abroad).

Figure 4 and Figure 5 present the overall collaboration pattern for all Canadian biotechnology and nanotechnology inventors.

Figure 4: Collaboration pattern in Canadian biotechnology

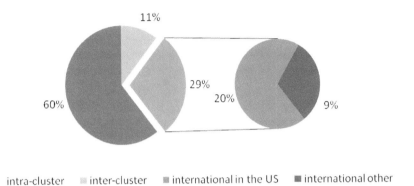

Figure 5: Collaboration pattern in Canadian nanotechnology

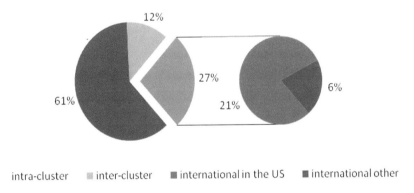

The majority (60% in biotech and 61% in nanotech) of the all collaboration instances take place within clusters and over a quarter (29% in biotech and 27% in nanotech) are distant ties directed abroad. Most of the foreign collaborative ties are linked to American inventors. Only a relatively small part (11% in biotech and 12% in a nanotech network) of all the collaboration involves inventors from other Canadian clusters or from elsewhere in Canada. So this broad brush overview of the collaborative behaviour of inventors detects very little differences between biotechnology and nanotechnology. Let us therefore take a magnifying glass and investigate in greater detail the knowledge flows within these clusters.

5. Local Collaboration in the Cluster-based Subnetworks

It has been suggested and empirically supported that firms in clusters are more innovative (see Baptista, Swann, 1998; Beaudry, 2001; Beaudry, Breschi, 2003; Beaudry, Swann, 2009). The companies co-located in a close geographical proximity enjoy numerous benefits, as discussed above. Biotechnology and nanotechnology knowledge is largely tacit, which limits knowledge diffusion over long distances. In fact, the transmission of tacit information and knowledge spillovers is usually associated with face-to-face contact. Collaboration among the inventors working in biotechnology and nanotechnology clusters is thus strongly encouraged by the benefits of acquiring knowledge that the subjects located within short geographical distance spill over.

This section analyses these local collaborations carried out entirely within clusters. We have divided both Canadian biotechnology and nanotechnology innovation networks into geographically based subnet-works, where each subnetwork strictly includes inventors who reside in one particular cluster, while excluding the ones that do not. Out-of-cluster and foreign inventors are therefore eliminated for the time being. For each of the subnetworks created in this manner, several network characteristics were calculated. The remaining part briefly discusses several of the basic structural properties of the network and explains the indicators used in this chapter to measure them. We show how these characteristics could be related to efficiency in knowledge diffusion among the inventors within the clusters and suggest the possible impact on innovation creation in the cluster.

5.1. Collaboration characteristics in the subnetworks

As Table 5 shows, 18-50% of collaborative relations between pairs of biotechnology inventors residing in the same cluster (and 20-47% between nanotechnology inventors) involve repetitive instances of collaboration. Biotechnology inventors in Toronto and Calgary tend to pursue collaborative relations with the same partners more often than the biotechnology inventors in Montreal, Vancouver or Edmonton. In Halifax, half of the collaborative ties of the local biotechnology inventors include repetitive collaborative relationships. As for the nanotech-nology inventors, those in Toronto, Montreal and Ottawa collaborate with the same partners much more often than inventors in Vancouver or Edmonton. With regards to the smaller nanotechnology clusters, in Kingston almost half of the collaborative ties of the local inventors include repetitive collaborative relationships and the repetitiveness is also high in Calgary.

In the biotechnology and nanotechnology networks, the strongest collaboration link – the most frequently repeated collaborative relation – concerns two pairs of inventors in Toronto (one in biotech and one in nanotech). They repeated their collaboration 60 (biotech) or 50 (nanotech) times. In smaller clusters, the maximum number of repeated collaborations is lower. Within the biotech subnetworks it is still relatively low for the larger clusters of Montreal (11) and Vancouver (10), where, on average, innovative activities involve slightly more co-inventors who collaborate with each other less often. The maximum number of repeated collaborations in the nanotechnology subnetworks is relatively high for Montreal (29), but surprisingly low for the similarly-sized Ottawa (6) and somewhat smaller Vancouver (12). On average, the innovative activities of nanotechnology inventors in Toronto involve considerably more co-inventors who collaborate with each other more often than in any other nanotechnology cluster studied.

Table 5: Collaboration characteristics in biotechnology and nanotechnology cluster-based subnetworks

| Cluster-based sub-network | Biotechnology | | | Nanotechnology | | |
	Number of collaborating pairs	% of repeated collaborations	Max number of repeated collaboration	Number of collaborating pairs	% of repeated collaborations	Max number of repeated collaborations
Toronto	1120	43%	60	1295	38%	50
Montreal	1027	36%	11	201	36%	29
Vancouver	568	37%	10	199	20%	12
Ottawa	343	36%	19	218	35%	6
Edmonton	334	37%	14	112	24%	6
Calgary	91	41%	16	41	41%	8
Quebec	155	18%	7	53	21%	3
Kingston	96	33%	10	36	47%	4
Saskatoon	259	28%	8	-	-	-
Winnipeg	54	19%	3	-	-	-
Halifax	20	50%	5	-	-	-
Sherbrooke	10	20%	3	-	-	-
Network	9731	36%	60	4920	34%	50

5.2. Fragmentation of the subnetworks

In order to assess the fragmentation of the subnetworks, we identified the network components and determined their major characteristics – each of which will be described in the following paragraphs (see Table 6). A *component* is defined as the maximal connected subnetwork (see Wasserman, Faust, 1994). It is a part of the network that includes a maximum number of vertices which are all directly or indirectly connected by links. A network may then be composed of a number of distinct components that have no links between each other. The largest component (in absolute value) of the biotechnology subnetworks is found in the Montreal cluster (109 interconnected inventors, which comprises 16% of inventors), even though Toronto has almost twice as many inventors (the largest component size is 98, which is only 11% of inventors). In nanotechnology, the largest component in Toronto consists of 155 inventors, or around 32% of all the Toronto nanotechnology inventors. Even though the Toronto nanotechnology cluster shows a surprisingly high interconnectedness of the inventors, the size of the largest components of the rest of the clusters are much smaller.

The *second largest components* of the biotechnology subnetworks in Montreal and Toronto are of similar sizes, with that of Vancouver being much smaller. The cluster of Vancouver is in general more fragmented than the other two. In Saskatoon, even the second largest component is composed of (proportionately) many inventors. Regarding the nanotechnology subnetworks, the second component in Toronto is more than 10 times smaller than the first largest component. In contrast, for the other three nanotechnology clusters, the second largest components are around half the size of the largest ones; and in Edmonton, they are almost of the same size. These nanotechnology cluster subnetworks are overall more fragmented than the Toronto one.

The *average component size* is fairly small for all of the biotechnology and nanotechnology clusters (around two to three inventors). As hinted at in the previous paragraph, Saskatoon, which comprises components of a large relative size, scores the highest on the average number of interconnected inventors (4.32 inventors). The second rank is occupied by Montreal and Ottawa (both have on average 3.2 connected inventors), but Toronto has a mean of only 2.71 inventors in a component. In nanotechnology, on the other hand, the Toronto subnetwork stands out: it includes components of a larger relative size – the mean number of interconnected inventors is 3.69. Moreover, half of the inventors form only around 20% of all the components, whereas this percentage is much larger for all the other nanotech clusters. The remaining nanotechnology subnetworks have on average comparable numbers of connected inventors (around 2.5-2.9 inventors).

The *counts of isolate vertices* (inventors with no links to other inventors) in both biotechnology and nanotechnology subnetworks are proportionately comparable for the large clusters (15%-19% of all the vertices) and relatively high for the smaller clusters (e.g., in Sherbrooke almost half of the biotech inventors are isolated). The Toronto nanotechnology subnetwork has the lowest percentage of isolate vertices (11%) of all the clusters. Many inventors have collaborators outside their clusters or outside Canada, which contribute to indirectly linking up inventors from the same cluster. In analysing the cluster-based subnetworks we therefore omit these out-of-cluster links. We hence consider only cooperation based on close personal contacts, which are limited by geographical distance.

Taking all of the above into account, we can conclude that the biotechnology network seems to be slightly less fragmented than the nanotechnology network. However, in nanotechnology there appears to be a well interconnected network component in Toronto, but the rest of the Canadian nanotechnology inventors are working in a relatively disconnected groups. Even when we consider the full network values, disregarding the geography, the average component size in nanotechnology is somewhat smaller (5.11 in biotech and 4.84 in nanotech), while the share of the components that include 50% of all the inventors is much higher in the nanotechnology network (only 10% in biotech but 26% in nanotech networks). The percentage of isolates is comparable in both networks (4% for both biotechnology and nanotechnology).

This result was to be expected. On the one hand, the specialisation fields within biotechnology are quite close in their scientific nature and are often overlapping. Inventors in the biotechnology network should thus be more interconnected between each other. Nanotechnology, on the other hand, includes many disparate fields, where the inventors understandably work in more separated groups. Nanotechnology would therefore appear more as a brand name than a "single" technology so far.

Table 6: Fragmentation in biotechnology and nanotechnology cluster-based subnetworks

Cluster-based subnetwork	Biotechnology							Nanotechnology						
	Number of components	1st largest component Size	As %	Ratio 2nd/1st	Average comp. size	Share of comp. with 50% inventors	Isolates as % of inventors	Number of components	1st largest component Size	As %	Ratio 2nd/1st	Average comp. size	Share of comp. with 50% inventors	Isolates as % of inventors
Toronto	342	98	11%	0.36	2.71	13%	19%	132	155	32%	0.08	3.69	21%	11%
Montreal	218	109	16%	0.31	3.20	11%	15%	73	21	12%	0.48	2.47	34%	19%
Vancouver	134	38	9%	0.47	3.07	15%	16%	52	21	15%	0.43	2.73	31%	18%
Ottawa	70	75	33%	0.15	3.2	9%	17%	68	23	13%	0.43	2.63	29%	18%
Edmonton	67	49	23%	0.43	3.13	11%	17%	27	15	19%	0.93	2.93	26%	15%
Calgary	39	15	16%	0.60	2.33	18%	24%	17	8	24%	0.50	1.94	35%	30%
Quebec	44	11	9%	0.82	2.89	21%	15%	19	6	13%	1.00	2.47	47%	17%
Kingston	38	8	9%	0.75	2.47	24%	18%	17	5	14%	1.00	2.06	53%	29%
Saskatoon	34	54	37%	0.67	4.32	6%	13%	-	-	-	-	-	-	-
Winnipeg	44	7	9%	0.86	1.75	25%	36%	-	-	-	-	-	-	-
Halifax	20	6	18%	0.67	1.65	30%	39%	-	-	-	-	-	-	-
Sherbrooke	18	3	12%	1.00	1.44	33%	46%	-	-	-	-	-	-	-
Network	894	579	13%	0.32	5.11	10%	4%	407	336	17%	0.09	4.84	26%	4%

5.3. Structural cohesion of the subnetworks

Structural cohesion refers to the degree to which vertices are connected among themselves. The most common measure of cohesion is the *density of a network*, which is the number of existing lines in the network expressed as a proportion of the maximum number of possible lines. Table 7 shows the subnetwork densities for each biotechnology and nanotechnology cluster. It is evident that for networks of smaller sizes the density is higher and vice versa. Even though density is an indicator often used in social network analysis, it is more suitable to compare networks of similar sizes, since density is inversely related to network size. De Nooy *et al.* (2005) explain that this is because the number of possible lines increases rapidly with the number of vertices, whereas the number of social ties that each person can maintain is limited. Therefore we measured the density by the average degree of a network. The *degree of a vertex* is the number of lines that are directly connected to the vertex (see Wasserman, Faust, 1994). It represents the number of direct collaborators with whom an inventor cooperated on at least one patent. The more co-inventors the inventors have, the tighter is the network structure. The *average degree of a network* then denotes the average of the degrees of all vertices and in fact it also shows the average number of co-inventors in each subnetwork, which we discussed earlier.

Accordingly, the biotechnology innovation subnetworks in the clusters of Saskatoon (average degree of subnetwork of 3.52), Edmonton (3.18) and Ottawa (3.06) are the densest, and Montreal (2.94) and Vancouver (2.76) are still relatively dense. The innovation subnetwork in the nanotechnology cluster of Toronto is by far the densest in both Canadian biotechnology and nanotechnology (average degree of subnetwork of 5.32). The nanotechnology inventors in Toronto have direct or indirect access to a larger amount of information and a greater number of inventors than in any other cluster. Consequently, the possibility of two inventors getting in touch through a chain of personal acquaintances is higher as well. Other larger nanotechnology clusters have much lower average degree values (Montreal 2.23, Ottawa 2.44 or Vancouver 2.8).

Since the biotechnology network is older, contains more inventors and is hence more developed, we also expected to find it to be denser, while we assumed that the connections between the subjects in the nanotechnology network would be much looser. However, this was not confirmed, mainly because of the very high cohesion among the nanotechnology inventors in the Toronto subnetwork. Moreover, the average degree value for the full Canadian network also shows a higher value (5) for nanotech than for biotech (4.26).

5.4. Cliquishness in the subnetworks

Cliquishness is a property of a local network structure that refers to the likelihood that two vertices connected to a specific third vertex are also connected to one another. Cliquish networks have a tendency towards dense local neighbourhoods, in which individual inventors are better interconnected with one another. Such networks exhibit a high transmission capacity, since a great amount of knowledge could be diffused rapidly (see Burt, 2001). Moreover, a high degree of cliquishness in an innovation network supports friendship and trust-building, and hence facilitates collaboration between innovators. Uzzi and Spiro (2005) and Schilling and Phelps (2007) argue that higher cliquishness enhances system performance and knowledge diffusion. However, Cowan and Jonard (2003) point out the existence of negative effects of cliquishness stemming from the loss due to repetition, as the knowledge exchanged in highly cliquish neighbourhoods is often redundant. Moreover, empirical findings of Fleming *et al.* (2006) confirm the negative impact of higher cliquishness in the network on innovative productivity. The role of a high degree of cliquishness in innovation production is still not obvious and the optimal degree will apparently depend on a variety of factors.

In this chapter we measured the degree of local cliquishness for each vertex with the egocentric density of a vertex, which is the fraction of all pairs of the immediate neighbours of a vertex that are also directly connected to each other, and then we calculated the *average egocentric density of a subnetwork*. The results are presented in Table 7. Cliquishness is quite comparable among the larger biotechnology subnetworks (Saskatoon, Ottawa, Vancouver and Montreal) or larger nanotechnology subnetworks (Vancouver, Edmonton, Ottawa and Toronto). The subnetworks of the smaller sizes in both networks seem to be less cliquish.

Our results are, however, not in agreement with Newman (2001a), who found that the degree of network cliquishness in biomedicine is much lower than in other fields (clustering coefficient of 0.066), which he explained by the differences in social organisation between biomedical and other research communities. The values for his other databases correspond to our results. The differences are probably caused by the distinct kinds of studied networks (as we mentioned before, he created his networks based on the co-authorship of the scientific articles and not the co-inventorship of patents). Both biotechnology and nanotechnology show quite comparable results regarding the cliquishness of the full networks.

Table 7: Structural cohesion and cliquishness in biotechnology and nanotechnology cluster-based subnetworks

| Cluster-based subnetwork | Biotechnology | | | Nanotechnology | | |
| | Structural cohesion | | Cliquishness | Structural cohesion | | Cliquishness |
	Subnetwork density	Average degree	Average egocentric density	Subnetwork density	Average degree	Average egocentric density
Toronto	0.003	2.42	0.44	0.011	5.32	0.54
Montreal	0.004	2.94	0.56	0.012	2.23	0.49
Vancouver	0.007	2.76	0.57	0.020	2.80	0.64
Ottawa	0.014	3.06	0.59	0.014	2.44	0.56
Edmonton	0.015	3.18	0.55	0.036	2.84	0.59
Calgary	0.022	2.00	0.29	0.078	2.48	0.45
Quebec	0.019	3.06	0.55	0.049	2.26	0.52
Kingston	0.022	2.04	0.47	0.061	2.06	0.45
Saskatoon	0.024	3.52	0.64	-	-	-
Winnipeg	0.018	1.40	0.32	-	-	-
Halifax	0.038	1.21	0.24	-	-	-
Sherbrooke	0.031	0.77	0.23	-	-	-
Network	0.001	4.26	0.71	0.003	5.00	0.76

5.5. Centrality of vertices

The *centrality of a vertex* indicates whether the position of an individual inventor within the subnetwork is more central or more peripheral. Inventors who are more central have better access to knowledge and better opportunities to spread information. Moreover, we expect that inventors who occupy the most central positions in the subnetworks will be the most influential and probably the most prolific (star scientists). We measured two indicators of the vertex centrality: degree centrality and betweenness centrality.

The simplest definition of centrality is the *degree centrality of a vertex*, which is in fact equal to the degree of the vertex defined above. Inventors in more central positions in the subnetwork are those directly connected to other inventors and thus have more sources of knowledge at their disposal.

Table 8 shows the maximal centralities in all the subnetworks. The most connected inventors for both networks live in Toronto (the biotechnology one has 51 co-inventors while the nanotechnology one 42 co-inventors), but Montreal's most connected inventor has only 16 (biotech) or 15 (nanotech) direct collaborators. Other well connected inventors are located in Vancouver (27 biotech co-inventors and 16 nanotech co-inventors) and among the biotechnology subnetworks also in Saskatoon (25 co-inventors).

Betweenness centrality of a vertex is defined as a proportion of all the shortest distances between pairs of other vertices that include this vertex (see De Nooy *et al.*, 2005). An inventor is more central if a lot of shortest paths between pairs of other inventors in the subnetwork have to go through him. Betweenness centrality is therefore based on the inventor's importance to other inventors as an intermediary and it measures his control over the interactions between other inventors and thus over the flow of knowledge in the subnetwork. The highest betweenness centrality values come from the biotechnology inventors in Saskatoon (0.074) or Ottawa (0.068), whereas they are much lower for the nanotechnology inventors, where the highest is in Edmonton (0.02).

In sum, Saskatoon's most central biotechnology inventor occupies his position based on all three centrality measures. In nanotechnology, Toronto benefits from several quite central inventors (surpassing others, particularly in degree centrality), but so does Edmonton, with its most central inventor enjoying high maximum centrality levels as well.

5.6. Centralisation of the subnetworks

Contrary to centrality, which refers to positions of individual inventors, centralisation characterises an entire network. A highly centralised network has a clear boundary between the centre and the periphery. The centre of a centralised network allows a more efficient transmission of knowledge, which consequently spreads fairly easily in highly centralised networks. A network is hence more centralised if centralities of the vertices vary substantially. The *centralisation of a network* is defined as the variation in the degree centrality of vertices, divided by the maximum degree variation that is possible in a network of the same size (see De Nooy *et al.*, 2005). Similarly, as with centrality, we used two main measures of network centralisation: degree centralisation and betweenness centralisation.

Degree centralisation of a network is based on the variation in degree centrality of vertices in a network. The Saskatoon, Halifax and Calgary subnetworks show the highest degree centralisation scores for the biotechnology clusters, while the Edmonton and Calgary subnetworks show the highest degree centralisation scores for the nanotechnology clusters, which correspond to the same concepts.

Analogous to degree centralisation, *betweenness centralisation of a network* is based on the variation in betweenness centrality of vertices in the network. The results are shown in Table 8. It is again Saskatoon and Ottawa that previously showed the highest maximal betweenness centralities of the vertices and now score the highest in betweenness centralisation of all the biotechnology subnetworks as well. Among the nanotechnology clusters, Edmonton, with the highest maximal betweenness centralities of the vertices, also has high values for betweenness centralisation.

**Table 8: Centrality and centralisation in biotechnology
and nanotechnology cluster-based subnetworks**

Cluster-based subnetwork	Biotechnology				Nanotechnology			
	Vertex centrality		Subnetwork centralisation		Vertex centrality		Subnetwork centralisation	
	Max degree	Max between-ness	Degree	Between-ness	Max degree	Max between-ness	De-gree	Between-ness
Toronto	51	0.008	0.05	0.008	42	0.009	0.08	0.009
Montreal	16	0.011	0.02	0.011	15	0.005	0.07	0.005
Vancouver	27	0.005	0.06	0.005	16	0.013	0.09	0.013
Ottawa	16	0.070	0.06	0.068	9	0.008	0.04	0.007
Edmonton	20	0.019	0.08	0.019	14	0.021	0.15	0.020
Calgary	12	0.011	0.11	0.011	7	0.000	0.15	0.000
Quebec	8	0.003	0.04	0.003	5	0.008	0.06	0.008
Kingston	6	0.003	0.04	0.003	4	0.005	0.06	0.005
Saskatoon	25	0.076	0.15	0.074	-	-	-	-
Winnipeg	6	0.002	0.06	0.002	-	-	-	-
Halifax	5	0.010	0.13	0.010	-	-	-	-
Sherbrooke	2	0.000	0.05	0.000	-	-	-	-
Network	66	0.009	0.01	0.009	54	0.006	0.02	0.006

In general, the biotechnology network has more highly central inventors then the nanotechnology network. For the centralisation measures, the degree centralisation indicator favours the nanotechnology network, whereas the betweenness centralisation indicators show the reverse. As betweenness centralisation refers to the positions of its inventors as intermediaries, we would not expect the nanotechnology network to score higher because of its well-known disciplinary fragmentation. And, indeed, the highest value is obtained in Edmonton, where the National Institute for Nanotechnology has been located since 2001. It has a much smaller score than Ottawa and Saskatoon, which host similar National Institutes of the National Research Council of Canada for biotechnology.

5.7. Geodesic distances in the subnetworks

The shortest path between two vertices is referred to as geodesic. The *geodesic distance* is then the length of a geodesic between them, which depends on the number of intermediaries needed for an inventor to reach another inventor in the subnetwork. A short path length in innovation networks should improve knowledge production and knowledge diffusion (see Cowan, Jonard, 2004; Fleming *et al.*, 2004), since knowledge can move to the different parts of a network more quickly and spread rapidly among inventors. Moreover, as Cowan and Jonard

(2004) suggest, decreased path length will cause knowledge to degrade less by bringing new sources of ideas and perspectives from the farthest parts of the network to the inventors.

The longest geodesic in a network (the longest shortest path) is called the *diameter of a network*. It quantifies how far apart the two farthest vertices are in a network and it is a rough indicator of the effectiveness of a network in connecting pairs of inventors. In general, the diameters in our subnetworks seem to be fairly long when compared to the overall size of the components (see Table 9). This suggests quite a low connectedness in our subnetworks. The largest diameter among the biotechnology subnetworks is found in the Montreal and Ottawa clusters, where an inventor transmitting knowledge needs as many as 10 intermediaries. In nanotechnology, it is also Ottawa that has the longest diameter. The exchange of knowledge is much easier in Vancouver (both among biotechnology and nanotechnology inventors) and obviously also in many other smaller clusters.

An indicator of the *average distance of a network*, which denotes an average of all the distances of all the vertices in the subnetwork, is a more global measure of efficiency in communication. Nevertheless, the distance between two unconnected vertices is not defined (does not exist) and the average distance could be measured only in fully interconnected networks. We therefore calculated the average distance only between reachable vertices (directly or indirectly connected). This measure shows similar results as the subnetwork diameter. The largest average distances are again found in the Montreal (4.27) and Ottawa (4.95) biotechnology clusters, and in the Ottawa nanotechnology cluster (2.58). Obviously, the geodesic distances are also lower in smaller clusters. Moreover, it should be taken into consideration that the fact that the distances are calculated only between reachable vertices may bring a certain bias to our results, since any small or highly disconnected subnetwork should yield lower scores for geodesic distances. Therefore it is necessary to evaluate this measure more globally – while considering how many inventors could be reached within the cluster.

**Table 9: Geodesic distances in biotechnology
and nanotechnology cluster-based subnetworks**

Cluster-based subnetwork	Biotechnology			Nanotechnology		
	Subnetwork diameter	Avg distance (reachable vertices)	Max reach	Subnetwork diameter	Avg distance (reachable vertices)	Max reach
Toronto	9	3.26	97	7	2.56	154
Montreal	11	4.27	108	4	1.67	20
Vancouver	5	1.98	37	3	1.61	20
Ottawa	11	4.95	74	10	2.58	22
Edmonton	7	2.50	48	3	1.60	14
Calgary	5	1.75	14	1	1.00	7
Quebec	4	1.48	10	3	1.22	5
Kingston	3	1.31	7	2	1.08	4
Saskatoon	6	2.75	53	-	-	-
Winnipeg	3	1.25	6	-	-	-
Halifax	2	1.23	5	-	-	-
Sherbrooke	1	1.00	2	-	-	-
Network	17	6.55	578	17	4.16	335

The *reach of a vertex* is defined as the number of vertices that can be reached from this particular vertex.

Table 9 shows the maximal reach for each subnetwork: the maximum number of reachable inventors within a subnetwork. Evidently, more inventors could be directly or indirectly reached in larger networks. In the Montreal biotechnology subnetwork, 108 inventors can reach one another, while in the larger Toronto biotechnology cluster only 97 inventors are connected among themselves. In nanotechnology, however, the maximal reach in the Toronto cluster is 154. The clusters with shorter maximal reach are likely to be more disconnected and thus show lower scores of geodesic distances, whereas the clusters with higher numbers of reachable vertices are more connected and should show longer geodesic distances. The exception among the biotechnology subnetworks seems to be Saskatoon, which, with a relatively long maximal reach, does not show a very long average shortest distance. The Toronto nanotechnology subnetwork has a maximal reach many times longer than that of other nanotechnology clusters, but the average shortest distance of the Toronto subnetwork is not considerably longer than that of the other clusters; and, in fact, it is even slightly shorter than that of the much smaller cluster of Ottawa. The geodesic characteristics of the Saskatoon biotech subnetwork and the Toronto nanotech subnetwork are thus indicative of network structures that enable more efficient knowledge diffusion.

As expected, the biotechnology subnetworks show longer geodesic distances but also a much longer maximal reach. This is also evident in full Canadian networks (biotech has the average distance of 6.55 and maximal reach of 578 inventors, whereas nanotech has the distance of 4.16, but maximal reach of only 335 inventors). Knowledge should thus flow faster in nanotechnology cluster subnetworks.

5.8. Summary of the network properties

We observed that in order to enhance the efficiency of each network in terms of knowledge diffusion, the network should be cohesive (which means that inventors are closely interconnected), cliquish (which fosters trust and close collaboration), it should have a long reach within large components (which enables bringing fresh and non-redundant knowledge from distant locations) and it should have a centralised structure (which supports fast knowledge transmission).

In biotechnology, the closest to these properties is the Saskatoon subnetwork. It is the densest, most cliquish and most centralised of all Canadian biotechnology clusters. It has on average the largest components and lowest share of isolates of all clusters. Despite the great size of the components, the diameter is still only of an average size. Inventors from both the Ottawa and Edmonton biotechnology clusters also benefit greatly from quite large components and fairly dense, relatively cliquish and rather centralised biotechnology subnetworks. The long geodesic distances, however, make it more difficult to bring new knowledge quickly to all researchers. In contrast, we found that the structural properties of the subnetworks of Calgary, Quebec and Toronto are not very suggestive of efficient knowledge transmission and innovation generation. Both the Calgary and Quebec subnetworks are quite sparse and consist of the components of rather small sizes, suggesting great disconnectedness among inventors. Calgary, however, is quite centralised, which supports a more efficient transmission of knowledge, but it has a high share of researchers working in geographical isolation. Quebec is fairly cliquish and hence better interconnected. In both clusters, relatively short geodesic distances increase the speed of knowledge transmission. The biotechnology subnetwork of the Toronto cluster is rather sparse, neither very cliquish nor centralised, and comprises components of relatively small sizes, many of which are completely isolated inventors. The Montreal biotechnology cluster, on the other hand, contains relatively large components through which knowledge has to travel large distances. It is also denser and more cliquish than the Toronto one; researchers seem to be more interconnected and knowledge could still be diffused more rapidly. The subnetwork structure of the Vancouver biotechnology cluster is somewhere in between the two previous patterns. It is denser than the Toronto subnetwork and quite cliquish, but comprises smaller components and thus involves shorter geodesic distances.

The most efficient nanotechnology cluster-based subnetworks are found in Toronto, Edmonton and Vancouver. Toronto's is the densest network of the Canadian nanotechnology clusters, where researchers are better interconnected and knowledge can hence be diffused quite rapidly. It has on average the largest components and the lowest share of geographically isolated researchers of all the clusters. Despite the large mean size of the components, the path lengths are still only slightly higher than average. Information can thus spread through a great number of researchers in a timely manner. The Toronto nanotechnology subnetwork is, however, only moderately cliquish and centralised. In contrast, inventors from both Edmonton and Vancouver nanotechnology clusters benefit from fairly cliquish and rather centralised nanotechnology subnetworks, a structure that supports both trust-building among the researchers and a more efficient transmission of information through centrally located researchers. The larger-sized components with quite short geodesic distances make it easier to bring new information quickly to a relatively high number of inventors in both clusters. As for the nanotechnology clusters of Montreal and Ottawa, we found that the structural properties of their subnetworks are not very supportive of efficient knowledge diffusion and innovation generation. Both subnetworks are quite sparse and neither very cliquish nor centralised. They consist of the components of rather small sizes, which explains the relatively short path lengths measured in the networks. Also, a high percentage of researchers in both nanotechnology clusters work in geographical isolation. These characteristics suggest a great disconnectedness among the inventors in a cluster.

6. Conclusions

The purpose of this work was to study Canadian biotechnology and nanotechnology clusters and collaborative networks of inventors, created by mapping the co-inventorship of biotechnology and nanotechnology patents registered at the USPTO. The innovation networks constructed in this way revealed not only the main patterns of collaborative behaviour of Canadian biotechnology and nanotechnology inventors inside and outside clusters, but also allowed us to evaluate the efficiency of networks in knowledge diffusion and its role in the creation of innovation.

Biotechnology and nanotechnology patenting in Canada has followed distinct paths. The base year for the start of biotechnology innovation in Canada could be considered the year 1976, but the patenting really only significantly accelerated after 1987. However, following the year 2001, Canadian biotechnology patenting has started to decrease. In the case of nanotechnology, which is at an earlier stage of the industry life cycle, it is the year 1986 that could be considered as its base year, after which Canadian nanotechnology patent productivity has been almost always increasing. The annual patent production in 2004 reached almost comparable levels for biotechnology and nanotechnology. Biotechnology patenting is strongly based on publicly funded research, with public institutions leading the league table of the most prolific assignees. In contrast, the patent market is much more concentrated in nanotechnology, with a high number of industrial patents (owned by firms). The outstanding number of patents assigned to Xerox – to which Canadian inventors have contributed – certainly impacts on the ability of Canada to develop its own nanotechnology niches.

Innovative activity in Canada is concentrated in several locations, which roughly correspond to the larger metropolitan areas. We have identified twelve biotechnology and eight nanotechnology clusters. In biotechnology, more than half of all Canadian inventors reside in three largest clusters – Toronto, Montreal and Vancouver – but in nanotechnology it is mainly the Toronto cluster that dominates the industrial sector, with around a quarter of all Canadian inventors residing there. However, most of the innovations created by the Toronto nanotechnology inventors are owned by foreign assignees (mainly US companies). Almost half of all the innovations authored or co-authored by Canadian nanotechnology inventors are assigned to foreign subjects. Although Canadians do the research, the fruit of their labour is not appropriated within Canada. Canada therefore appears as a research subcontractor of patents in nanotechnology. This is not conducive to the creation of a healthy interconnected network of inventors where multidisciplinarity and diversity fosters invention.

We also investigated the collaborative behaviour of the biotechnology and nanotechnology inventors inside and outside their clusters. The majority of all of these collaborations takes place within the biotechnology or nanotechnology clusters and over a quarter are distant ties directed abroad. Most of the foreign collaborative ties are again linked to American inventors. Only a relatively small number of all the collaborations involve cooperation among the inventors from different clusters or with out-of-cluster Canadians.

The intra-cluster collaborations within the cluster-based subnetworks were examined in depth. We measured several structural network properties corresponding to each cluster and related them to the likely efficiency of each subnetwork in the knowledge diffusion and the innovation creation. Moreover, we carried out a comparative analysis of the properties of the full networks and cluster-based subnetworks of biotechnology and nanotechnology and found the collaborative structure within each sector to be quite distinct. The biotechnology innovation network is larger and more developed than the nanotechnology one. We discovered that the biotechnology network is also less fragmented. The specialisation fields within biotechnology are quite close in their scientific nature and are often overlapping. The inventors in the biotechnology network are thus more interconnected between each other. Nanotechnology, however, includes many quite disparate fields, where the inventors understandably work in a larger number of separated groups. A notable exception here is the Toronto nanotechnology cluster, which involves highly interconnected inventors with quite close collaboration ties and a dense subnetwork structure. The geodesic distances in biotechnology networks are longer, but so is the maximal reach, which enables the bringing of fresh and non-redundant knowledge from distant locations. The cliquishness of both networks is, however, quite comparable, but its exact role in knowledge creation and innovation generation still remains to be determined.

The National Research Council of Canada (NRC) has five national biotechnology institutes throughout the country, but only one in nanotechnology, a field much more fragmented. Our analysis clearly shows that biotechnology cluster-based subnetworks are better developed and organised in a number of clusters in Canada, and especially in those hosting the five NRC institutes (Montreal, Vancouver, Ottawa, Saskatoon and Halifax – although the latter is a much smaller cluster). These institutional effects have a positive influence on the organisation of innovation in these clusters. In contrast, in nanotechnology, two poles are present: Toronto and Edmonton, which is still emerging. Regarding the National Institute for Nanotechnology, institutions are put in place to insure that discoveries are spun off or licensed to local firms (prioritised) in order to generate the synergies needed for the evolution of a successful cluster. Although the majority of innovation capability lies in Toronto, we have seen that the majority of the intellectual property leaves the country. Other nanotechnology clusters are emerging and their local network of inventors are still fragmented.

This chapter represents another step towards understanding the influence of knowledge networks on the innovative activities of inventors located within high technology clusters. We intend to continue exploring the exact role played by networks, and their importance in the chain of knowledge creation with a focus on the networks of Canadian biotechnology and nanotechnology scientists, the authors or co-authors of the scientific articles. This will enable us to investigate the influence of the nature and the structure of the networks of various innovators (inventors and scientists) on the propensity to innovate firms in clusters. We intend to merge the two databases (patents and articles) to gain a full picture of the production of innovation in Canadian biotechnology and nanotechnology.

Bibliography

Acs, Z. J., Audretsch, D. B., Feldman, M. P., "Real effects of academic research: Comment", in *The American Economic Review*, 1992, 82 (1), p. 363-367.

Acs, Z. J., Audretsch, D. B., Feldman, M. P., "R&D spillovers and recipient firm size", in *The Review of Economics and Statistics*, 1994, 76 (2), p. 336-340.

Audretsch, D. B., Feldman, M. P., "R&D spillovers and the geography of innovation and production", in *The American Economic Review*, 1996, 86 (3), p. 630-640.

Balconi, M., Breschi, S., Lissoni, F., "Networks of inventors and the role of academia: an exploration of Italian patent data", in *Research Policy*, 2004, 33, p. 127-145.

Baptista, R., Swann, P., "Do firms in clusters innovate more?", in *Research Policy*, 1998, 27, p. 525-540.

Beaucage, J.-S., Beaudry, C., "The importance of knowledge networks within Canadian Biotechnology clusters", International Schumpeter Conference, Sophia-Antipolis 2006.

Beaudry, C., "Entry, growth and patenting in industrial clusters", in *International Journal of Economics of Business*, 2001, 8, 3, p. 405-436.

Beaudry, C., Breschi, S., "Are firms in clusters really more innovative?", in *Economics of Innovation and New Technology*, 2003, 12, 4, p. 325-342.

Beaudry, Swann, "Firm-level growth in industrial clusters: a bird's eye view of the United Kingdom", in *Small Business Economics*, 2009, 32, 4, p. 409-424.

Breschi, S., Lissoni, F., "Mobility and social networks: localized knowledge spillovres revisited", in *CESPRI*, Working Papers, 2003, 142.

Breschi, S., Lissoni, F., "Knowledge networks from patent data: methodological issues and research targets", in *CESPRI*, Working Papers, 2004, 150.

Burt, R., "Bandwidth and echo: trust, information, and gossip in social networks", in A. Casella and J.E. Rauch (eds.), *Networks and Markets: Contributions from Economics and Sociology*, Russel Sage Foundation, New York, 2001.

Cantner, U., Graf, H., "The network of innovators in Jena: an application of social network analysis", in *Research Policy*, 2006, 35, p. 463-480.

Cockburn, I. M., Henderson, R. M., "Absorptive capacity, coauthoring behavior, and the organization of research in drug discovery", in *The Journal of Industrial Economics*, 1998, 46 (2), p. 157-182.

Cowan, R., Jonard, N., "The dynamics of collective invention", in *Journal of Economic Behaviour and Organization*, 2003, 52, p. 513-532.

Cowan, R., Jonard, N., "Network structure and the diffusion of knowledge", in *Journal of Economic Dynamics and Control*, 2004, 28, p. 1557-1575.

Cowan, R., Jonard, N., Ozman, M., "Knowledge dynamics in a network industry", in *Technological Forecasting and Social Change*, 2004, 71, p. 469-484.

Cowan, R., Jonard, N., Zimmermann, J.-B., "Bilateral collaboration and the emergence of innovation networks", in *Management Science*, 2007, 53, 7, p. 1051-1067.

Dahl, M. S., Pedersen, C. O. R., "Knowledge flows through informal contacts in idustrial clusters: myth or reality?", in *Research Policy*, 2004, 33, p. 1673-1686.

De Nooy, W., Mrvar, A. and Batagelj, A., *Exploratory Social Network Analysis with Pajek*, Cambridge University Press, Cambridge, 2005.

Ducor, P., "Intellectual property: Coauthorship and coinventorship", in *Science*, 2000, 289 (5481), p. 873-875.

Ejermo, O., Karlsson, C., "Interregional inventor networks as studied by patent coinventorships'", in *Research Policy*, 2006, 35, p. 412-430.

Ernst & Young, "Beyond Borders: The Canadian Biotechnology Report 2002", Toronto, 2002.

Fleming, L., King, C., "Juda, A., Small worlds and innovation", *SSRN* Working Papers, IV., 2006.

Gauvin, S., "Networks of innovators: evidence from Canadian patents", Group Decision and Negotiation, 1995, 4, p. 411-428.

Gittelman, M., "Does geography matter for science-based firms? Epistemic communities and the geography of research and patenting in biotechnology", *DRUID* Summer Conference on Knowledge, Innovation and Competitiveness, Dynamics of Firms, Networks, Regions and Institutions, Copenhagen, Denmark, 2006.

Jaffe, A. B., "Real effects of academic research", in *The American Economic Review*, 1989, 79 (5), p. 957-970.

Jaffe, A. B., Trajtenberg, M., & Henderson, R., "Geographic localization of knowledge spillovers as evidenced by patent citations", in *Quarterly Journal of Economics*, 1993, 108, p. 577-598.

Krugman, P., *Geography and Trade*, MA: The MIT Press, Cambridge, 1991.

Lamoreaux, N.R., Sokoloff, K.I., "Location and technological change in the American glass industry during the late 19th and early 20th century", *NBER*, Working Papers, 1997, 5938.

Mariani, M., "Networks of inventors in the chemical industry", *MERIT* Research Memorandum, 2000.

Marshall, A., *Principles of Economics*, Macmillan, London, 1920.

Morone, P., Taylor, R., "Knowledge diffusion dynamics and network properties of face-to-face interactions", in *Journal of Evolutionary Economics*, 2004, 14, p. 327-351.

Munn-Venn, T., Mitchell, P., "Biotechnology in Canada: a technology platform for growth", the report from the Conference Board of Canada, 2005. Available on-line: http://www.agwest.sk.ca/biotech/documents/115-06-Biotechnology%20in%20Canada.pdf.

Newman, M. E. J., "Scientific collaboration networks. I. Network construction and fundamental results", in *Physical Review*, 2001a, 64 (016131).

Newman, M. E. J., "Scientific collaboration networks. II. Shortest paths, weighted networks, and centrality", in *Physical Review*, 2001b, 64 (016131).

Newman, M. E. J., "Clustering and preferential attachment in growing networks", in *Physical Review*, 2001c, 64 (025102).

Newman, M. E. J., "The structure of scientific collaboration networks", in *Proceedings of National Academy of Sciences*, 2001d, 98 (2), p. 404-409.

Newman, M. E. J., Watts, D.J., Strogatz, S.H., "Random graph models of social networks", in *Proceedings of the National Academy of Sciences*, 2002, 99, p. 2566-2572.

Niosi, J., Bas, T. G., "The competencies of regions – Canada's clusters in biotechnology", in *Small Business Economics*, 2001, 17 (1-2), p. 31-42.

Niosi, J., *Canada's Regional Innovation Systems. The Science-based Industries*, McGill-Queen's University Press, 2005.

Niosi, J., "Success factors in Canadian Academic Spin-Offs", in *Journal of Technology Transfer*, 2006, 31, p. 451-457.

OECD, "A Framework for Biotechnology Statistics", 2005, Available on-line: http://www.oecd.org/dataoecd/5/48/34935605.pdf.

Porter, M. E., *On Competition*, Harvard Business School press, Boston, 1998.

Putsch, F., "Analysis and modeling of science collaboration networks", *Working Paper*, 2006.

Rasmussen, B., "An analysis of the biomedical sectors in Australia and Canada in a National Innovation Systems Context", Centre for Strategic Economic Studies, Victoria University of Technology, Working Paper Series, 2004, No. 21, Available on-line: http://www.cfses.com/documents/pharma/21-biomedical_Sect_Aust_&_Can_Innovation_Rasmussen.pdf.

Rose, A., "A challenge for Mmeasuring biotechnology activities", in *The Economics and Social Dynamics of Biotechnology*, 2000.

Schiffauerova, A., Beaudry C., "Canadian nanotechnology innovation networks: intra-cluster, inter-cluster and foreign collaboration", in *Journal of Innovation Economics*, 2009, 2 (2), p. 119-146.

Schiffauerova, A., Beaudry, C., "Innovation in Canadian biotechnology clusters", Submitted to the *International Journal of Biotechnology*, 2009.

Schilling, M. A., Phelps, C. C., "The impact of large-scale network structure on firm innovation", in *Management Science*, 2007, 53 (7), p. 1113-1126.

Singh, J., "Collaborative networks as determinants of knowledge diffusion", in *Management Science*, 2005, 51 (5), p. 756-770.

Statistics Canada, Practices and Activities of Canadian Biotechnology Firms: Results from the Biotechnology Use and Development Survey, 1999, 2001. Available on-line: http://www.statcan.ca/english/research/88F0006XIE/88 F0006XIB2001011.pdf.

Statistics Canada, Overview of the Biotechnology Use and Development Survey, 2003. Available on-line: http://www.statcan.ca/english/research/88F0006XIE/88F0006XIE2005009.pdf.

Statistics Canada, Preliminary Results of the Biotechnology Use and Development Survey -2005, Available on-line: http://www.statcan.ca/Daily/English/070130/d070130c.htm.

Strachan, G., "The impact of regulations on the growth and evolution of Canadian commercial biotechnology", in *Current Opinion in Biotechnology* 1995, 6, p. 261-263.

Uzzi, B., Spiro, J., "Collaboration and creativity: the small world problem", in *American Journal of Sociology*, 2005, 111 (2), p. 447-504.

Wasserman, S., Faust, K., *Social Network Analysis*, Cambridge University Press, Cambridge, 1994.

Appendix A – BIOTECHNOLOGY:
Single factor ANOVA for the differences in population means

(average number of co-inventors per patent in each cluster)

SUMMARY

Groups	Count	Sum	Average	Variance
TRT	850	2476	2.912941	2.536581
MTL	471	1521	3.229299	3.849438
VAN	260	792	3.046154	2.33763
EDM	162	531	3.277778	3.667702
CAL	130	337	2.592308	1.390638
SAS	104	342	3.288462	3.158701
WIN	35	74	2.114286	4.045378
KIN	65	174	2.676923	1.253365
OTT	292	863	2.955479	2.626877
QUE	66	187	2.833333	2.079487
HAL	20	45	2.25	1.881579
SHE	16	39	2.4375	1.595833
out	51	151	2.960784	3.158431

ANOVA

Source of Variation	SS	Df	MS	F	P-value	F crit
Between Groups	127.1085	12	10.59237	3.797459626	9.33492E-06	1.756024811
Within Groups	6998.433	2509	2.789332			
Total	7125.542	2521				

Appendix B – NANOTECHNOLOGY:
Single factor ANOVA for the differences in population means

(average number of co-inventors per patent in each cluster)
SUMMARY

Groups	Count	Sum	Average	Variance
Toronto	169	486	2.87574	1.942801
Montreal	162	497	3.067901	2.287286
Ottawa	103	297	2.883495	2.20198
Vancouver	103	298	2.893204	2.410051
Edmonton	57	184	3.22807	2.929198
Quebec	23	87	3.782609	2.359684
Kingston	14	48	3.428571	1.956044
Calgary	34	116	3.411765	7.40107
out	52	136	2.615385	1.653092

ANOVA

Source of Variation	SS	Df	MS	F	P-value	F crit
Between Groups	39.00393	8	4.875491	1.989548	0.045233	1.951464
Within Groups	1734.99	708	2.450552			
Total	1773.994	716				

CHAPTER VIII

Identifying Clusters in the Puget Sound Region

Paul SOMMERS and William B. BEYERS

1. Introduction and background

This chapter was undertaken out of curiosity about how clusters would be defined through the use of a formal statistical procedure, with an input-output model of our regional economy. It was also undertaken to see if the clusters that emerged from this analysis were similar to those developed by consultants for our local regional planning organisation, the Puget Sound Regional Council (PSRC).

The chapter starts with a brief background and literature review, followed by a discussion on the development of the data base for this chapter. Results of the analyses are then presented, and compared with those developed by the PSRC. The chapter ends with some concluding comments.

Industry clusters have become an important instrument of economic development policy. Hundreds of cluster initiatives have been identified in countries around the world (see Sövell, Lindqvist, Ketels, 2003). Scholars have developed methods for identifying clusters, and practitioners have gathered in a variety of venues to discuss strategies for implementing cluster initiatives. This chapter experiments with the technique of hierarchical cluster analysis to define sectoral clusters for the Central Puget Sound region in western Washington. It compares the cluster structure identified by this analysis to the structure used in the cluster initiative developed by the Puget Sound Regional Council (Puget Sound Regional Council, 2005) in a regional economic development process called the Prosperity Partnership, and to clusters identified by the City of Seattle's Office of Economic Development (Office of Economic Development n.d.). Our purpose is to compare the clusters identified by an explicit analytic algorithm to those developed through diverse methods, including consultations with industry experts as well as analytic processes. The comparisons may reveal additional opportunities for new cluster initiatives, or they may confirm the structures identified by consulting expert opinion.

Competing cluster definitions, whose derivation are not clear, have been used for regional and city-level cluster initiatives. It seemed to us that a more rigorous attempt to define clusters would be useful. Methodologies based on analysis of inter-industry relationships depicted in input-output tables have been recommended by several authors. The inter-industry purchase coefficients in an appropriate input-output model are subjected to either principal components or hierarchical cluster analysis to identify groupings of industries that are relatively similar in terms of their input requirements (see Feser, Bergman, 2000, and Hill, Brennan, 2000). Cluster competitiveness is typically assessed using location quotients based on employment in the geographic region of interest, compared to the nation of which the region is a part, a methodology suggested by Porter (see Porter, 2003).

Cluster analysis is a statistical method that uses algorithms to classify data. Like principal components analysis, it is a formal statistical procedure. We should emphasise that cluster analysis and the concept of industry "clusters" as described by Porter are totally different concepts. There are many cluster analysis algorithms that can be used with data of a widely varying nature to classify groups with statistical similarity based on the cluster algorithm being used. We have used one such method that is well-suited to scaled data, such as the coefficient structure of an input-output model. Index numbers such as location quotients are also amenable to grouping algorithms in cluster analysis. It is by chance that we are using a statistical technique named cluster analysis to help define industry clusters of the type conceptualised by Porter and other scholars focused on regional competitiveness and regional development.

2. Development of a Data Base and Resulting Clusters

Based on the existing literature on cluster definition methods, we decided to identify clusters for the Central Puget Sound (CPS) region, a four-county region identified in federal statistics as the Seattle-Tacoma-Bremerton Consolidated Metropolitan Statistical Area. For data on inter-industry relationships, we acquired data on these four counties for the year 2004 from IMPLAN, and constructed a regional input-output model using the IMPLAN software for the CPS region. IMPLAN is an input-output modeling system offered by a commercial company. The IMPLAN model is based on a national transactions table with over 500 industry sectors; this model can be configured for any county in the

U.S., or for multi-county regions.[1] We extracted a direct requirements matrix from this model for the CPS region. This matrix consisted of 427 distinct industrial sectors, a number too large for the SPSS hierarchical cluster procedure we planned to use to identify clusters in the CPS region. Upon inspection of the regional direct requirements matrix, we also discovered that many of the 427 industries were very small. Accordingly, we decided to aggregate the matrix to combine very small industries defined at the equivalent of four digit NAICS industries into two or three digit aggregated industries. The resulting matrix had 145 input sectors. The full 427 industry sectors were retained in the model, resulting in a 427 sector by 145 input-requirements matrix, which was subjected to hierarchical cluster analysis using Ward's algorithm. The analysis resulted in 28 distinct clusters, some of which were subsequently subdivided to produce more homogenous cluster groups.

Ward's algorithm groups sectors according to the similarity of their structure, given the basis for the grouping. In this case, the basis for grouping was the 145 direct requirements coefficients for each sector. The clustering algorithm creates a figure called a dendrogram; Figure 1 is an aggregated version of this dendrogram. Interpretation of such a detailed dendrogram is a complex task. In order to see reasons for the grouping of individual sectors, it is necessary to order the data in the same sequence as the dendrogram, and to then look for patterns in the input-data. We literally printed out the 427 sector-x-145 direct requirements coefficient matrix to be able to inspect this data for these patterns. Figure 1 is divided into two broad parts: services (retail up through cluster 2d funds and trusts) and a manufacturing focused set of clusters (wood products through trucking and trucking-dependent). The cluster algorithm produces patterns that are with some "noise", and the interpretation of the clusters is also somewhat subjective. No two sectors have identical input structures, yet the clustering algorithm places those that are statistically similar adjacent to each other in the dendrogram.

---

[1] For more information about IMPLAN, see www.implan.com.

Figure 1: Dendrogram of Puget Sound Region Clusters

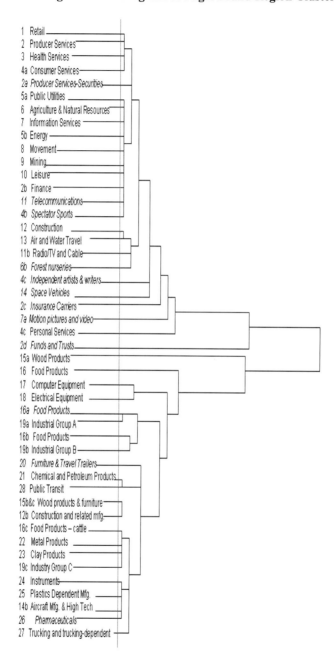

In the process of interpreting the dendrogram, we created Figure 1. The labels in this figure are based on our interpretation of the basis for clustering. The stem structure in the dendrogram is as shown in the output from the statistical package used for this analysis: SPSS. This statistical package creates this stem structure in a way so that clusters are differentiated by their "uniqueness" within the overall structure of the data set. Those with similar structures are adjacent to each other in the dendrogram and the cluster analysis routine aggregates the individual clusters in a hierarchical manner, so that clusters with increasing structural difference are brought into the dendrogram at the higher levels of aggregation. The cluster routine also creates "isolates", clusters with only one sector. Some clusters appear to be dominated by intra-sectoral transactions. These are identified in italics in figure 1. For example, the telecommunications cluster (11a) had an intra-industry coefficient of .096, a far higher direct requirement coefficient for use of telecommunications than any other industry in the direct requirements matrix.

The bases for clustering are illustrated in Table 1 for several of the clusters. These are presented as illustrative, and are not definitive of all the clusters identified in this analysis.

Table 1: Bases of specialisation in selected clusters

Cluster	Cluster Name	Structural Concentration
1	Retail	Similar pattern of use across many sectors, with relatively small variation in coefficients. For example, telecommunications ranged from .0046 to .0069; insurance from .00077 to .00116; real estate from .027 to .041; legal services from .00155 to .00233
2	Producer Services	Wholesale, postal, producer services, and food services
3	Health Services	Wholesale, real estate, producer services, food services
4	Consumer and research	Real estate, telecommunications, producer services (especially employment services)
5	Agriculture & Natural Resources / Restaurants & Bars	Agriculture-forestry services, petroleum products, wholesale
6	Information Oriented	Producer services, esp. employment services, one with motion pictures (sound recording)
8	Movement	Petroleum products, wholesale
10	Leisure	Petroleum products, wholesale, and intra-industry

3. Analysis of Results

Following Porter's suggestion, we calculated location quotients using regional employment compared to national employment in each of the cluster groups identified in our analysis to assess cluster strength. The results are shown in Table 2. The clusters with the greatest competitive strength by this measure are: utilities, aerospace, metal products and public transit. We also calculated Export percentages for these sectors, from the IMPLAN data base. Public transit and utilities do not have high export percentages. In contrast, many sectors with relatively low location quotients are estimated to be quite export oriented, such as mining, cement and clay products.

Table 2: Location Quotients and Export Percentages by Cluster

Cluster	Export %	LQ
1 Retail	17.8%	0.91
2 Producer Services	38.7%	0.95
3 Health Services	0.8%	0.86
4 Consumer Services	42.0%	1.02
5 Utilities	21.0%	2.64
6 Agriculture & Natural Resources	22.8%	0.86
7 Information Oriented Services	59.8%	1.23
8 Movement	37.9%	0.93
9 Mining	92.1%	0.50
10 Leisure	24.3%	0.85
11 Telecommunications	67.1%	1.32
12 Construction	20.8%	1.01
13 Air and Water Travel	77.0%	1.89
14 Aerospace	74.4%	5.29
15 Wood Products	53.9%	0.82
16 Food Products	44.2%	0.38
17 Computer Equipment	28.2%	0.75
18 Electrical Machinery	50.2%	1.37
19 Industrial Group	47.3%	0.88
20 Furniture & Travel Trailers	23.2%	0.99
21 Chemical & Petroleum Products	57.9%	0.34
22 Metal Products	43.6%	2.33
23 Cement & Clay Products	66.7%	0.79
24 Instruments	64.1%	0.51
25 Plastics Dependent Mfg.	31.1%	0.70
26 Pharmaceuticals	11.8%	0.32
27 Trucking & trucking dependent	33.0%	0.72
28 Public Transit	8.2%	9.89

We can see the relative importance of exports and location quotients by sector in Figure 2. This scatterplot indicates the lack of correlation between these two measures; in fact, for this distribution the correlation is -.129. A further perspective on exports and location quotients is given in Table 3. This table presents a two-way classification of location quotients and exports, with quadrants defined for location quotients above and below 1.0, and exports above and below the mean (42.2%). Clusters in group 1 have strong local markets, and location quotients below 1.0. This group includes several consumer services, including retailing and health care. Group 2 includes clusters with location quotients above 1, but exports below average. This group includes a number of regionally focused sectors, such as construction and utilities. Quadrant 3 includes sectors with relatively strong exports, but location quotients below 1.0. This group includes some sectors quite important in the overall Washington state economy, but with a lesser concentration in the services-rich Central Puget Sound region economy, such as wood and food products. Quadrant 4 includes sectors with location quotients above 1, and exports greater than the average percentage. Aerospace leads this group in size and concentration, but with port functions and information oriented services also playing an important role.

Figure 2: Export Percentages and Location Quotients

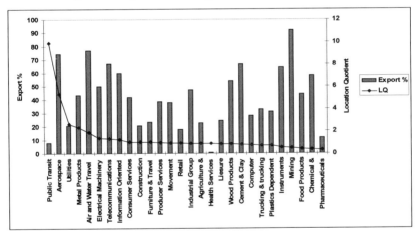

Table 3: Two-way classification of exports and location quotients

Group 2 LQ>1 Exports< Mean	Export	LQ	Group 4 LQ>1 Exports > Mean	Export	LQ
4 Consumer Services	42.0%	1.02	Information Oriented Services	59.8%	1.23
12 Construction	20.8%	1.01	Telecommunications	67.1%	1.32
22 Metal Products	43.6%	2.33	Air and Water Travel	77.0%	1.89
28 Public Transit	8.2%	9.89	Aerospace	74.4%	5.29
5 Utilities	21.0%	2.64	18 Electrical Machinery	50.2%	1.37
Group 1 LQ<1 **Exports < Mean**			**Group 3 LQ<1** **Exports > Mean**		
1 Retail	17.8%	0.91	9 Mining	92.1%	0.50
2 Producer Services	38.7%	0.95	15 Wood Products	53.9%	0.82
3 Health Services	0.8%	0.86	16 Food Products	44.2%	0.38
6 Agriculture & Natural	22.8%	0.86	19 Industrial Group	47.3%	0.88
Resources			21 Chemical & Petroleum	57.9%	0.34
8 Movement	37.9%	0.93	Products		
10 Leisure	24.3%	0.85	23 Cement & Clay Products	66.7%	0.79
17 Computer Equipment	28.2%	0.75	24 Instruments	64.1%	0.51
20 Furniture	23.2%	0.99			
& Travel Trailers					
25 Plastics Dependent Mfg.	31.1%	0.70			
26 Pharmaceuticals	11.8%	0.32			
27 Trucking & trucking	33.0%	0.72			
dependent					

Another two-way classification is presented in Table 4. This table contrasts exports and local purchases shares, similar to the classification suggested by Chenery & Watanabe (see Chenery, Watanabe, 1958). Sectors with weak exports and weak local purchases shares are in group 1. In this table, local purchases are local inter-industry purchases, excluding local payments of labour income. Clusters included in group 1 include several consumer oriented services, such as retailing and health services. Group 2 includes sectors with strong exports but weak local linkages. The data for aerospace included here reports higher local purchases than recorded in the 2002 Washington State input-output model for aerospace, a likely artifact of relatively high intra-industry purchases in the aerospace sector in the US input-output model upon which the IMPLAN model was based. Group 3 reports clusters with relatively strong backward linkages, but relatively weak exports. This group includes some clusters with strong regional final demand, such as construction. Group 4 includes the clusters with strong exports and strong local purchases. This group includes some clusters with back-ward linkages to regional natural resources, such as wood products, food products, cement and clay.

Table 4: Two-way classification of exports and local purchases

Group 1	Group 2
Exports < 42.2%, Local Purchases < 22.9% Weak Exports, Weak local Purchases 1 Retail 17.8%, 20.7% 3 Health Services 0.8%, 20.6% 5 Utilities 21.0%, 11.4% 8 Movement 37.9%, 7.9% 10 Leisure 24.3%, 19.1% 28 Public Transit 8.2%, 17.2%	Exports > 42.2%, Local Purchases < 22.9% Strong Exports, Weak Local Purchases 7 Information Services 59.8%, 21.7% 9 Mining 92.1%, 13.0% 11 Telecommunications 67.1%, 24.0% 14 Aerospace 74.4%, 22.4% 19 Industrial Group 47.3%, 20.8%
Group 3	**Group 4**
Exports < 42.2%, Local Purchases > 22.9% Weak Exports, Strong Local Purchases 2 Producer Services 38.7%, 24.1% 4 Consumer Services 42.0%, 23.1% 6 Agriculture & Natural Resources, 22.8%, 23.6% 12 Construction 20.8%, 24.3% 17 Computer Equipment 28.2%, 48.9% 20 Furniture & Travel Tr, 23.2%, 37.8% 25 Plastics Dependent Mfg., 31.1%, 23.4% 26 Pharmaceuticals 11.8%, 32.7% 27 Trucking & Tr. Dep. 33.0%, 29.8%	Exports> 42.2%, Local Purchases > 22.9% Strong Exports, Strong Local Purchases 13 Air and Water Travel 77.0%, 32.8% 15 Wood Products 53.9%, 35.7% 16 Food Products 44.2%, 37.1% 18 Electrical Machinery 50.2%, 31.7% 21 Chemical & Petroleum 57.9%, 28.2% 22 Metal Products 43.6%, 23.1% 23 Cement & Clay 66.7%, 25.7% 24 Instruments 64.2%, 31.7%

From a regional development perspective, clusters with strong exports, relative concentration and strong backward linkages could be considered more robust than clusters with weak exports, a lack of regional concentration and weak backward linkages. Two clusters (air and water travel, and electrical machinery) have relatively high values on all three measures. Several clusters have high export levels and are concentrated in the region, but they have relatively weak backward linkages (aerospace, information oriented services, telecommunications).

This analysis demonstrated the feasibility of creating regional economic clusters through the use of formal cluster analysis algorithm, with a regional input-output model. The model used in this application may have some structural differences from a survey-based model for the larger Washington economy (see Beyers, Lin, 2008), but it has far more detail than the survey-based Washington input-output model. This richness of the sectoring structure has allowed the cluster analysis algorithm to produce a richer array of clusters than would have been possible with the Washington model.

We can clearly use the clusters based on inter-industry linkages to produce taxonomies of clusters, based on classification schemes such as reported in Tables 3 and 4. Other metrics could have been derived from the IMPLAN system to further classify the clusters, such as earnings per worker and size of employment by cluster.

4. Comparison with Puget Sound Regional Council clusters

The PSRC has also recently developed a cluster approach to regional development in the Central Puget Sound region. They hired The Economic Competitiveness Group and Global Insight to develop measures of clusters (Economic Competitiveness Group and Global Insight, 2005; Puget Sound Regional Council, 2007). In a two-page discussion of their methodology, a location quotient analysis is featured, along with interviews with local experts, an assessment of employment growth, and an evaluation of linkages among industries in terms of common suppliers and common markets. No data on interview results or common suppliers and markets is provided in the report; it is not clear to the reader exactly how clusters were identified nor how their strength was assessed other than the two metrics of location quotients computed using employment data and employment growth. The precise basis for the industry groupings labelled as "clusters" in the charts and tables of this report is not explained. Rather, data is presented on the characteristics of these "clusters" with no clear basis for identifying these industry groupings as clusters.

Figure 3: Regional cluster size and growth

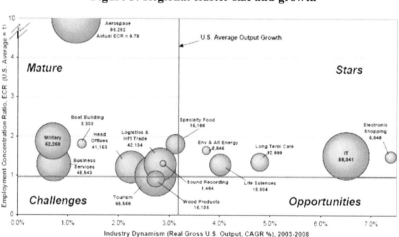

Source: Prosperity Partnership (http://www.prosperitypartnership.org/clusters/index.htm).

Figure 3 summarises the results of the analysis. The bubbles in the chart represent employment levels in each cluster; the elevation of the bubble on the vertical axis labelled 'employment concentration' shows location quotients that are familiar to regional scientists, and the bubble's position on the horizontal axis shows expected future growth of each cluster. In addition, the report notes that just 34% of total employment in the Puget Sound region falls into clusters, with the remaining 66% consisting mainly of industries presumed to have local markets. Thus, there is an implicit fourth criterion defining the clusters – a tendency of the clustered industries to exports goods or services outside the region.

Table 5: Prosperity Partnership cluster size, employment concentration and dynamism

Cluster	Industry Dynamism, CAGR, U.S. Real Gross Output 2003-2008	Employment Concentration Ratio 2001	Employment 2001	Change in Employment, CAGR 1996-2001
Aerospace	1.15%	9.78	96,292	11.0%
Boat Building	1.28%	1.81	3,303	-2.1%
Business Services	0.72%	1.30	48,543	4.6%
Insurance	-1.09%	1.03	19,304	2.9%
Architectural & Engineering Services	4.10%	1.47	19,278	5.5%
Marketing, Advertising, & PR	4.77%	1.79	9,961	6.3%
Electronic Shopping	7.39%	1.49	5,348	24.8%
Environment & Alternative Energy	3.74%	1.64	2,845	4.6%
Head Offices	2.25%	1.22	41,153	-1.7%
Information Technology	6.50%	1.51	88,341	10.1%
Software	3.65%	3.34	30,601	14.2%
Telecom	6.42%	1.59	27,177	5.8%
Computer & On-Line Services	7.25%	1.17	24,539	15.1%
Computer & Electronic Manufacturing	8.57%	0.54	6,024	-0.6%
Life Sciences	4.02%	1.28	18,804	-1.7%
Logistics & International Trade	2.82%	1.29	42,134	1.2%
Air Transport	4.18%	2.18	18,341	4.5%
Truck Transport	2.44%	0.76	8,313	0.8%
Support Activities	2.66%	0.93	6,513	-1.5%
Sea Transport	2.94%	3.58	5,780	-2.7%
Warehousing	3.50%	1.09	1,732	-2.4%
Rail Transport	-0.05%	0.49	1,424	-0.2%
Trade Finance	-0.75%	0.11	32	14.7%
Long-Term Care	4.80%	1.35	12,999	1.2%
Military	0.70%	1.87	52,250	-1.1%
Sound Recording	2.87%	1.31	1,464	-0.5%
Specialty Food	3.12%	1.80	15,166	-2.9%
Seafood	2.70%	7.46	7,209	-5.6%
Beverages	3.91%	1.16	3,491	-0.4%
Baked Goods	1.71%	1.21	3,242	-0.9%
Dairy Products	3.60%	0.81	854	-2.6%
Frozen Specialty Food Manufacturing	1.07%	0.52	370	44.0%
Tourism	2.73%	1.00	68,556	2.7%
Food	2.96%	1.00	29,714	2.5%
Accommodation	2.06%	0.70	16,358	1.9%
Entertainment	3.03%	1.35	16,040	4.4%
Transportation	2.39%	2.07	6,444	1.6%
Wood Products	2.73%	0.95	15,135	-1.0%
Total			**512,333**	

Source: *Global Insight, 2004*
Note: *CAGR=compound annual growth rate. In the case of the Military cluster, industry dynamism represents U.S. national military employment growth.*

(Reproduced from Prosperity Partnership, Economic Analysis of the Central Puget Sound Region, September 2005, http://prosperitypartnership.org/pubs.htm (September, 2007).

Table 5 provides data on the variables depicted in the bubble chart and gives some detail about the industries included in each cluster. However, no data are presented indicating the level of export-orientation for the 15 clusters selected by these consultants, and they also do not report the level of export markets in other industries not selected.

Other attempts have been made to identify clusters in the Puget Sound based on informal methods. The Global Insight report notes a prior effort by the Puget Sound Regional Council in 2003. The City of Seattle's Office of Economic Development has also identified a long list of clusters and sub-clusters.[2] Some of the city's clusters resemble those identified by Global Insight (e.g., aerospace and information technology), but the city's list contains others that were not identified by Global Insight (e.g., music), as well as other clusters that are constructed in different and conflicting ways (e.g., the maritime cluster in the city's list, which embraces fishing and marine construction *vs.* the logistics and trade cluster in the Global Insight list – which does not include fishing and marine construction but features links between land and water based transportation industries). The basis for the city's cluster list is not apparent although the city did commission several cluster studies by independent consultants in 2003, and the city's list may have been derived from these studies (see Berk, Associates, 2004; Beyers, Bonds, Wenzl, Sommers, 2004; Sommers, Andreoli, 2004).

Many differences in cluster structure can be identified by comparing this analysis with the work of the PSRC consultants. Aerospace is the largest manufacturing sector in Washington, consisting principally of the commercial aircraft and space/missile manufacturing facilities of Boeing, plus a number of smaller manufacturers, many of whom are subcontractors to Boeing. Labelling this industrial agglomeration as a cluster in the PSRC list seems a bit of a misnomer since the reality is that Boeing itself constitutes over 80% of employment in the NAICS industry category "aerospace", and Boeing's principal partners or subcontractors in building these products are scattered around the nation and the world, but are not located in the Puget Sound. The total value-added contributed by the subcontractors in the aerospace industry in the Puget Sound is a very small percentage of the value of Boeing's products. Our cluster analysis using IMPLAN data embeds the aircraft industry (using IMPLAN's industry label) in a cluster with other high-tech manufacturing industries, including semiconductors and medical products. This construct seems on logical grounds to meet the definition of a cluster; more than one industry is included and there is evidence of

---

[2]   Mimeo from the City of Seattle Office of Economic Development, n.d.

inter-industry transactions and reliance on a skilled workforce, including engineers, machinists and others with common skill sets.

Information technology provides a contrasting case. The PSRC cluster with this title joins software publishing with several computer-related manufacturing industries. This construct could be challenged by experts knowledgeable about the business practices of leading firms in these industries. In particular, the Microsoft Corporation, which is by far the largest software publisher in the Puget Sound, has for many years collaborated closely with leading computer hardware manufacturers, including IBM and Intel, producing operating systems that work with the latest computer designs introduced by these manufacturers. However, IBM and Intel have no significant facilities in the Puget Sound; IBM was located in New York during the early years of the personal computer industry when Microsoft was strategically allied with IBM, and Intel was based in Silicon Valley in California and later developed a significant presence near Portland, Oregon. No computer manufacturers of equivalent stature or strategic importance to Microsoft are located in the Puget Sound region. Thus the cluster structure used in the PSRC report is meaningful at a national level but has no practical significance within the Puget Sound.

Interestingly, the cluster analysis in this chapter places software publishing in a cluster with other information oriented industries, including custom computer programming and other computer services. Industries that are not conventionally thought of as information industries are also included in this cluster, such as sound recording and advertising. However, due to significant industry convergence, these industries are making extensive use of computer technology. Musical recordings get distributed via the internet or are played live via streaming digital services on the internet. Advertising has become an important component of internet sites such as Google or Yahoo. Thus this cluster construct appears to be capturing important features of evolving industry structures.

Table 6: Comparison of clusters derived from IMPLAN and Prosperity Partnership clusters

Cluster Name	Cluster	Key Industries	Comparable Prosperity Partnership Cluster	Key Industries
Retail	1	All retail sectors		
Producer Services	2	Consulting, accounting, rental services, management of companies, photography, travel arrangement, legal		
Health Services	3	Hospitals, health practitioner offices, social services, child care	Long Term Care	
Consumer and Research Services	4a	Dry cleaning, laundry, death care, performing arts, recreation, other educational services, research and development	Life Sciences, Tourism	
Securities- commodity contracts- investments	2a	Securities, commodity contracts, investments		
Public Utilities	5a	Federal and local government owned utilities, other government enterprises	Clean Tech/Alternative Energy	Utilities, waste management and remediation
Agriculture and Natural Resource Production/ Restaurants and Bars	6	Fishing, farming, nurseries and greenhouses, food service and drinking places		
Information oriented services	7	Software publishing, custom computer programming, other computer services, advertising, office administration, facilities support, investigation, sound recording	Information Technology, Sound Recording	Info. Tech. includes software and custom computer programming plus computer related manufacturing
Energy	5b	Oil & gas extraction, refineries, natural gas distribution, electric power generation and distribution	Clean Tech/Alternative Energy	
Movement	8	Scenic & sightseeing transportation, postal service, employment services, support activities for oil & gas extraction, sewage and water services	Tourism	

Cluster Name	Cluster	Key Industries	Comparable Prosperity Partnership Cluster	Key Industries
Personal services	4c	Other personal services, civic and professional organisations, museums, fitness, colleges & universities, elementary and secondary schools, grantmaking and religious organisations		
Funds- trusts- and other financial vehicles	2d	Funds, trusts, and other financial vehicles		
Wood Products	15a	Sawmills, secondary wood products, pulp and paper mills	Wood Products	Lumber and paper mills, doors-windows-engineered products
Food Products	16	Dairy industries, slaughtering except poultry		
Computer equipment	17	Computer, irradiation, and electronic equipment manufacturing	Information Technology	Info. Tech. includes software and custom computer programming plus computer related manufacturing
Electrical Machinery	18	Instruments, audio & video equipment, office equipment, watches		
Milling	16a	Flour mills, secondary processing of non-ferrous metals		
Industrial Group A	19a	Misc. manufacturing incl. wineries, industrial controls, & musical instruments		
Food Products	16b	Coffee, tea, breweries, soft drinks	Specialty Food	Seafood; beverages; baked, dairy and frozen specialty foods
Industrial Group B	19b	Misc. manufacturing (pumps, valves, metal buildings, tanks, etc.)		
Wood Furniture and Travel Trailers	20	Wood Furniture and Travel Trailers		
Chemical and Petrol Products	21	Plastics, organic chemicals, asphalt		

Cluster Name	Cluster	Key Industries	Comparable Prosperity Partnership Cluster	Key Industries
Mining	9	Stone, gravel & sand mining, coal mining		
Leisure	10	Insurance brokers, hotels, couriers, auto rental, railroads	Tourism	Transportation Services, Eating & Drinking Places, Lodging, Entertainment Services
Finance	2b	Monetary authorities, nondepository credit intermediaries, lessors of non-financial intangible assets		
Telecommunications	11a	Telecommunications		
Specator Sports	4b	Spectator sports	Tourism	Transportation Services, Eating & Drinking Places, Lodging, Entertainment Services, Performing Arts
Construction and related design	12	All construction industries, architecture and environmental consulting		Utilities, waste management and remediation, management and environmental consulting
Air and Water Travel	13	Air and water transportation	Logistics/International Trade	Marine ports, railroads, trucking, airports, warehousing, trade finance
Radio/TV and Cable	11b	Radio & television broadcasting, cable networks		
Forest nurseries- forest products- and timber	6a	Forest nurseries- forest products- and timber		
Independent artists- writers- and performers	4c	Independent artists- writers- and performers		
Propulsion units and parts for space vehicles	14	Propulsion units and parts for space vehicles		
Insurance carriers	2c	Insurance carriers		
Motion picture and video industries	7A	Motion picture and video industries		

Cluster Name	Cluster	Key Industries	Comparable Prosperity Partnership Cluster	Key Industries
State and local government passenger transit	28	State and local government passenger transit		
Wood Products	15b	Doors, windows, engineered wood products, prefabricated wood buildings	Wood Products	Lumber and paper mills, doors-windows-engineered products
Furniture	15c	Mattresses, furniture, blinds and shades		
Construction & Mfg related to construction	22	New residential structures, architectural woodwork, cabinets, manufactured homes		
Food products – cattle	16c	Meat processing, ranching, poultry		
Metal Products	23	Machinery, rolling mills, forging		
Cement and clay products	24	Concrete and clay products, waste management and recycling	Clean Tech/Alternative Energy	Utilities, waste management and remediation, management and environmental consulting
Industry Complex C	19c	Dental laboratories, printing and publishing, wholesale trade, ambulatory health services, automotive repair, shipbuilding, truck manufacturing, etc.	Long Term Care	Other ambulatory health care services
Instruments	25	Industrial and laboratory instruments, magnetic and optical media manufacturing		
Plastics Dependent Mfg.	26	Plastic products, toys, toiletries, opthalmic goods		
Aircraft Mfg. & Hi Tech	27	Aircraft, semiconductors, medical products	Aerospace, Life Sciences	Aerospace; scientific research and development, Pharmaceuticals
Pharmaceutical and medicine manufacturing	27a	Pharmaceutical and medicine manufacturing		
Trucking and trucking (and energy) dependent	28	Trucking, concrete, gypsum		
Miscellaneous industries	29	Industrial gases, primary aluminum, rendering		

Another interesting contrast is apparent looking at the air and water transportation industries. The PSRC cluster called Logistics and International Trade links these industries to land based transportation and related services, focusing on the movement of goods by sea to the ports in the Puget Sound and trans-shipment of these goods via rail or truck to other urban markets throughout the United States. The cluster analysis in this chapter links air and water transportation in a cluster in the middle of the dendrogram, but land based transportation industries are located at the lower end of the dendrogram and there is no linkage between these widely separated clusters until one reaches the very highest level of linkage. This dendrogram suggests very different patterns of inter-industry linkages for air/water and land-based transportation systems. The PSRC analysis highlights the importance of land-based transportation to the ports, but the dendogram suggests that the land-based transportation industries have stronger linkages to industries other than water transportation. These differences in cluster structures actually highlight a key problem of the ports and their international shipping clients, namely obtaining sufficient support from the rail industry to keep the container-based shipping industry competitive, and sufficient investment from the government to provide adequate highway infrastructure. The challenges faced by the ports may be precisely because prevailing industry structures cause land transportation industries to focus more on other clients' needs.

Life sciences is a distinct cluster in the PSRC structure, consisting of scientific research and development services, an industry category often used for start-up biotech companies and private research institutes focused on research activities; and pharmaceutical manufacturing, the industry for which many of the start-up companies are developing products and into which the start-up companies themselves sometimes move. The PSRC cluster also includes medical product manufacturing (instruments, diagnostic and therapeutic equipment), mirroring the membership of an industry association in Seattle that includes both biotech and biomedical product companies. No single life science cluster emerged from our analysis of the IMPLAN data. Scientific research and development is embedded within a set of consumer oriented service industries. Pharmaceutical manufacturing shows up as an isolated industry, located between the aircraft and high-tech cluster, one that contains truck transportation, and several industries requiring substantial inputs from truck transportation including concrete, gypsum, and gravel. Medical product manufacturing is included in a broad electrical machinery cluster. In this case, entirely different industry linkages are highlighted by the two analyses of industrial structure in the Puget Sound. The PSRC approach mirrors the way these industries have organised themselves through an association; thus the PSRC cluster definition may reflect the result of expert interviews that were one component in their methodology. On the other hand, the IMPLAN analysis reflects current inter-industry relationships that may be dominated by non-biotech, chemical-based pharmaceutical products, explaining the different placement of the pharmaceutical industry; few of the biotech companies are manufacturing products at this point. Most are engaged in intensive research and development work and are therefore placed in the scientific research and development industry, an industry that also includes companies doing research and development that is not at all related to biotechnology.

Three very diverse manufacturing clusters are identified in the IMPLAN analysis, each containing a number of very small industries. These broad collections of manufacturing companies in some way resemble the broad manufacturing cluster with a series of sub-clusters identified in the cluster list provided by the City of Seattle. This list reflects an analysis of manufacturing industries carried out for the Office of Economic Development by a consultant who suggested that while the products are quite different, there is a broad similarity of skills and processes within the many smaller manufacturing sub-sectors located in Seattle's industrial districts (see Berk, Associates, 2004). The IMPLAN analysis also identifies two construction clusters, one focused on residential construction and related wood-based manufacturing of cabinets and architectural woodwork, and a second cluster with many specialised industries such as non-residential structures, roads, bridges, water and sewer systems, and architectural services. This cluster structure fits with the city's scheme, which lists construction and contracting as a single sub-cluster within the Basic Industries cluster, which also includes many manufacturing industries. Finally, some of the similarities between broad industrial groupings in the IMPLAN analysis and the city's approach suggest that the PSRC structure may be ignoring some important features of the local economy. PSRC's approach of linking computer-related manufacturing with software publishing does not seem to reflect local circumstances. The IMPLAN analysis does not show any such linkage. The cluster objects or structures used by PSRC reflect industry groupings defined elsewhere, perhaps at a national level, and then augmented by a review by local experts. This process could perhaps have been improved by an original analysis of data on this region to make sure that the industry groupings used in subsequent analysis and in cluster initiatives actually reflect local structures that local business leaders perceive.

A single tourism cluster does not emerge from the IMPLAN analysis; spectator sports is called out as an isolated industry with significant competitive strength; eating and drinking places are grouped with agricultural industries; lodging is linked to other leisure services such as travel agents and car rental companies. The city's tourism cluster includes lodging and food services. The PSRC tourism cluster links eating and drinking places with lodging, transportation services, and entertainment industries.

Finally, a music cluster is a major focus of city policy, including entertainers plus sound and lighting industries, music publishing, as well as musical instrument manufacturing and repair. Neither the PSRC structure nor the IMPLAN analysis reveals a comparable music cluster. Independent artists and performers emerge as an isolated industry in the IMPLAN cluster analysis, and musical performances are part of the tourism cluster in the PSRC structure.

Clearly, reliance on an explicit statistical procedure results in different cluster structures than a blended methodology reflecting independent consultants studying different clusters (city cluster list) or a blend of analytic procedures and expert opinion (the PSRC cluster list). Which of these is better probably depends on local circumstances. Local experts who are sensitive to actual transaction-based relationships in a metropolitan economy may be aware of inter-industry relationships that may be weighted differently or based on different phenomena than the input-output model captures. For example, one of the authors was told that a particular hardware store should be included in the maritime cluster because it had a larger and broader inventory of special products needed by vessel owners than any other hardware store in the city, and that recreational boating companies should not be included in the maritime cluster focused on fishing, marine transportation and related industries such as marine construction. These fine distinctions may reflect the self organisation of industries but cannot be captured in an analysis of input-output data unless, for example, the recreational boating and industrial maritime industries fell into separate industry categories. Since they are in fact mixed in several industry categories, the recreational and industrial components cannot be easily disentangled, nor can a single even fairly large hardware store be identified in the coefficients expressing the fishing or marine transportation industries' relationship with wholesale or retail trade. On the other hand, the analysis of IMPLAN data emphasises the movement of people by the water and air transportation industries, a facet of transportation services that is not addressed by the logistics and international trade cluster in the PSRC initiative. The formal cluster analysis may be suggesting some missed opportunities for additional cluster initiatives. The varied placement of the industries comprising the city and PSRC tourism clusters in the analysis of IMPLAN data suggests very differently-structured industries. In this case, the formal analysis may provide a cautionary signal to organisers of a future cluster initiative focused on tourism. Some of these industries are strongly linked to local consumers, others not. Some show significant competitive strength, others not. The diversity of these industries may make organisational efforts quite difficult.

This chapter was an experiment designed to identify patterns in the structure of the Puget Sound regional economy through the use of a formal method of classification. Our goal was to undertake this classification out of curiosity as to what kind of industry groups would be articulated, and to then compare these groups with those identified by consultants to our local metropolitan planning organisation, the Puget Sound Regional Council, and by the City of Seattle. Our methodology is summarised in Table 7.

Table 7: Summary of analytic methodology for identifying clusters

Comprehensive	All industries eligible for inclusion in clusters
Detailed	Based on a database with 440 sectors
Geographic concentration	Database describes all of a single metropolitan region
Inter-industry relationships	Clusters defined by patterns of inter-industry transactions
Explicit methodology	Wards' algorithm used to identify groups of industries with similar inter-industry patterns as depicted in a dendogram
Analyst judgement	Analysts made adjustments to final dendogram based on subjective factors such as prior knowledge of industry groupings
Replicable	IMPLAN data available for any U.S. metropolitan area

Through the use of detailed input-output data generated by the IMPLAN system, we were able to develop a direct requirements matrix that could be analysed through the use of hierarchical cluster analysis. This methodology produced groupings of local industries with similar industrial structure, which we have labelled as industry clusters. In some cases, this methodology has produced intuitive groupings, and in other cases the groupings are less intuitive. Based on our knowledge of local industry structure gained through decades of experience in analysing economic trends in this region, some of the less intuitive groupings produced by the algorithm were re-arranged, resulting in the final cluster structure presented in this chapter.

The principal difference between the groupings produced in our analysis and those developed by PSRC and by the City of Seattle is that our analysis covers the entire economy, while the two governmental lists of clusters cover only portions of the regional industry structure. Consultants to the PSRC and the city used different, more subjective methodologies to develop their industry clusters (location quotients, expert opinion, advisory group recommendations), so it is not surprising that there are major differences between our cluster list and those developed by the two government-sponsored initiatives. Our analysis suggests somewhat different implications for cluster initiatives that these governmental organisations could consider in refining their programmes.

This approach to cluster identification could be replicated in other US urban areas, since IMPLAN data are available for any US county, or combinations of counties representing coherent metropolitan areas. The inter-industry relationships in the IMPLAN model are based on a national input-output table, and the unique county level data sets are constructed by appropriately varying the size of each of the 440 industries represented in the model. Thus, it would be interesting to try this approach in other urban areas to see if different cluster structures emerge, given the differences in industry size but constant inter-industry relationships for any given industry inherent in the IMPLAN system.

Analysts with access to other input-output models with a similar level of detail for other metropolitan areas could also substitute their own model and follow our methodological approach to see if different clusters emerge when the inter-industry relationships themselves are altered. We have made one experiment in this direction using the Washington State Input-Output Model, but the Washington model is very aggregated (only 52 sectors) so no useful findings can be reported from that experiment. More detailed models are required for this approach to be useful. IMPLAN itself allow analysts to partially or completely replace IMPLAN's inter-industry structure with an alternative inter-industry matrix of the analyst's choice, thereby facilitating such a strategy.

In other recent work for the State of Washington, we have developed clusters defined on the basis of relatively large location quotients and inter-industry ties, again using the IMPLAN database (see Sommers, Beyers, Wenzl, 2008). This work was undertaken separately for King, Pierce, and Snohomish counties, while Kitsap county was analysed in a region also including Clallam, Jefferson and Island counties. This spatial structure was dictated by the state agency that commissioned the work, and the differences in spatial organisation preclude direct comparisons to the findings in this chapter. Unlike the current analysis that includes all industries in the economy as a part of some cluster, the work for the state only focused on clusters that were concentrated beyond a certain threshold level in the region. Thus, another useful direction for future work would be to compare dendograms developed from comprehensive datasets, as in this chapter, to dendograms created using data subjected first to the threshold tests we used in the State of Washington work. Many analysts have applied such thresholds in identifying clusters, but we have not seen a systematic comparison of results with and without such thresholds.

Future research could help sharpen regional economic development strategies by developing longitudinal measures of growth of clusters. The development of longitudinal data for measures such as employment for the clusters defined in this analysis would reveal clusters that are growing, stable and declining; different policy measures could be developed for clusters with varied development trajectories. The IMPLAN system could be used to define the export-orientation of the clusters developed in this chapter, allowing better understanding of their contribution to the regional economic base. Further analysis of the forward and backward linkages of each cluster could help in identifying key inter-industry linkages that could become the focus for cluster initiatives.

We conclude that use of explicit algorithms for identifying industry clusters in regional economies is a useful strategy for identifying economic structures and for facilitating discussions about local economic development policy. The variations in analytical approaches discussed in this concluding section suggest that a great deal of additional research is needed to identify the advantages and disadvantages of these alternatives. Systematic comparisons with data representing several different regional economies is a recommended next step.

Bibliography

Berk and Associates, "Basic industries cluster analysis study", Office of Economic Development, Seattle, 2004.

Beyers, W., Bonds, A., Wenzl, A., Sommers, P., "The economic impact of Seattle's music industry", Office of Economic Development, Seattle, 2004.

Beyers, W., Lin, T.-W., "The 2002 Washington State Input-Output Model", Office of Financial Management, 2008. http://www.ofm.wa.gov/economy/io/2002/default.asp.

Chenery, H. Watanabe T., "International Comparisons of the Structure of Production", in *Econometrica*, 1958, 26 (4), p. 487-521.

Economic Competitiveness Group and Global Insight, "Economic Analysis of the Central Puget Sound: Part III - Puget Sound's Industry Clusters", Puget Sound Regional Council, Seattle, 2005.

Feser, E. J., Bergman, E. M., "National Industry Cluster Templates: A Framework for Applied Cluster Analysis", in *Regional Studies*, 2000, 34 (1), p. 1-19.

Hill, E. W., Brennan, J.F., "A Methodology for Identifying the Drivers of Industrial Clusters: The Foundation of Regional Competitive Advantage", in *Economic Development Quarterly*, 2000, 14 (1), p. 65-96.

Office of Economic Development, "City of Seattle Clusters – Office of Economic Development" (n.d.).

Porter, M., "The Economic Performance of Regions", in *Regional Studies*, 2003, 37 (6-7), p. 549-578.

Puget Sound Regional Council, "Prosperity Partnership", 2007.

Puget Sound Regional Council, "Seattle: Report for the Puget Sound Regional Council", http://www.prosperitypartnership.org/pubs.htm.

Sommers, P., Andreoli, D., "Seattle's maritime cluster: characteristics, trends and policy issues", 2007, Office of Economic Development, Seattle, 2004.

Sommers, P., Beyers, W., Wenzl, A., "Industry cluster analysis for Washington State workforce development areas", Olympia, Washington State Workforce Board, 2008.

Sövell, Ö., Lindqvist, G., Ketels, C., "The cluster initiative greenbook", 2003, http://www.cluster-research.org/greenbook.htm.

Authors

Catherine **BEAUDRY**, Rhodes Scholar, has a Ph.D. in economics from the University of Oxford. She is an associate professor at École Polytechnique de Montréal, a member of CIRST and a researcher at CIRANO. Her main research interests are industrial clusters, collaboration, innovation networks, innovative firm performance and survival. Her current research focuses on the impact of university funded research in biotechnology and nanotechnology. Recent selected publications include Beaudry, C. and Schiffauerova, A. "Who's right, Marshall or Jacobs? The localisation versus urbanisation debate", in *Research Policy*, 2009, 38 (2), p. 318-337.

William B. **BEYERS** is Professor of Geography at the University of Washington. He received his BA and PhD from the University of Washington. His research interests include regional structural change, the role of producer and cultural industries in regional development, and the geography of high-tech industry. A recent publication: "Determinants of change in service industry employment in the United States 1998-2005: findings based on a new classification of industries" *The Service Industries Journal*, 30 (4), 2010, p. 531-547.

Sophie **BOUTILLIER*** is Associate Professor in Economics, has a Ph.D in both Economics and Sociology (Université of Paris X Nanterre) and is Director of Research. She is member of the research unit Laboratoire de recherche sur l'Industrie et l'Innovation (Université du Littoral Côte d'Opale). She is also Visiting Professor at Seattle University (USA), at the University of Yucatan (Mexico) and at the Wesford Business School (Grenoble, France) and Dean of Department of Economics and Management (University of Littoral Côte d'Opale). Specialised in entrepreneur theory, labour economics and economics of innovation, Sophie Boutillier also works on the Greek economy. She teaches at the Institut National des Langues et Civilisations Orientales (Paris).

Thierry **BURGER-HELMCHEN***, has a PhD in Management Science, University Louis Pasteur, France, and is Researcher at BETA, University of Strasbourg. His research topics are strategic entrepreneurship and evaluation using real options and the development of empirical implementation methods of real option analysis notably in the video game industry. He teaches strategy and structure of SMEs and managerial economics at the University of Strasbourg.

Maryann P. FELDMAN is the S.K. Heninger Distinguished Chair in Public Policy at the University of North Carolina, Chapel Hill. Her research and teaching interests focus on the areas of innovation, the commercialisation of academic research and the factors that promote technological change and economic growth. A large part of Dr. Feldman's work concerns the geography of innovation – investigating the reasons why innovation clusters spatially and the mechanisms that support and sustain industrial clusters. Recent publications include Feldman, M. P. and G.D. Santangelo, *New Perspectives in International Business Research*, Emerald Books, Connecticut, 2008.

Abdelillah HAMDOUCH* is Associate Professor of Economics and Director of Research at the CLERSE-MESHS-CNRS Research Unit, University of Science and Technology, Lille. He is also Affiliate Professor at the ESC Dijon Bourgogne Business School and is an expert for the DG Research of the European Commission. His ongoing research is focused on territorial innovation dynamics, especially in biopharmaceuticals and environmental industries.

Cao HUAN graduated from Southwest Normal University and obtained a master's degree in psychology in 2004. She joined the University of Electronics, Science and Technology as both a teacher and a PhD student, majoring in knowledge management and human resource management.

Blandine LAPERCHE* is Associate Professor and Director of Research at the Research Unit on Industry and Innovation (ULCO). She is co-editor of the journal *Innovations, Cahiers d'économie de l'innovation*, and of the *Journal of Innovation Economics*. She is also head of the Forum « The Spirit of Innovation ». Her Research mainly focuses on the following topics: technological innovation and intellectual property rights, management of innovation and corporate strategies and innovation networking. Recent publications include *The Genesis of Innovation. Systemic Linkages Between Knowledge and the Market*, Edward Elgar, Cheltenham, 2008 (eds. with Dimitri Uuznidis and N. Von Tunzelmann) and *Powerful Finance and Innovation Trends in a High-Risk Economy*, Palgrave Macmillan, London, 2008 (eds with D. Uzunidis).

Francis MUNIER* is Associate Professor and scholar at a prominent laboratory in the domain of technological innovation (BETA, Strasbourg) and is the author of numerous publications, His research concerns the field of innovation economics and knowledge with both empirical and conceptual applications.

Andrea SCHIFFAUEROVA has recently completed her PhD studies at the École Polytechnique de Montréal. Her doctoral studies involved research on innovation in clusters, innovation networks, knowledge diffusion and collaboration in biotechnology and nanotechnology. Currently she is an assistant professor at Concordia University in Montreal where she concentrates on the dynamics of innovation. Recent selected publications include Beaudry, C. and Schiffauerova, A. "Who's right, Marshall or Jacobs? The localisation versus urbanisation debate", in *Research Policy*, 2009, 38 (2), p. 318-337.

Paul SOMMERS* is Professor at Seattle University, teaching in the master's level Public Management Program and in the Department of Economics. His research focuses on clusters, economic development strategy and economic impact estimation. A recent publication is: Sommers, P. Clumps or Clusters – A Case Study of Biotechnology and Life Sciences in the Seattle Area; In Laperche, Blandine, Dimitri Uzunidis and Nick von Tunzelmann (eds.), *The Genesis of Innovation, Systemic Linkages Between Knowledge and the Market*, Edward Elgar, Cheltenham, 2008.

Dimitri UZUNIDIS* is Professor of economics at the Technical University of Crete (Greece) and Director of the Research Unit on Industry and Innovation at the University of littoral (France). He is President of the Research Network on Innovation and editor of the journal *Innovations. Cahiers d'économie de l'innovation*, of the *Journal of Innovation Economics* and of the series L'esprit économique, L'Harmattan, Paris. He is also an expert for several international institutions. Specialised in international industrial economics and economics of innovation, Dimitri Uzunidis focuses his research on the political economy of globalisation, on the innovative strategies of firms in the context of globalisation, on the dynamics of innovation in innovative milieu and on the place of the entrepreneur in the dynamics of capitalism.

*Members of the Research Network on Innovation, http://rri.univ-littoral.fr.